71-96/69 7

Frontispiece : Sarcophagus of King Ahiram (in the period 1250-1000 B.C.

The inscription on the lid of the sarcophagus is the earliest form of the Phoenician alphabeti
script which has been discovered. The inscription reads:

THE COFFIN WHICH ITTOBAAL, SON OF AHIRAM, KING OF BYBLOS, MADE FOR HI
FATHER AS HIS ABODE IN ETERNITY. AND IF ANY KING OR ANY GOVERNOR OR AN
ARMY COMMANDER ATTACKS BYBLOS AND EXPOSES THIS COFFIN, LET HIS JUDICIA
SCEPTER BE BROKEN, LET HIS ROYAL THRONE BE OVERTHROWN, AND LET PEACE FLE
FROM BYBLOS; AND AS FOR HIM, LET A VAGABOND EFFACE HIS INSCRIPTIONS!

NINA JIDEJIAN

BYBLOS
THROUGH THE AGES

With a Foreword by
MAURICE DUNAND

DAR EL-MACHREQ PUBLISHERS ⊔ BEIRUT

To my husband

Acknowledgments

This book could not have been written were it not for the lifetime dedication of a great man and scholar, Maurice Dunand. My indebtedness to Mr. Dunand is apparent on every page. I have referred to all of his preliminary reports and books on the excavations at Byblos from 1926 to the present.

The desire to publish a book on Byblos in the English language came to me while doing graduate work in ancient history at the American University of Beirut. Because of the constant necessity of referring to the excavation reports of Pierre Montet and Maurice Dunand, it occurred to me that it might be useful to correlate the archaeological material with ancient inscriptions and texts. My aim is not to present a continuous history but rather to collect what is known about Byblos from these sources. Short historical surveys of the Near East have been included to clarify periods poorly represented by archaeological data. Where opinions of scholars remain divided, I have presented the major opposing views.

To Dr. Dimitri C. Baramki, Director of Museums of the American University of Beirut, I wish to express my thanks for advice on archaeological periods covered by this book. I am deeply indebted to Dr. William A. Ward, Associate Professor of History at the American University of Beirut, for his valuable assistance in clarifying problems concerning the relations of Byblos with Egypt. I am grateful for his kindness in reading the manuscript and making helpful suggestions. To Dr. John Pairman Brown, formerly Associate Professor of Classical Languages at the American University of Beirut, I am in debt for his guidance and counsel in my research.

I wish to express my appreciation to Dr. William M. Bickers for the care with which he has read and edited this book.

Acknowledgment is made to Emir Maurice Chehab, Director General of Antiquities of Lebanon, for kind permission to publish pictures of the treasures of Byblos. These pictures have been made available by courtesy of the Beirut National Museum. I wish to express my appreciation to Dr. James B. Pritchard, Professor of Archaeology and Curator of the University Museum, University of Pennsylvania, for permission to publish his photograph of Ahiram's sarcophagus for the frontispiece of this book. I am indebted to Dr. Raif Nassif, Director of the School of Medicine of the American University of Beirut, for the photographs taken at Byblos which illustrate the text and for the aerial view of the temples taken on May 17, 1968. I wish to thank Mr. Guy Abela for allowing me to reproduce several lithographs from his collection of works of nineteenth century travellers to Lebanon.

Grateful acknowledgment is made to the National Council of Tourism of Lebanon for permission to publish pictures taken from the files of the Photographic Department. Acknowledgment is made with thanks to the Institut Français d'Archéologie, Beirut, and to the Jafet Library of the American University of Beirut for the facilities given me in my research.

Last, but not least, I wish to thank my husband without whose understanding and encouragement this book could not have been completed.

Foreword

Présenter ce livre au lecteur est une tâche agréable. Il donne un résumé rapide de la très longue histoire de Byblos depuis le début des temps néolithiques jusqu'à la fin des Croisades, en suivant les divisions chronologiques les plus unanimement admises dans les études orientales.

Les quatre premiers millénaires de cette histoire sont allégrement franchis : une trentaine de pages y suffisent. Les textes font défaut, la documentation est essentiellement archéologique. L'intérêt en est faible pour le lecteur non spécialisé auquel ce livre est destiné. Le dépouillement attentif des *Fouilles de Byblos* amène l'auteur à présenter les monuments et documents les plus importants qui balisent le cours de l'histoire. Les connexions avec l'Égypte assurent la séquence chronologique.

A partir de l'époque des tablettes d'El-Amarna les textes devenus nombreux permettent de mettre en chaîne continue les maillons de l'histoire. Le précieux recueil des textes orientaux de Pritchard est à cette fin d'une valeur incomparable. Madame Nina Jidejian a su en extraire et ordonner les faits de base qui marquent le cours des événements et ceux moins importants mais évocateurs du détail pittoresque qui éveillera l'attention. Les références aux récits bibliques sont fréquentes et opportunes. Elles éclairent l'histoire de Byblos dans la mesure où celle-ci

se raccorde avec celle des régions méridionales en contact avec Israël, le pays de Tyr en particulier.

Depuis le Ve siècle, les historiens grecs, latins et le grand recueil de F. Jacoby ont été abondamment exploités. On retrouve dans ces pages l'exposé rapide qui clarifie toutes choses et ne donne que l'essentiel. Le lecteur s'y meut aisément.

Les temps byzantins et ceux de la *mamluqiya arabiya* sont rapidement survolés. C'est une histoire difficile et à Byblos le document évocateur est rare. Pour l'époque des Croisades, un peu d'histoire, la présentation du château franc, de l'église Saint-Jean, des remparts — tout au moins leur fondation — donnent le coup de gong qui termine l'histoire de Byblos avant l'éveil de la Syrie.

Quelques pages sur le culte d'Adonis, d'autres sur les forêts et leur exploitation, celles-ci particulièrement bien documentées, intéresseront le lecteur.

Un choix d'objets sortis du tertre de Byblos est présenté. La reproduction du sarcophage du roi Ahiram est la meilleure qui ait jamais été donnée. Les monuments principaux exhumés au cours des fouilles apparaissent jusque dans les détails dans une excellente vue d'avion.

Je souhaite à ce livre une large et longue audience: il la mérite. Je souhaite aussi que Madame Nina Jidejian ne s'arrête pas dans son travail. Elle a un don de recherche patiente, un talent de présentation qui font vivement désirer une suite à ce premier ouvrage. Il lui serait aisé de présenter d'autres sites phéniciens et syriens. Je pense à Aradus et Symira, à Ougarit et Lattaquieh, à Damas. A cette fin on peut faire confiance à ses maîtres de l'American University de Beyrouth. Le professeur Dimitri C. Baramki et le professeur William A. Ward qui ont su orienter Madame Jidejian dans ses recherches sauront l'encourager à les poursuivre.

MAURICE DUNAND

Preface

Byblos has until recently been the special concern only of scholars and archaeologists. Since the city has been excavated it has become a site of interest for the general public. The most widely read book in the world, the Bible, derives its name from βύβλος (Bublos) "papyrus scroll", a name used by the Greeks for the city. Apart from scholars and students of history few people know why. Other interesting facts about Byblos are the inscriptions, texts and testimonies of travellers in antiquity found in obscure or technical journals to which access is difficult. The excavation reports which contain the archaeological basis for facts and conclusions put forward in this work are specialized and difficult for the general public to understand. The purpose of this book is to make available to the reader all that is known about Byblos from the earliest times and to serve as a guide to the sources should a fuller study be desired. All sources which have been consulted are cited in the footnotes and bibliography.

The story of Byblos, however fragmentary, covers a span of seven thousand years. Archaeological evidence has revealed that a small fishing community existed here as early as 5000 B.C. The Phoenicians considered Byblos the most ancient city on their coast. Philo of Byblos who lived

during the second century of our era wrote in Greek but referred to older texts in Phoenician of which no traces remain. According to Philo, "Kronos put a wall about his habitation and founded Byblos of Phoenicia, the first city."[1] In the ancient world the founding of a city was attributed to a god. The massive walls of the Early Bronze Age built ca. 2800 B.C. reflect this tradition as recorded by Philo. Thus there is both archaeological evidence and a text to indicate that Byblos even in the minds of the ancients was a city existing from remote times.

As the excavations continue outside the ancient city walls more archaeological evidence will appear. Several problems concerning Byblos are yet to be resolved. The lack of more records leaves many periods at Byblos in the dark and open to conjecture. There is no native literature of Phoenicia for the period covering the first millenium B.C. which has been preserved. The few fragments extant of Philo of Byblos are insufficient to give a comprehensive idea of the religious, political and sociological background of the city.

Reference has been made to the reports of Pierre Montet who was responsible for the excavations from 1921-1924, and to Maurice Dunand who has conducted the excavations from 1925 until the present time. Ancient texts, inscriptions, passages from the Old Testament and the works of classical authors have been consulted. Inscribed monuments of Egyptian origin found at Byblos have been included in an effort to corroborate the archaeological material with texts and inscriptions. From this evidence it can be seen that Byblos was a great city and deserves attention even though more emphasis has been given to Tyre and Sidon because of frequent mention in Old Testament and classical texts. Byblos was important as the timber and shipbuilding center of the Eastern Mediterranean world

[1] Felix Jacoby, *Die Fragmente der Griechischen Historiker*, Dritter Teil C, Leiden, E.J. Brill, 1958, No. 790. Extracts of Philo of Byblos have been preserved in Eusebius' *Praeparatio Evangelica*.

during the third and second millenia B.C. The first example of monumental architecture in Phoenicia is seen at Byblos. Around 2800 B.C. the earliest foundations of a temple to the city goddess, Baalat-Gebal, were made corresponding to the period monumental architecture appeared in Egypt. From the third millenium B.C. to the Roman period the city held an important place in the ancient world as a commercial center. Byblos also became the religious center for the worship of Adonis in the Graeco-Roman world. True to her early traditions as a temple city Byblos continued to attract pilgrims during several centuries until at long last her temples were abandoned and fell into ruins.

It is hoped that this account of the city will guide the reader through the ages when Byblos lived and prospered.

N. J.

List of Abbreviations

The following abbreviations are used throughout this work:

ANET	Ancient Near Eastern Texts relating to the Old Testament. Ed. James B. Pritchard. 2nd edition 1955.
BASOR	Bulletin of the American Schools of Oriental Research.
BMB	Bulletin du Musée de Beyrouth.
JAOS	Journal of the American Oriental Society.
JEA	Journal of Egyptian Archaeology.
Kemi	Kemi. Revue de philologie et d'archéologie égyptiennes et coptes.
Syria	Syria. Revue d'art oriental et d'archéologie.

Contents

Map of Jebeil.
Ernest Renan, *Mission de Phénicie*,
Atlas (1864), Plate XIX

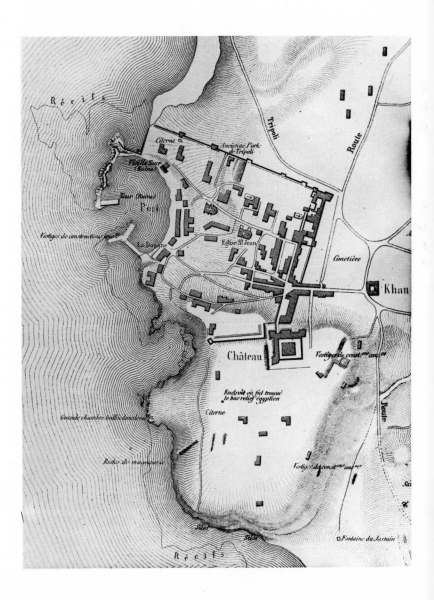

1   The Site

[1] *ANET*, p. 227.

Situated on the Lebanese coast twenty-five miles north of Beirut the ancient seaport of Byblos developed into an important commercial center in the Eastern Mediterranean world. As early as the beginning of the third millenium B.C., after the unification of Egypt, the pharaohs of the Old Kingdom needed timber for shipbuilding and took steps to develop close ties with Byblos. Sea-going ships were built which towed rafts of tree trunks along the coast to the harbors of the Nile Delta. During the reign of Senefru, a pharaoh of the Fourth Dynasty (ca. 2650 or 2600 B.C.), an Egyptian inscription states that forty ships filled with cedar logs were brought to Egypt.[1] The site of Byblos as a timber and shipbuilding center was determined by two factors: an acropolis with a small but adequate harbor and its position on the coast where timber bearing mountains came down nearest to the sea. No other port on the Phoenician coast enjoyed such advantages. Due to its geographical situation the ancient city prospered.

Byblos, modern Jebeil, was written *Kpny* or *Kbny* which stood for *Gubla* in ancient Egyptian and cuneiform inscriptions. It was referred to as Gebal in the Old Testament (1 Kings 5.18 and Ezekiel 27.9) and its Biblical name has been preserved in the present day city of Jebeil. During the second millenium B.C. commercial exchanges existed between the Aegean world and the Eastern Mediterranean. Middle Minoan pottery found at Byblos is an important piece of evidence of this trade.[2] Reference to Phoenician sailors in the Aegean is found in Homer (*Iliad* 23.744-745). "Byblos" was the name given to the city by the Greeks probably at the end of the second millenium B.C. It must be borne in mind that both

[2] Claude F.A. Schaeffer, *Stratigraphie comparée et chronologie de l'Asie Occidentale, Syrie, Palestine, Asie Mineure, Chypre, Perse et Caucase,* Londres, Oxford University Press, 1948, p. 66.

"Byblos" and "Phoenicia" are Greek terms referring to the city and coastal area from 1200 B.C. onward. For the preceding periods the terms Gubla and Gebal were applied to the city and the term Canaan to the coast. To avoid confusing the reader the city will be referred to as Byblos during all periods.

During the first millenium B.C. Byblos was the center of an extensive papyrus trade with Egypt and the Greek world. The word used by the Greeks for papyrus was βύβλος *(bublos)*. In addition to stone and potsherds one of the writing materials used in Greece in the first millenium B.C. was papyrus of Egyptian origin. The Greek word for papyrus and the Greek name for the Phoenician city of Gubla are the same.[3] This indicates that papyrus came to Greece not direct from Egypt but through Phoenician intermediaries. Evidence can be found of this trade in several texts. The Wen-Amon papyrus (eleventh century B.C.) relates the adventures of the Egyptian envoy Wen-Amon to Byblos to procure cedar wood. This was at a period when the city enjoyed political and economic independence from Egypt. In this account it is stated that five hundred rolls of papyrus and five hundred coils of rope were sent from Egypt to the king of Byblos in payment for shipments of cedar wood. At a corresponding period there is also evidence of the presence and use of papyrus in the Greek world. In the *Odyssey* 21.390-391 Homer refers to a ship's cable made of papyrus. This text is evidence that papyrus rope was used for sailing purposes by the Greeks. Papyrus rolls were used for writing material at a later period (ca. 800 B.C.) when the Greeks adopted the Phoenician alphabet. It is probable that Byblos imported papyrus from Egypt which was then transhipped to the Aegean. During the late seventh century B.C. Egypt developed direct trade routes by establishment of the Greek trading colony at Naukratis.

Until the middle of the nineteenth century all knowledge of the history of Phoenicia was derived from the Old Testament and the works of Greek and Latin authors. The exact location of Byblos was lost to history for many centuries. In describing the city Strabo, a Greek geographer of the first century of our era, stated that "the city is situated on a height only a slight distance from the sea".[4] Here in 1860 Ernest Renan located the site dominating the ancient port of Jebeil. The entire site at that time was covered by houses and orchards.

[3] Hjalmar Frisk, *Griechisches Etymologisches Wörterbuch*, Heidelberg: Carl Winter, 1960, s.v. βίβλος earlier βύβλος . According to Frisk the cortex of the papyrus shrub and later the papyrus shrub itself was called after the Phoenician port of Byblos (Gubla) whence the cortex after processing was exported to the Greeks. The English word "Bible" is derived through medieval Latin from Greek τὰ βιβλία *(ta biblia)* which means "the books" or more specifically a particular collection of books.

[4] Strabo, *The Geography of Strabo*, 16.2.18.

2

[5] Ernest Renan, *Mission de Phénicie*, Paris, Imprimerie Impériale, 1864, p. 1.

Renan had been commissioned by Napoleon III, Emperor of France, to make a survey of the historical sites of Phoenicia. Civil war between the Maronite and Druse factions in the country had brought the French army to Lebanon in 1860.[5] Renan made an analogy between his mission and that of the French scientists who followed Napoleon I into Egypt in 1798. The houses built over ancient Byblos proved to be a great hindrance for the excavations. Renan was obliged to make superficial soundings in the gardens between the houses. Nevertheless he made a careful survey and published his findings and every inscription he unearthed in *Mission de Phénicie* in 1864. Most of the inscriptions were in Greek. He found these not only in surface excavations but also in nearby villages where stones from Byblos had been taken for the construction of houses. It must be kept in mind that there had been free access to the site. Thus Byblos had served as a "quarry", not only for Jebeil but also for the immediate neighborhood. Large stone blocks could be retrieved just below the surface. Renan found stone blocks in the walls of several houses. Some of these displayed inscriptions in hieroglyphic, Greek or Latin letters. Digging wells and reservoirs for houses at Byblos had brought to the surface many ancient fragments from the lower levels. Little attention was paid at the time to their historical value. Some found their way into the hands of art dealers if they were made of precious metal, others were cast aside. Clandestine excavations carried out by the inhabitants of the region contributed incalculable damage to the site. Renan stated: "Never has one seen so well as in this circumstance how the limited curiosity of the amateur can be the enemy of the greater curiosity of the scholar."[6]

[6] *Mission de Phénicie*, p. 155.

In addition to Greek inscriptions Renan found a fragment of bas-relief which he believed was Egyptian. On it is a representation of a goddess with the solar disc between cow's horns set on her head which is a characteristic of the Egyptian goddess Hathor. Of the hieroglyphic inscription only one word, translated by M. de Rougé as "eternally", remains.[7] Although Renan did not realize it at the time the goddess no doubt was Baalat-Gebal, the "Lady of Byblos". This fragment has been called the "Renan bas-relief" and is presently in the Louvre *(Fig. 106)*.

[7] *Mission de Phénicie*, p. 179.

At the time of Renan's visit to Jebeil the Crusader castle, although partly buried by debris, still occupied the dominating

3

position on the site. From a close examination of the castle he concluded that the granite columns used as binders and the bossed masonry in the construction were of the Roman period and had been re-used by the Crusaders *(Fig. 125)*. The re-use of architectural elements and stone building blocks of earlier periods is characteristic of Byblos and has done much damage to earlier archaeological levels. What the Crusaders alone did was enough to render future excavations a complex and difficult undertaking. In their search for large building blocks for the castle they destroyed the Arab and Byzantine levels to reach the Roman levels underneath. After extracting the stone and columns they needed they threw back the debris from the deep foundations of the castle and its surrounding moat.

To Ernest Renan credit must be given for the first published records of surface excavations at Byblos. The same may be said of Tyre, Sidon and Aradus. Although his work was supplemented by systematic excavations at Byblos carried out sixty years later, *Mission de Phénicie* has preserved interesting information for the historian and archaeologist.

For many years illegal excavators had been providing antique dealers and private collectors with objects of value from Byblos. The bust of Osorkon I, a pharaoh of the Twenty-second Dynasty (924-889 B.C.), presently in the Louvre is an example. In addition to its great artistic value this beautiful sandstone bust has two important inscriptions. The cartouche of Osorkon I in Egyptian hieroglyphs is engraved in the center of the bust. Surrounding the cartouche like a necklace is another inscription of three lines which is a dedication in Phoenician letters by King Elibaal of Byblos.[8] The Egyptologist Wiedemann discovered the bust in Naples in 1881, although it is not known how it got there. It is mentioned in his *Histoire Egyptienne* in 1884. He published the inscription in hieroglyphs but did not mention the presence of the Phoenician alphabetic script. An antique dealer, by name Canessa, put the bust up for sale in Paris in 1910 and made note of the alphabetic inscription. The sale catalogue stated that the inscription was Carian and had been subsequently added to the hieroglyphic script. The alphabetic inscription therefore was considered a forgery. The bust eventually came into the possession of an amateur in Paris, Joanny Peytel. At his death his nephew, André Peytel, donated the statue to the Louvre when convinced of its exceptional importance. René Dussaud

[8] René Dussaud, "Dédicace d'une statue d'Osorkon par Elibaal, roi de Byblos", *Syria* VI, 1925, pp. 101-110. The term "cartouche" is applied to names and titles of Egyptian pharaohs engraved within an oblong separating them from the rest of the inscription.

4

identified the alphabetic script as Phoenician and it has been accepted that this statue came from Byblos. It had been set up in the sanctuary of Baalat-Gebal during the tenth century B.C. by Elibaal, king of Byblos.

A second attempt to excavate Byblos was undertaken by Pierre Montet, the well-known French Egyptologist. In 1919 Montet visited Jebeil and was struck by the fact that fragments of stone with hieroglyphic inscriptions were being found within a well defined area. Using this as a starting point he carried out four campaigns during the years 1921-1924. During the first he came across the foundations of a temple which had been ravaged by fire, levelled off and covered with flagstones. In these ruins he found many fragments of alabaster offering dishes of Egyptian origin bearing the cartouches of pharaohs of the Old Kingdom as well as artifacts which could be dated to the Middle Kingdom.[9] Until this time scholars had suspected that a connection existed between Egypt and Byblos because of a similarity in religious myths. Plutarch, a priest of the Pythian Apollo at Chaeronia, Boeotia, wrote a treatise *On Isis and Osiris* during the first century A.D. In this treatise he related how the Egyptian goddess Isis travelled to Byblos to find the body of her slain lover-brother Osiris. This legend presupposed contact between Egypt and Byblos. Montet's excavations confirmed this fact and further proved that close trade relations existed between Egypt and Byblos as far back as the third millenium B.C.

At the time of Montet's excavations twenty-nine houses and gardens occupied the site. More than once an excavated area had to be abandoned due to the presence of a house which prevented further digging. Thus the archaeologist did not realize that the flagstones he uncovered belonged to a temple of the Roman period built over different architectural stages of the temple of Baalat-Gebal. Believing he had discovered two separate temples built side by side he named one the "Egyptian temple" and the other the "Syrian temple".

In 1922 a landslide on the sea-side slope of the excavations revealed a royal tomb. The burial chamber contained the sarcophagus of a king of Byblos contemporary with Amenemhat III (ca. 1800 B.C.). Here were found rich funerary gifts from the pharaoh. This led to the discovery of other tombs in the necropolis totalling nine royal tombs of the kings of Byblos. The most important was the tomb

[9] Pierre Montet, *Byblos et l'Egypte,* Quatre campagnes de fouilles à Gebeil 1921, 1922, 1923, 1924, Paris, Librairie Orientaliste Paul Geuthner, 1928, pp. 68-74.

and sarcophagus of Ahiram bearing the earliest archaic inscription of the Phoenician alphabet.[10] In the Ahiram burial chamber there were two other plain stone sarcophagi dating to an earlier period.

When M. Dunand took charge of the excavations in 1925 he was faced with innumerable problems. The stratification of the site had been much disturbed. Hellenistic potsherds in a Chalcolithic jar burial were found even though several thousand years separated the objects. In 1930 funds were allocated by the government for the expropriation of all the houses built over the site. Extending the excavations in the vicinity of Montet's "Egyptian" and "Syrian" temples Dunand concluded that the temple was a large building complex of the Roman period built over the foundations of earlier successive stages of the temple of Baalat-Gebal. He named the two parts of the temple *Bâtiment* I and *Bâtiment* II. From the Early Bronze Age down through the Roman period the city goddess of Byblos was worshipped in this temple under different names and titles: Baalat-Gebal, Hathor, Isis and Astarte.

Dunand continued the excavations within the Early Bronze Age city walls and at present has extended his excavations to include other parts of Jebeil. His excavation reports give a detailed description of his work and a catalogue of the artifacts found has been published in *Fouilles de Byblos* I and II.[11] Dunand has also published for the layman a short history of the site.[12]

Little was written specifically about Byblos during the last century. In 1899 Jules Rouvier published a lecture which gives a good outline of the city's history.[13] John Kenrick's *Phoenicia*[14] and George Rawlinson's *History of Phoenicia*[15] are full histories of Phoenicia. F.C. Movers' important work in German *Die Phönizier*[16] is considered an excellent reference to ancient texts. These works were written during the second half of the nineteenth century and depend mainly upon literary sources. George Francis Hill in his introduction to the *Catalogue of the Greek Coins of Phoenicia*[17] gives a short account of the history of Byblos. In the light of the excavations of Montet and Dunand the interpretations of these scholars in some cases must be revised.

In 1926 G. Contenau, Honorary Curator of Oriental Antiquities in the Louvre, published a book covering the various contributions of the Phoenicians to civilization. This book republished in 1949 is called *La Civilisation Phénicienne*.[18] Technical studies on Byblos

[10] *Byblos et l'Egypte,* pp. 215-238.

[11] M. Dunand, *Fouilles de Byblos* I and II, Paris, Librairie Orientaliste Paul Geuthner, 1939.

[12] M. Dunand, *Byblos, son histoire, ses ruines, ses légendes,* Beyrouth, 1963.

[13] Jules Rouvier, "Gébal-Byblos, son histoire dans l'antiquité et sa nécropole phénicienne", Conférence donnée à l'Association Bibliographique de Beyrouth le jeudi 23 mars 1899.

[14] John Kenrick, *Phoenicia,* London, B. Fellowes, 1855.

[15] George Rawlinson, *History of Phoenicia,* London, Longmans, Green & Co., 1889.

[16] F.C. Movers, *Die Phönizier* I & II, Berlin, Ferdinand Dümmler's Berlagsbudhandlung, 1856.

[17] George F. Hill, *Catalogue of the Greek Coins of Phoenicia,* London, Longmans & Co., 1910.

[18] G. Contenau, *La civilisation phénicienne,* rev. ed., Paris, Payot, 1949.

in the periodical literature have been listed in the bibliography at the end of this book.

Byblos is visited by thousands of tourists each year from all over the world. However, it is not only during the twentieth century that visitors have come to be impressed with what they see. There have been tourists of the distant past who have marvelled at the sights. Lucian, a Syrian born in A.D. 125 in Samosata, the capital of Commagene, travelled to Byblos during the second century of our era. In his treatise *De Dea Syria* he described Byblos as an important temple city, a place of pilgrimage in the ancient world where the rites of Adonis were performed.[19]

Nassiri Khosrau, a Persian traveller, passed through Byblos in A.D. 1047 and reported that he saw a great number of columns. "No one," he wrote, "knows what purpose they served nor from where they were brought."[20] The granite columns Nassiri Khosrau wondered about can be seen today incorporated as binders in the Crusader castle and the port. Some granite columns also can be seen lying under the shallow water in the harbor. During the Roman period a colonnade surrounded the city. During the reign of Justinian (A.D. 551) a severe earthquake was responsible for the devastation of the coastal cities of Phoenicia. Many buildings in Byblos were destroyed and the columns shattered. At the time of the Persian's visit many columns still lay fallen. Two hundred years after Nassiri Khosrau passed by Byblos a Spanish traveller, Benjamin de Tudèle, visited the city. De Tudèle referred to a temple in the city in which there were three seated colossi covered in gold.[21] Whether he actually saw the statues or was told of their existence in the past by the inhabitants is open to conjecture. In 1921 Pierre Montet discovered three seated stone colossi, badly mutilated, at the entrance of the building he had named the "Egyptian" temple. The colossi dating from an earlier period had been re-used in this temple of the Roman period.[22] Montet's discovery is another clear instance where archaeology has been able to corroborate literary texts.

It is thanks to Emir Maurice Chehab, Director General of Antiquities of Lebanon, that tourists of the future will be able to visit and appreciate the historical sites of ancient Phoenicia. Emir Maurice Chehab has devoted a lifetime to archaeological research and it is under his tireless supervision that the sites of the Phoenician city-states are being excavated and preserved for posterity.

[19] Lucian, *The Syrian Goddess*, trans. by Herbert A. Strong, London, Constable & Co., Ltd., 1913, § 6-9.

[20] *Sefer Nameh, Relation des voyages de Nassiri Khosrau*, trans. by C. Schefer, Paris, 1881, p. 46.

[21] R. Dussaud, "Le sanctuaire phénicien de Byblos d'après Benjamin de Tudèle", *Syria* VII, 1927, pp. 248-249.

[22] *Fouilles de Byblos* I, pp. 71-72. Dunand believes that the seated colossi belong to the Persian period (ca. fifth century B.C.). It is possible that gold leaf was used to cover the statues due to the poor quality of the local limestone.

Stone idol of the Neolithic Age (ca. 4500 B.C.)

2   The Stone Age

The Neolithic Settlements (5000-4000 B.C.)

Like Europe and parts of Africa the Near East was inhabited by an unknown species of man as early as 500,000 years ago during the Second or Mendel-Riss interglacial period. This species of man had the ability to fashion tools out of flint. The fashioning of the first flint tools was an important step in the cultural history of mankind. It was the first step in the direction of industrial production permitting man to reach the stage where he could put his imagination to work.

During the Paleolithic Age in Lebanon primitive man sought cover in natural caves and rock shelters in certain regions along the coast. A rock shelter at Ksar 'Akil near Antelias shows stratified occupation levels. From the flint tools he left behind we know that during this period man established stations near Batroun, Nahr Ibrahim (the ancient Adonis River), Nahr-el-Kelb (the ancient Lycus River), Furn esh-Shubbak and Bir Hassan in Beirut. The caves in the foothills of Jebeil also served as shelters. At this food-collecting stage man hunted and gathered seeds and berries in order to survive. From the ninth to the early seventh millenium B.C. the Natufian sites of Palestine are evidence that the incipient food-producing era had been introduced in this general area.[1] Man had become less dependent on hunting and food gathering as a source of subsistence. As early as the first half of the seventh millenium B.C. there is evidence that village-farming communities had been established in north Syria and north Mesopotamia.[2] Sickles made of small flint blades set in curved branches or jawbones of animals prove that man was

[1] W.F. Albright, "Some Remarks on the Archaeological Chronology of Palestine before about 1500 B.C.", in Robert W. Ehrich (ed.), *Chronologies in Old World Archaeology*, Chicago, University of Chicago Press, 1954, p. 49.

[2] Patty Jo Watson, "The Chronology of North Syria and North Mesopotamia from 10,000 B.C. to 2000 B.C.", *Chronologies in Old World Archaeology*, pp. 61-64.

9

cultivating his crops. The chipped-stone industry (flint and obsidian) comprising punches, burins, lance heads and other projectile points is found in the Pre-Pottery Neolithic Age which lasted from the early seventh to the late sixth millenium B.C. Man had settled in the plains on plots of land which he cultivated. The development and refinement of flint and bone tools enabled man during the Pottery Neolithic Age (late sixth to end of fifth millenium B.C.) to make pottery for storing food, to weave and to make wickerwork baskets. On the coast, in addition to growing his crops, he also hunted and fished. It is at this stage that the earliest settlement at Byblos appeared.

Reference has been made to M. Dunand's preliminary reports for the information concerning the Neolithic settlements at Byblos.[3] It is presumed that the houses of the earliest settlement, of which no architectural traces remain, were flimsy shelters consisting of one room built over a stone foundation of pebbles gathered from river beds. Branches of trees plastered with mud served to roof these huts. About 4500 B.C. the inhabitants of Byblos started to make floors of crushed limestone *(Fig. 7)*. First a substructure was laid composed of fist sized pebbles held together by clay. Crushed limestone was made into a paste and spread on the floor of the monocellular hut to be polished probably by means of a large stone. Quarrying was unknown. A low wall consisting of one or two layers of stones surrounded the floor and supported curved poles which held up the roof of branches and animal skins. Metal was unknown as indicated by the absence of any traces above and beneath this level.

The deceased were buried in shallow graves. The skeletons found in four such graves were disturbed and originally had either been lying on their backs or in half flexed position. In one of these graves a pottery bowl with an incised decoration was found.[4] This indicates that there existed at the time some sort of belief in a future life that led to an attempt to protect the body of the dead.

During this period at Byblos there is evidence of another settlement. These houses had floors of beaten earth instead of crushed limestone. A new type of burial was introduced. The dead were buried in cradle or cist graves. The skeletons lay in semi-flexed or flexed positions in "cradles" made of upright stones suggesting that more care was being taken in the disposal of the dead.[5] Two such graves, that of a young man in a very flexed position and that of a child in a semi-flexed position, contained bowls within reach.

[3] M. Dunand, "Rapport préliminaire sur les fouilles de Byblos en 1948", *BMB* IX, 1949-1950, pp. 65-74. See also *BMB* XII, 1955, pp. 7-12 and 13-20; and *BMB* XVI, 1964, pp. 69-73, 75-79 and 81-85.

[4] Dunand, *BMB* IX, 1949-1950, Plate III, 1.

[5] Dunand, *BMB* IX, 1949-1950, pp. 68-73. Dunand believes that the graves belonging to the crushed limestone floors settlement are of a slightly earlier period.

It is probable that once the body was laid in the grave it was covered with earth and stones because to reach the graves the excavators had to remove the tumulus. The presence of a large number of bone fish-hooks in the vicinity is clear evidence that the early settlement at Byblos was a fisherman's village.

Pottery was made by hand towards the end of the Neolithic Age. Up to that time receptacles were of limestone or diorite and animal skins. These were used to store food. Originally pottery was made by laying a flat base and putting together lumps of clay. Later man proceeded to make rings of clay in different sizes, graduating from bottom to top, pasting the outside of the vessel with clay before baking it. Fine flint grits were used as temper. Man also developed an artistic sense, well illustrated in the pottery of this period at Byblos. Incisions on the pottery started to have patterns and designs suggested by straw. Designs on pottery were made by fingernail, circles by reeds and incisions with twigs. A certain type of decoration (the term "chicken scratching" is used to describe it) was made with the edge of a sea shell. In time the crude incision gave way to a definite pattern, the herringbone pattern, which later is seen as a functional element in the architecture of houses in Byblos *(Fig. 5)*.

Furthermore man began to believe in a powerful force that controlled him and his environment. The earliest idol of Byblos was a large pebble which an inhabitant crudely engraved after his own image. This large pebble is the first known god of Byblos.

The Chalcolithic Settlement (3500-3100 B.C.)

Sometime during the fourth millenium B.C. a new folk entered the western horn of the Fertile Crescent and settled at Byblos ca. 3500 or 3450 B.C. They introduced the potter's wheel, a new type of dwelling and new burial rites. The newcomers were acquainted with the use of metal as evidenced by bronze weapons in the burials and elsewhere at this level.

The mode of burial consisted of tying the body in a very flexed position immediately after death. It was then placed into a large burial jar *(Fig. 9)*. An area on the shoulder of the jar was marked out by periphereal pricking to form a flap. The flap was removed temporarily to allow the insertion of the body *(Fig. 10)*. With the body in some cases was buried a three jar pottery group — a jar,

11

a cruze and a carinated bowl — which no doubt contained food and drink. This indicates that there was during this period a definite belief in an after-life. The relatives of the deceased wished him to be accompanied with the necessary comforts. In the Beirut National Museum several of these jar burials are displayed. During the excavations Dunand unearthed a large Chalcolithic necropolis. At the time of the publication of the excavation reports in 1952, one thousand two hundred and seven jar burials had been discovered.[6] One jar contained the skeleton of a woman of small stature. Lying around her were some earthly possessions to be used in the next life: a globular pot at her feet, a vase of buff clay by her head, two silver hair bands, a gold ring with a carnelian bead held in place with fine twines, two earrings, each one consisting of two silver rings, fourteen small silver beads, twenty-one carnelian beads, a bone bead, a limestone bead, a bone amulet, four pierced shells and fragments of teeth. Another jar burial contained five copper daggers with three rivets in each, a silver hair band, seven hollowed out gold beads, twenty carnelian beads, a cylindrical bead in blue stone, twenty-two olive shaped silver beads, four silver necklaces, a piece of bone studded with silver, and three slabs of rectangular bone forming a necklace.[7] Another jar contained the skeleton of a man and over this was placed a smaller jar containing the skeleton of a dog.[8] No doubt the man was a hunter deeply attached to his dog and companion. Another jar burial contained a stone mace head which had been laid beside the body in addition to the three-jar tomb group of pottery. The deceased was probably a warrior or a hunter. The Chalcolithic necropolis, containing such a large number of jar burials, is evidence that the settlement was growing in size. The dead at this period were buried in one locality some distance from the houses. One of the jar burials was found lying directly on a crushed limestone floor of the older Neolithic settlement which had by this time been completely covered up and occupied by the Chalcolithic necropolis. During this period at Byblos, side by side with monocellular huts, several houses were found built on a rectangular plan with rounded corners to the exterior *(Fig. 8)*. Some of the larger houses were divided into two parts by a partition. The floors of these dwellings were made of beaten earth. In some cases floors were crudely covered with small flat pebbles.

[6] Dunand, *BMB* XII, 1955, p. 22.

[7] Dunand, *BMB* XVI, 1964, pp. 78-79.

[8] Dunand, *BMB* IX, 1949-1950, p. 67.

The Proto-Urban Settlement at Byblos (3100-2900 B.C.)

The proto-urban period (which is also called by some archaeologists Early Bronze Phase I, 3100-2900 B.C.) saw a new type of house plan introduced at Byblos. In some cases houses were built on a rectangular plan and had a partition set at one third the length of the building. The floors were of beaten earth. The stones used in the walls of these constructions were no longer rocks and pebbles from riverside beds but were small slabs of sandstone prized from the parent rock found nearby. These stone slabs were placed in the walls in a herringbone pattern *(Fig. 11)*. The larger foundation stones were limestone. At this early stage of building the inhabitants of Byblos were faced with one of the fundamental problems of architecture. They had to devise a method to prevent walls from fissuring and falling while at the same time supporting the roof of their houses. As the angles of the walls were subjected to the stress of lateral thrust the cornerstones had to be solidly entrenched. To resist the stress on the walls large irregular shaped foundation stones of unhewn rock were placed, partly buried, at the corners of the building.

Early Bronze Age pottery figurines

3 The Early Bronze Age
(2900-2300 B.C.)

Byblos and the Egyptian Old Kingdom

The first urban settlement at Byblos (also called Early Bronze Phase II, 2900-2600 B.C.) is characterized by more solidly built houses of sandstone. There are few remains of buildings dating to this period. Some of the larger houses are designed with rooms surrounding a courtyard. The essential characteristic of architecture at Byblos during this period is the use of wooden posts. Stone bases were placed along the walls of the houses to support the wooden posts which held up the roof. The houses usually contained seven posts. In Proverbs 9.1 one can see an analogy to this type of building even though this passage refers to a much later period:

> WISDOM HAS BUILT HER HOUSE
>
> SHE HAS SET UP HER SEVEN PILLARS.

Six of the wooden posts were placed along opposite walls of the house but never in the corners. The seventh was placed one third of the length on the axis of the house in order to support the ridge pole. The reason for this specific positioning of the seventh post was that the ridge pole, which ran the length of the house, was made from a tree trunk. The tree trunk was naturally thicker at the base and gradually diminished in diameter towards its top. The architect of Byblos at the beginning of the third millenium B.C. had to devise a plan to avoid the danger of the roof collapsing from sheer weight and to prevent the ridge pole from breaking. He estimated no doubt by observation, and trial and error, that the probable breaking point of the ridge pole would be one third of the distance from the weakest part, that is, the top of the tree. He therefore set the seventh post at

15

this point in the room. At a later period (Early Bronze Phase III, 2600-2300 B.C.) the stone bases for wooden posts were placed in the corners of the house.[1]

Byblos was no longer a small rural community. Around 2800 B.C. the foundations for the Temple of Baalat-Gebal were laid. Baalat-Gebal, or Baalat-Gubla, the "Lady of Byblos", was to preside over the city's destiny throughout the succeeding ages. One of the earliest attempts at city planning in world history was now conceived. The city was surrounded by a massive wall for the first time. There were two entrances to the city, the Land Gate and the Sea Gate. At this early stage of city life a narrow winding street led from the center to the outer walls. From this street secondary lanes branched off taking irregular paths among the houses. It is interesting to see that precautions had been taken in laying out streets so that access to the city walls from the center of the city and the residential area would be easy and rapid in case of attack.[2] There was a system of canals to drain off excess rain water. The well at Byblos which was to become the center of activity in the city was already being used to supply water. It is at this point in its history that Byblos emerges as a city of importance. This is the beginning of a period of prosperity, wealth and intense commercial activity.

Contact between Egypt and Byblos during the Protodynastic period (First and Second Egyptian Dynasties, ca. 3200-2800 B.C.) has been well documented. Small Egyptian objects found here such as a gold bead, a bird figurine, two playing pieces and a small ape statuette give ample evidence.[3] Byblos and its relations with the pharaohs of the Old Kingdom can be reconstructed from examination of the artifacts found in the ruins of the Temple of Baalat-Gebal. The first inscription of Egyptian origin is a fragment of diorite with the cartouche of Khasekhemui, the last pharaoh of the Second Dynasty.[4] This fragment was not found *in situ* but in the debris near the temple and was originally part of an offering plate from the pharaoh. The pharaohs of the Second Dynasty undertook expeditions abroad and the inscription of Khasekhemui found here indicates his interest in the city.

During the Old Kingdom military expeditions were sent to Nubia to procure gold and to Sinai to mine copper and turquoise. Egypt enjoyed a period of peace and stability and this was reflected at Byblos. The pharaohs of the Fourth and Fifth Dynasties found it

[1] Dunand, "Rapport préliminaire sur les fouilles de Byblos en 1948", *BMB* IX, 1949-1950, pp. 53-64, especially p. 54. See also Haroutune Y. Kalayan, *L'habitation au Liban* I, Beirut, Syco Press, 1966, pp. 9-10.

[2] *Fouilles de Byblos* I, p. 363.

[3] William A. Ward, "Egypt and the East Mediterranean from Pre-Dynastic Times to the End of the Old Kingdom", *Journal of Economic and Social History of the Orient* VI, 1963, pp. 1-57, especially p. 18.

[4] *Fouilles de Byblos* I, p. 26, No. 1115. See also *Syria* IX, 1928, p. 181.

[5] Pierre Montet, "La IVe dynastie à Byblos", *Kemi* XVI, 1962, pp. 86-89.

[6] *ANET*, p. 227.

expedient to send offerings to the Temple of Baalat-Gebal.[5] Fragments of alabaster jars and plates with the inscriptions of Cheops, Khephren, Mycerinus, Unas and Sahura were found in the excavations. What inspired the interest of the pharaohs of the Old Kingdom in the temple of a city goddess of a distant land? What caused Byblos to develop from an obscure settlement on the coast of Canaan at the beginning of the Early Bronze Age into a prosperous city protected by walls? The answer lies in an inscription on the Palermo Stone found in Egypt. During the reign of Senefru, a pharaoh of the Fourth Dynasty (ca. 2650-2600 B.C.) an important shipment of cedar wood was sent to Egypt from Byblos. The inscription shows the use to which the timber was put:[6]

> BRINGING FORTY SHIPS FILLED (WITH) CEDAR LOGS
> SHIPBUILDING (OF) CEDARWOOD,
> ONE "PRAISE-OF-THE-TWO-LANDS" SHIP 100 CUBITS (LONG)
> AND OF MERU-WOOD; TWO SHIPS, 100 CUBITS (LONG)
> MAKING THE DOORS OF THE ROYAL PALACE (OF) CEDARWOOD.

The pharaohs of the Old Kingdom needed the timber essential for shipbuilding, tomb construction and funerary ritual. Although Egypt had trees such as the acacia and the dum palm which could be used for building houses and boats, it was not suitable for long wooden beams. Only the coniferous trees from the mountains of Lebanon could provide Egypt with this. Egypt also used wood products such as cedar oil in mummification. This provided a strong religious motivation for maintaining trade with Byblos.

Transport of timber to Egypt was safer by sea than by land since the desert was a greater barrier than the sea. The Sinai peninsula and southern Palestine were infested with nomads who harassed overland caravans to Egypt. Several expeditions were undertaken by pharaohs of the Fifth and Sixth Dynasties against these elusive tribes though they were only partially successful.[7] Thus the port of Byblos flourished as the center of the timber trade.

[7] *ANET*, p. 227. An inscription at Abydos in the tomb of Uni, an official of the Sixth Dynasty, records his activities as a military commander against the Asiatics under Pepi I.

The Temple of Baalat-Gebal and the Early Bronze Age Temple

The Temple of Baalat-Gebal was built ca. 2800 B.C. It is the first example of monumental architecture in Phoenicia and went through several architectural stages of construction *(Fig. 12 and 14)*.

17

The earliest foundations (called *Bâtiment 40* by Dunand) are contemporary to the reign of Djoser (Third Dynasty). A later architectural stage is contemporary to the Sixth Dynasty; a still later stage corresponds to the period covered by the Middle Kingdom. A description of the successive stages this temple underwent would require a study in itself. It suffices to say that from the Early Bronze Age through the Roman period the temple was in use.

There are two pieces of evidence which illustrate that over a period of two millenia Baalat-Gebal was represented in art in a manner similar to the Egyptian Hathor-Isis. The first, a cylinder seal of a ruler of Byblos of the third millenium B.C. which Montet has dated to the early Memphite period (Third Dynasty), was found in the foundations of the temple. In addition to the inscription in hieroglyphic there are the figures of a god and goddess on the seal. The goddess, who appears to be Baalat-Gebal, is represented as the Egyptian Hathor-Isis. She is garbed in a long narrow tunic, on her head is the solar disc and cow's horns. The god is referred to as *Khau-ta* of the country of Negau *(Fig. 15)*.[8] The date of the cylinder seal and the reading of the inscription have been discussed at length. H. Goedicke places this seal in the reign of Unas (Fifth Dynasty), basing his view on the form of the signs in the inscription.[9] Nevertheless, it is the earliest representation in art of Baalat-Gebal or her Egyptian counterpart Hathor-Isis found at Byblos. The second piece of evidence is the stele of Yehawmilk (fifth century B.C.). The inscription in Phoenician letters states that Yehawmilk, king of Byblos, built a portico with columns for the temple, an altar of bronze and offered objects of gold to the goddess. At the top of the stele there are the figures of the goddess of Byblos and the king. Baalat-Gebal is seated on a throne wearing a tunic like the Egyptian Hathor-Isis. On her head is a mortar on which is set the solar disc and cow's horns. The goddess is holding a staff with a lotus flower in her left hand. Her right hand is raised in an attitude of blessing. The king of Byblos is wearing a long tunic and tiara in the Persian fashion. His left hand is raised in salutation, in his right hand he holds a libation bowl *(Fig. 104)*.[10] During the fifth century B.C. at the height of Persian influence in the Near East Baalat-Gebal retained her traditional Egyptian characteristics.

There are few architectural remains seen today to illustrate the successive stages of construction the Temple of Baalat-Gebal

[8] Pierre Montet, "Le pays de Negaou près de Byblos et son dieu", *Syria* IV, 1923, p. 181. See also *Byblos et l'Egypte*, pp. 62-68.

[9] Hans Goedicke, "A Cylinder Seal of a Ruler of Byblos of the Third Millenium", *Mitteilungen des Deutchen Archäeologischen Instituts Abteilung Kairo* XIX, 1963, pp. 1-5. On this reading see *BASOR*, No. 176, 1964, pp. 44 ff. Albright suggests: "ruler of the land of Byblos named Hasrurūm (?) son of Rūm." Goedicke, "The Cylinder Seal of a Ruler of Byblos Reconsidered", *Journal of the American Research Center in Egypt* V, 1966, pp. 19-21 now reads the name: "Ba'alat-rūm's son . . . rūm, the chief of the (foreign) land of Byblos, given life eternally, beloved by the foreign-sun-(god), Ba'alat and *Khau-ta*.

[10] *Byblos et l'Egypte*, pp. 41-44.

11 *Byblos et l'Egypte,* p. 68,
No. 45; p. 69, No. 46; pp.
70-74, Nos. 47-51, 56, 57
and 62.

12 *Byblos et l'Egypte,* pp.
111-125. For a study of the
"Montet jar" see O. Tuf-
nell and W.A. Ward, "Relations between Byblos, Egypt
and Mesopotamia at the
End of the Third Millenium
B.C.", *Syria* XLIII, 1966,
pp. 165-241. See also Kathleen M. Kenyon, *Amorites
and Canaanites,* London,
Oxford University Press,
1966, pp. 48-50.

underwent after its founding. There is evidence that the temple was destroyed by fire during the Amorite invasions (2300-2100 B.C.). It was rebuilt and repaired during successive periods by the kings of Byblos. The Romans at the time of building their temple levelled off the ruins of the building. They covered up the floors with large flagstones and thus inadvertently sealed off for posterity important artifacts of the Early and Middle Bronze Ages which lay buried in the debris and ashes of the older stages of the temple. When Montet removed the flagstones of the "Syrian" temple (*Bâtiment* II) he came across a variety of objects lying loose in the sand over the ash layer of the Early Bronze Age stage of the temple. Fragments of stone vases bearing the names in hieroglyphic characters of pharaohs of the Old Kingdom are evidence of their respect for this particular temple. Fragments of alabaster with the cartouches of Mycerinus (Fourth Dynasty), of Unas (Fifth Dynasty) and several fragments of two Sixth Dynasty pharaohs, Pepi I and Pepi II were found *(Figs. 17 and 18).*[11] Other objects of interest were beads, scarabs, bronze scissors and a variety of bronze, stone and ivory statuettes of human figures and animals. During his second campaign Montet unearthed a large painted pottery jar with its lid in place buried upright in the sand about one meter below the flagstones of the "Syrian" temple. The lid of the jar has an applied loop handle consisting of a roll of clay with one end modelled into the head of a snake. The "Montet jar" is made of red ware and contains both light and dark grits of uneven size. The decoration consists of roughly drawn hatched chevrons in red paint on the shoulder of the jar with a series of painted bands below interrupted in two places by wavy lines. This closed deposit from Byblos has yielded nearly a thousand objects. The "Montet jar" contained a large number of seals, seal amulets, scarabs, cylinder seals, pendants, baboon figurines and bronze ornaments. Over forty bronze and silver torques were found in the jar. The metal bar was bent to shape by beating and hammering and the two ends were flattened and then curled. More than forty complete pierced toggle pins with expanded heads were also found in the jar *(Figs. 34 and 35).* Of interest is the fact that the "Montet jar" which is now dated around 2130-2040 B.C. contained a variety of objects dating to an earlier period.[12] Could this be considered as evidence that the priests of the Temple of Baalat-Gebal buried valuables in earthenware jars as part of the temple

treasures? The excavations of Montet and Dunand turned up about forty deposits composed of thousands of metal figurines, jewelry, weapons and other cult objects. The majority of these were found in sealed pottery vessels. The deposits were found mainly in four areas: in the foundations of the "Syrian" temple, under the floors of the *pro-cella* of the Temple of the Obelisks and in two areas called by Dunand *Champ des offrandes* and *Enceinte sacrée*. Dunand believes that the deposits in the *Champ des offrandes* were connected with a temple that may have been built at the end of the Early Bronze Age and was used during the Middle Bronze Age. No attempt was made by Dunand to restore this temple due to the scarcity of architectural remains. The deposits were found in the ruins of a rectangular *cella* and courtyard *(Fig. 71)*. The custom of concealing valuables is known from other places in the ancient Near East, such as Ugarit, Mari and Tod.[13] This suggests that at Byblos assemblages of deposits were buried for the sake of hiding them.

[13] Ora Neghbi and S. Moskowitz, "The Foundation Deposits or Offering Deposits of Byblos", *BASOR*, No. 184, 1966, pp. 21-26.

There are a total of thirty-six inscriptions from Byblos bearing the names of Pepi I and Pepi II (Sixth Dynasty), the last pharaohs of the Old Kingdom to honor the Temple of Baalat-Gebal. A deposit of ash 0.50 m. thick lay over the floor of the Early Bronze Age temple and several inscriptions of Pepi II were found in the burnt material. The American University of Beirut Museum possesses several fragments of alabaster with Egyptian royal inscriptions. As these were acquired by purchase the exact location on the site of Byblos at which the fragments were found cannot be determined. Eight of them bear the cartouches of Pepi I and two of them display the name of Pepi II.[14]

[14] Harold H. Nelson, "Fragments of Egyptian Old Kingdom Stone Vases from Byblos", *Berytus* I, 1934, pp. 19-22.

Royal inscriptions of the tenth century B.C. relate how the kings of Byblos made repairs to the temple or dedicated statues to Baalat-Gebal. Yehimilk (950 B.C.) states that he restored the ruins of the temples of Baalat-Gebal and Baal-shamen. Abibaal (ca. 925 B.C.) inscribed a dedication to Baalat-Gebal on the statue of Pharaoh Sheshonk I. Elibaal (ca. 915 B.C.) inscribed a dedication to the goddess on a statue of Osorkon I. At the end of the tenth century B.C. Shipit-Baal built a wall in the temple dedicated to this goddess.[15]

[15] William F. Albright, "The Phoenician Inscriptions of the Tenth Century B.C. from Byblus", *JAOS* LXVII, 1947, pp. 155-158.

A large building complex of the Early Bronze Age was erected ca. 2600 B.C. facing the Temple of Baalat-Gebal and separated from it by the sacred lake *(Fig. 25)*. This temple called by Dunand *Temple en L* consists of two separate units and a court arranged

roughly in the shape of an L, lying in an east-west direction. The temple may have been dedicated to a male deity although no inscriptions have been found to substantiate this. The walls of the building are well built and consist of two marginal rows of large stones filled with smaller stones. The sanctuary, a small *cella,* is flanked by smaller rooms on either side *(Fig. 27).* It is built more or less in the center of the sacred court. A small obelisk was discovered leaning against the south wall of the *cella.* The inner room of the temple contains eight rectangular stone bases for wooden posts, one in each corner and three along the walls. The eighth stone base held the post which carried the main weight of the ridge pole. Similar stone bases for posts to support the wooden superstructure were discovered in all the rooms of the temple. The stone base for wooden posts was a characteristic of the architecture of the period. The *cella* and some of the rooms are paved with flagstones. The walls were originally covered with a crushed limestone plaster.

The use to which the north-eastern building was put is not certain. One of the rooms may have been the quarters of the high priest. Dunand believes that this building was part of the temple proper and that ritual sacrifices were performed here since four clay vessels set firmly in a ledge nearby could have been used to hold water *(Fig. 28).* The eastern room of this building was incorporated during the Middle Bronze Age into the Temple of the Obelisks. According to Dunand it became a "jewelers' workshop" associated with the temple proper. The Temple of the Obelisks was built over this temple and during the excavations had to be removed and rebuilt some distance away. As attested by a thick layer of ash the entire building complex of the Early Bronze Age was destroyed by a vast conflagration at the time of the Amorite invasions.[16]

The period ca. 2300-1900 B.C. was an era of chaos and disorder along the coastal area. A wave of new peoples, the Amorites according to Dunand, invaded Canaan and destroyed cities as they proceeded north. Byblos, like every city in Palestine, was destroyed by fire. It was also an age of troubles in Egypt. The period from the Seventh through the Tenth Dynasties saw a continual inner struggle for power. The country was divided into nomes, or provinces, and the nomarchs openly waged war against eachother. There was no central authority. Nubia became independent of Egyptian control. The quarries of Sinai were closed due to raids of nomadic tribes.

[16] *Fouilles de Byblos* II, Part 2, pp. 896-897 for plan of Early Bronze Age temple.

After the reign of Pepi II (end of the Sixth Dynasty) and until the Twelfth Dynasty, no royal Egyptian inscriptions have been found at Byblos. It would appear that during this period of confusion commercial relations between Egypt and Byblos were almost at a standstill.

According to Schaeffer during the period following the Amorite invasions and before the beginning of the Twelfth Dynasty (Middle Kingdom), a new people arrived in the Near East. They came from Anatolia and it is believed that they may have had some connection with the Hurrians. The newcomers were skilled in the art of metallurgy and introduced new techniques in that craft. They are identified by metal torques worn around the neck, toggle pins with an expanded head and pierced near the top, bi-conical bronze beads, socketed lance heads and crescent shaped socketed axe heads. These people, referred to as the "Torque Wearers" had a profound impression at Byblos.[17] All the metal articles mentioned above have been found here as well as in Ugarit *(Figs. 34 and 35)*. The large amount of gold and silver jewelry found in the royal tombs of the kings of Byblos of the Middle Bronze Age and the variety of bronze figurines, daggers, arms and fenestrated axes unearthed in the foundations of the Temple of the Obelisks are ample evidence that the artisans of Byblos had developed new techniques. Schaeffer believes that in addition to the timber trade, metallurgy formed an important part of the city's economy at this period.[18]

During the reign of Nebḥepetre Mentuḥotpe, a pharaoh of the Eleventh Dynasty (2134-1991 B.C.), there is a record of an Egyptian expedition to the Lebanon to cut cedar trees. The inscription, which is fragmentary, is on the funerary stele of the pharaoh's chief steward, Henenu: "(I) re(ached land bringing cedar) wood (of) the Plateau of Cedar."[19] From Egyptian records of a later date, it is firmly established that the phrase "Plateau of Cedar" refers to Lebanon, indicating that, in the Egyptian mind, the two terms were synonymous.

The name of a king of Byblos appears on a cuneiform text at the end of the third millenium B.C. and adds to our knowledge of relations between Mesopotamia and Byblos during the Third Dynasty of Ur period. An economic text in the Drehem archives lists among other rulers, "Ibdâdî, the *Ensi* of Byblos" contemporary with Amar-Suen of the Third Dynasty of Ur (ca. 2050 B.C.). This

[17] H. Hubert, "De quelques objets de bronze trouvés à Byblos", *Syria* VI, 1925, pp. 16-29. See also *Fouilles de Byblos* II, Part 2, p. 699. For a full discussion see Claude Schaeffer, *Ugaritica* II, Paris, Librairie Orientaliste Paul Geuthner, 1949, pp. 49-120.

[18] Schaeffer, *Ugaritica* II, p. 67.

[19] William C. Hayes, "Career of the Great Steward Henenu under Nebḥepetre Mentuḥotpe", *JEA* XXXV, 1949, pp. 43-49.

[20] E. Sollberger, "Byblos sous les rois d'Ur", *Archiv für Orientforschung* XIX, 1959-1960, pp. 120-122. On this reading of the name, see W.F. Albright, *BASOR* No. 163, 1961, p. 45, n. 44. See also W.A. Ward, "Relations Between Egypt and Mesopotamia from Prehistoric Times to the End of the Middle Kingdom", *Journal of Economic and Social History of the Orient* VII, Part 2, 1964, pp. 129-130.

is the earliest reference to Byblos in cuneiform sources. The title used for the king of Byblos in this text has given rise to the belief that Byblos was part of an Ur III "Empire". The title *Ensi* (ruler) is used in Sumerian texts of this period for independent rulers as well as for rulers who belonged to the Third Dynasty of Ur Empire.[20]

Sphinx covered in gold leaf from the Temple of the Obelisks
(the sphinx measures eight centimeters in length)

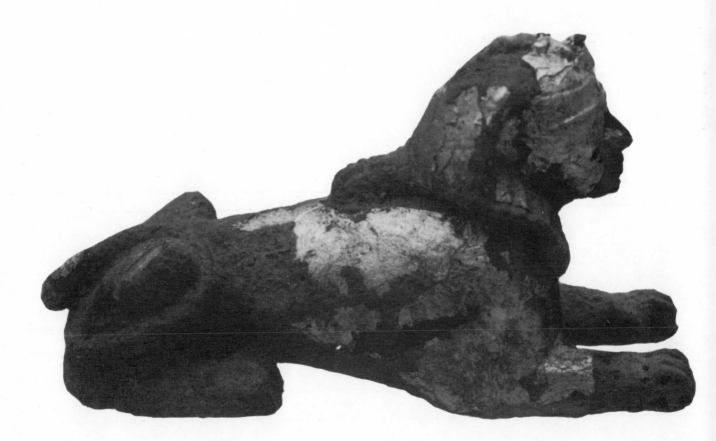

4   The Middle Bronze Age
(1900-1600 B.C.)

Byblos and the Egyptian Middle Kingdom

This period is well represented at Byblos. The excavation of the royal necropolis by Montet and the discovery by Dunand of an important temple of the Middle Bronze Age, the Temple of the Obelisks, have added to our knowledge of the material culture and the political and economic history of the city during the early second millenium B.C. Once again, after a period of nearly two hundred years, Byblos resumed close ties with Egypt although trade had never completely ceased. We have in our possession Egyptian sources which throw light on this period, namely the Si-nuhe chronicle and the Execration Texts (see pp. 39-41).

The Middle Bronze Age was a period of peace and prosperity in the Near East and this was reflected at Byblos. From an examination of the variety of objects found here, it can be seen that Byblos enjoyed extensive trade relations with Egypt and neighboring countries. The presence of a complete Kamaris pot and a few Kamaris potsherds show that trade relations existed with Crete at this time.[1]

Many royal inscriptions of the Twelfth Dynasty (1991-1786 B.C.) have been found at Byblos. Dunand discovered a small limestone fragment on which is engraved the figure of Isis seated on a low-backed seat and the cartouche of Sen-usert I, a bone cylinder inscribed with the name of Amenemhat II and a white spherical paste bead with the cartouche of Amenemhat III which had been used as an amulet.[2] In Tomb I of the royal necropolis, an obsidian vase in a setting of gold was found inscribed with the throne name of Amenemhat III.[3] In Tomb II an obsidian box with gold

[1] Dimitri C. Baramki, *The Archaeological Museum of the American University of Beirut,* Centennial Publications, Beirut, Société d'Impression et d'Édition Libanaise, 1967, Plate III.

[2] *Fouilles de Byblos* II, Part 1, pp. 196-197, No. 8503; *Fouilles de Byblos* I, p. 104, No. 1551; p. 185, No. 2905.

[3] *Byblos et l'Egypte*, p. 155, No. 610.

25

ornamentation was found with the throne name of Amenemhat IV inscribed on the lid.[4] Another inscription of Amenemhat IV was found in Tomb II on the lid of a grey stone vase.[5]

[4] *Byblos et l'Egypte*, p. 157, No. 611.

[5] *Byblos et l'Egypte*, p. 159, No. 614.

The Royal Necropolis of the Kings of Byblos

On February 16, 1922 a landslide on the steep shore side of Byblos ripped open a rock-cut tomb at a depth of twelve meters from the surface. The burial chamber contained a white stone sarcophagus with a broken lid *(Fig. 37)*.[6] This was indeed a case of nature coming to the aid of science and led to the discovery of a total of nine royal tombs. Tombs I, II and III had not been violated in antiquity. Tomb IV, at the time of excavation, appeared to be protected by a covering of flagstones but had been looted in more recent times. At the bottom of the sarcophagus in the burial chamber fragments of school paper were found with a few words in English and the date 1851. Tombs V-IX had been violated in antiquity.[7] The tombs consist of wide, square or rectangular shafts cut into the rock. Each shaft was covered with flagstone pavement and filled with earth, stone and ash. At the bottom of the vertical shaft a burial chamber was cut to one side where the sarcophagus and the funerary offerings were placed. After the burial a wall was built which divided the chamber from the shaft though this did not deter tomb robbers. Invariably, a tunnel was dug into the chambers through the layers of red clay under the rock. Since most of the looted tombs had been dug in the clay stratum, the overhanging rock forming the roof of the burial chamber was no protection against thieves.

Tombs I, II, III and IV belong to the period corresponding to the Egyptian Twelfth Dynasty (Middle Kingdom). A subterranean passage linked Tombs I and II. Tombs III and IV were separated by a wall of rock but were of the same type of construction. In Tomb I the sarcophagus was found in the center of the chamber with gifts for the dead inside and on top of the lid *(Figs. 38 and 39)*. Other objects such as pottery and bronze vessels were spread around the sarcophagus on the ground and against the walls. The skeletons of Tomb I consisted of a man and remnants of bones of several animals which were probably food offerings to the dead.[8] Tomb I also contained rich funerary gifts from the Egyptian Pharaoh

[6] Charles Virolleaud, "Découverte à Byblos d'un hypogée de la XIIe dynastie égyptienne", *Syria* III, 1922, pp. 273-290.

[7] P. Montet, "Un Égyptien, roi de Byblos, sous la XIIe dynastie", *Syria* VIII, 1927, p. 85.

[8] *Byblos et l'Egypte*, pp. 155-204 for full discussion of tombs I-IV. See also René Dussaud, "Les quatre campagnes de M. Pierre Montet à Byblos", *Syria* XI, 1930, pp. 164-187.

Amenemhat III. In the sarcophagus various precious articles were found including the obsidian vase of Amenemhat III *(Fig. 43)*. This vase contained perfume or incense, according to its hieroglyphic inscription. There were also found, among other objects, a silver mirror, a pair of silver sandals and a silver "tea pot" with a triangular beak provided with a strainer. This silver "tea pot" is similar to a receptacle found in the connecting Tomb II *(Figs. 40 and 41)*. The receptacle in Tomb II has a lid formed of a lotus flower resting on its opened leaves. These two pieces of silver-work indicate a high degree of perfection in craftsmanship. Nothing similar has been found in Egypt. Montet believes that the silver "tea pots" were made in Byblos. He bases his argument on the fact that during the Empire Egyptian wall paintings represent vases of equal artistic perfection as part of the booty brought home by pharaohs from expeditions into Syria.[9] Several bronze tridents were found in the tomb and appear to have had a double function in a manner similar to the early mace-heads. It is possible that they were used as a symbol of power and at the same time as a weapon *(Figs. 42 and 44)*.[10]

In Tomb II Montet found, in addition to the silver "tea pot", a gold pectoral set with inlaid polished stones on which is seen a falcon with extended wings and two representations of a pharaoh wearing the white crown of Upper Egypt *(Fig. 50)*. Also were found a box with gold ornamentation on which was inscribed the throne name of Amenemhat IV accompanied by his titles and a grey stone vase with an inscription of Amenemhat IV *(Figs. 47 and 48)*. The vase had been repaired in antiquity. The name of the occupant of Tomb II is known from a gold and bronze scimitar of the *harpé* type inscribed with the name of Ibshemuabi *(Fig. 55)*. The hieroglyphic inscription on the scimitar reads as follows:[11]

THE COUNT OF BYBLOS, IBSHEMUABI, WHO REPEATS LIFE, SON OF THE COUNT, ABISHEMU, THE TRIUMPHANT.

Ties between Egypt and Byblos were so close at the end of the Middle Kingdom that princes of Byblos used Egyptian hieroglyphic inscriptions and the Egyptian title *haty-a* "Count" which in Egypt was a title conferred by the pharaoh.[12] As Tomb II is connected with Tomb I by a subterranean passage, as was customary in the burials of fathers and sons, it can be accepted that Tomb I belonged to the father, Abishemu and Tomb II to the son, Ibshemuabi.

[9] *Byblos et l'Egypte*, p. 191. See also Helene Kantor, *The Aegean and the Orient in the Second Millenium B.C.*, Bloomington, Indiana, Principia Press, 1947, p. 20 with notes. Miss Kantor emphasizes the Aegean connections of these "tea pots".

[10] *Byblos et l'Egypte*, p. 96. Montet makes an analogy to the weapon seen on bas-relief from Zendjirli, Figure 43.

[11] *Byblos et l'Egypte*, p. 174, No. 653; *ANET*, p. 229 and n. 5; W.F. Albright, *The Vocalization of the Egyptian Syllabic Orthography*, New Haven, 1934, suggests the readings Yapashemu-abi and Abi-shemu for the two names.

[12] *ANET*, p. 229.

In Tomb II there was no stone sarcophagus. From the disorderly position in which the objects were found it is presumed that the sarcophagus was possibly made of wood and had broken down in the process of decay. In addition to a number of precious articles such as a silver mirror *(Fig. 46)*, a gold bowl and a gold necklace *(Figs. 53 and 54)*, there was also found a gold pendant set with precious stones *(Fig. 49)*. On top of the pendant a scarab is set between two uraei, the one to the right wears the white crown of Upper Egypt, the one to the left wears the red crown of Lower Egypt. Under the scarab is a cartouche in a horizontal position on which is engraved the name of Ibshemuabi, preceded by the title "Prince of *Kpn*" (Gubla).[13] Under the cartouche there is a falcon with extended wings holding a ring in each claw.

The floor of the burial chamber of Tomb III was paved and walls had been built to cover the crude rock. It did not contain a stone sarcophagus. The remains of two skeletons were discovered. A pectoral in gold in the form of a falcon with extended wings was found *(Fig. 62)*. The very thin gold leaf of which it was made indicates that it must have been overlaid on bone or wood which has not been preserved.

Tomb IV was cut out of the solid rock and at first sight Montet believed that it had not been violated. At the bottom of the sarcophagus, placed parallel to the entrance of the chamber, fragments of paper were found with the date 1851. The sarcophagus had no lid. Two fragments of an alabaster vase with a hieroglyphic inscription were discovered. The inscription was of particular interest to Montet because it led him to believe that he could identify the origin of two scarabs which were part of the LeClerq collection in the Louvre.[14] He believed that the two scarabs came from Byblos and had some connection with this royal burial. He concluded that the occupant of Tomb IV was an Egyptian who had reigned at Byblos during the Twelfth Dynasty. This theory has now been discarded by Montet.[15] No royal inscriptions of Egyptian pharaohs were found in Tombs III and IV.

In 1925 an antique dealer in Jerusalem came into possession of a collection of sixty-seven precious objects which, it is now believed, came originally from Byblos. This collection was then sold to the Oriental Institute of the University of Chicago who agreed to return the treasure to its country of origin. Eventually

[13] *Byblos et l'Egypte*, p. 165, No. 618.

[14] P. Montet, "Un Égyptien, roi de Byblos, sous la XIIᵉ dynastie", *Syria* VIII, 1927, pp. 85-92.

[15] Pierre Montet, "Dépôts d'offrandes à Byblos et à Tod", *Kemi* XVI, 1962, p. 93 and n. 1. See W.F. Albright, "Remarks on the Chronology of Early Bronze IV-Middle Bronze IIA in Phoenicia and Syria-Palestine", *BASOR*, No. 184, 1966, p. 29. Albright believes the occupant of Tomb IV was Prince Inten of Byblos, contemporary with Zimri-Lim of Mari (ca. 1730-1700 B.C.) and Neferhotep I, a pharaoh of the Thirteenth Dynasty.

[16] Maurice Chehab, "Un trésor d'orfèvrerie syro-égyptien", *BMB* I, 1937, pp. 7-21.

[17] P. Montet, *Kemi* XVI, 1962, pp. 92-94.

the Lebanese government bought the collection which is now in the Beirut National Museum.[16] As Tomb IV was violated during the nineteenth century it is possible that several of these artifacts came originally from the burial chamber. However it is difficult to believe that these articles would be sold seventy-five years after discovery. Montet suggests another possibility and concludes that these objects came from Byblos. He believes that during the period between the end of his excavations in January 1925 and the beginning of Dunand's campaigns in 1926 clandestine excavators may have found these precious objects in the region of the temples. Of interest is a gold pectoral on which there are two representations of the Egyptian goddess Hathor in the form of a cow with the solar disc between her horns *(Fig. 61)*.[17] The king is represented in the form of a child who is caressing the neck of the goddess and at the same time is kneeling and drinking her milk. Other objects of value in the collection are gold cow's hooves, gold pins, a faience vase in a gold setting, rings and bracelets.

Objects found in Tombs I, II, III and IV included plaquettes of ivory, faience, silver and bronze cups, plates, spoons, knives wrought of precious metal, carved animal heads used as handles for mirrors, rings and bracelets, pins and scissors of bronze, and alabaster vases. In addition to the inscriptions from these tombs a large quantity of Middle Bronze Age pottery, important for dating, places these tombs in the period corresponding to the Egyptian Middle Kingdom.

Tomb V is the most important royal tomb at Byblos. Three sarcophagi were discovered in the burial chamber: two plain ones with one and two tenons, respectively, and the sarcophagus of Ahiram which is strikingly different from any other found at this site. The sarcophagi of the royal necropolis are generally made of white limestone, polished inside and out with no sculptured reliefs or inscriptions. Ahiram's sarcophagus is richly carved. Tenons on the lids of sarcophagi at Byblos had a functional purpose. Long ropes were tied around the tenons, long enough to allow several turnings of the rope, so that the lid could be lowered into the shaft after the body was laid in the sarcophagus for burial.

During the excavation of the tomb of Ahiram potsherds, dated to the Late Bronze II and Early Iron Ages, were found in great number mixed with the earth in the upper part of the tomb shaft.

29

When this rubble was removed a short Phoenician inscription on the southern wall of the shaft was brought to light. The graffito on the wall of the shaft reads:[18]

[18] W.F. Albright, *JAOS* LXVII, 1947, p. 156.

> ATTENTION! BEHOLD, THOU SHALT COME TO GRIEF BELOW HERE!

Slightly below the inscription in the western and eastern sides of the shaft there were niches which had probably supported wooden beams carrying a second protective "roof" *(Fig. 93)*. It would appear that the builders of the tomb felt that the body of the king did not have sufficient protection. The flagstones which sealed off the opening of the shaft and the wall built to close the burial chamber were not adequate. For this reason a wooden "roof" was added to serve as a third obstacle for tomb robbers.

Below the niches no more potsherds were found in the debris of the shaft. At the bottom near the entrance to the burial chamber, several fragments of alabaster were found. One fragment bore the name and titles of Rameses II (1314-1292 B.C.). The wall at the entrance of the burial chamber had partially fallen in. The chamber itself was in disorder and was half-full of mud. A huge block of stone had fallen from the roof. The lid of the sarcophagus had been displaced. On the edge of the lid blocks of stone had been set up one on top of the other by the tomb robbers. Fearing the roof would collapse on their heads, the robbers took the precaution of removing stones from the wall at the entrance and setting them up on the lid to support the roof *(Fig. 92)*.[19]

[19] *Byblos et l'Egypte*, pp. 215-238.

After clearing out the mud from the burial chamber two other stone sarcophagi were found. They had been looted in antiquity and only contained the remnants of bones. The sarcophagus at the farther end of the chamber had its lid displaced; the second sarcophagus had its cover broken.

The sarcophagus of Ahiram is borne by four crouching lions. On the lid of the sarcophagus the tenons are formed by the protruding heads of two lions which are sculptured in low relief *(Fig. 96)*. On one side of the sarcophagus King Ahiram is represented seated on a throne guarded by winged sphinxes *(Fig. 94)*. In his left hand he holds a lotus flower. In front of him is a rich offering table towards which seven courtiers advance. The two ends of the sarcophagus have sculptured reliefs of four women; two beat their

breasts and two lift their arms above their heads in an attitude of grief *(Fig. 97)*. The other side depicts a procession of persons carrying offerings: two women with baskets on their heads, followed by two men carrying jugs on their shoulders. Then comes a man leading a sacrificial goat and finally three persons with hands lifted in salutation or grief *(Fig. 95)*. Above these reliefs there is a frieze of lotus flowers, alternately opened and closed, which shows strong Egyptian influence. Beneath the lotus flower motif there is a rope design running all around the sarcophagus which is of Syrian inspiration. The lions bearing the sarcophagus and the beasts on the lid betray Syrian influence and have no Egyptian prototypes. These Syrian motifs are found at Zendjirli on stelae and bas-reliefs. The scene on the Ahiram sarcophagus has many Egyptian analogies as well as north Syrian.[20] The "lotus-and-bud" pattern though originally Egyptian, has already been seen at Byblos on a vase fragment found by Montet.[21] It shows the lotus and bud linked with curving loops. By the time of the sarcophagus of Ahiram, the Phoenician form of the motif had been fully established. The sarcophagus illustrates another characteristic Phoenician motif adapted originally from Egyptian funerary art. This is the "procession to a seated figure".[22] The artisans of Byblos borrowed freely from Egypt and Mesopotamia but retained their own method of execution. Thanks to their imaginative faculties they created new combinations and styles from older designs.

The inscription on the lid of the sarcophagus is of utmost importance because it is the earliest form of the Phoenician alphabetic script yet to be discovered. It reads:[23]

> THE COFFIN WHICH (IT)TOBAAL, SON OF AHIRAM, KING OF BYBLOS, MADE FOR HIS FATHER AS HIS AB(O)DE IN ETERNITY. AND IF ANY KING OR ANY GOVERNOR OR ANY ARMY COMMANDER ATTACKS BYBLOS AND EXPOSES THIS COFFIN, LET HIS JUDICIAL SCEPTER BE BROKEN, LET HIS ROYAL THRONE BE OVERTHROWN, AND LET PEACE FLEE FROM BYBLOS; AND AS FOR HIM, LET A VAGABOND (?) EFFACE HIS INSCRIPTION (S)!

Ironically the graffito on the wall of the shaft and the inscription on the sarcophagus did not serve their purpose. Robbers entered the tomb by a passage dug into the clay stratum and looted the tomb in antiquity.

[20] R.D. Barnett, *A Catalogue of the Nimrud Ivories*, London, The Trustees of the British Museum, 1957, pp. 31-62. This chapter gives a summary on the origins and development of Syrian and Phoenician art.

[21] *Byblos et l'Egypte*, Atlas, Plate CXLVIII, Fig. 918. This vase fragment was found in a tomb of an individual and has been dated to the Middle Bronze Age.

[22] *A Catalogue of the Nimrud Ivories*, p. 57.

[23] W.F. Albright, *JAOS* LXVII, 1947, pp. 155-156.

There is scholarly disagreement over the dating of the Ahiram inscription. Briefly, the archaeological evidence supporting the opposing points of view is as follows. The discovery in 1868 of the Moabite stone with the inscription of King Mesha (2 Kings 3.4-27) confirmed the existence of a North Semitic alphabetic script in the middle of the ninth century B.C. Then came the discovery by Montet of the sarcophagus of Ahiram with an alphabetic text in this script. According to David Diringer, Director of the Alphabet Museum and Seminar at Cambridge University, it now seems reasonably certain that the sarcophagus can be placed in the eleventh century B.C.[24] Other North Semitic inscriptions have been discovered which belong to a slightly earlier or later period. Of these, three come from Byblos — the Yehimilk inscription according to Diringer can be placed in the eleventh century B.C., and the Abibaal and Elibaal inscriptions in the tenth century B.C. From an examination of the Byblian inscriptions, the Gezer calendar (1000 B.C.) and the Roueisseh spearhead inscription (eleventh to tenth century B.C.) it is apparent that there existed in the last centuries of the second millenium B.C. an early form of alphabetic writing consisting of twenty-two symbols written uniformly from right to left. This consonantal writing is now regarded as the direct ancestor of the Phoenician, Moabite, Hebrew, Aramaic and Greek scripts.

[24] David Diringer, *Writing*, London, Thames and Hudson, 1962, pp. 114-121 for a full discussion.

Pottery was found in Ahiram's tomb belonging to the second phase of the late Bronze Age (1400-1200 B.C.), such as fragments of Cypriote "milk-bowls" and other vessels and jugs with concentric circles. A fragment of an ivory plaque decorated with the figure of a bull being attacked by a griffin and a lion, betraying Mycenaean influence, was found at the bottom of the shaft *(Fig. 100)*. Two fragments of alabaster with the cartouche of Rameses II, one found in the shaft and one in the chamber, were also considered as evidence, in addition to the pottery finds, to date this tomb to the thirteenth century B.C. *(Figs. 98-99)*. Several scholars, including W.F. Albright, have contested this date basing their arguments on a comparison with the royal inscription of Abibaal, king of Byblos on a fragment of what appeared to be a seated statue of Sheshonk I (945-924 B.C.). The script of the Ahiram and Abibaal inscriptions is so nearly identical that it seemed quite evident to Albright that both fall within the tenth century B.C., the sarcophagus of Ahiram belonging to the beginning of the century.[25] The vase fragments bearing the cartouche

[25] W.F. Albright, *JAOS* LXVII, 1947, p. 154.

of Rameses II and the potsherds of the Late Bronze Age Phase II then would have to be considered as fragments of older debris. This is understandable at Byblos where digging and exploitation of the site within the ancient city walls have been carried out continuously for many centuries. An inscription of Rameses II was found near the colossi in the temple of the Roman period. Another inscription of this pharaoh was incorporated in the wall of a building of the Byzantine period. At Byblos many objects have not been found *in situ*. Tomb I was discovered in the royal necropolis as a result of the landslide in 1922 after torrential rain. Due to the landslide, the shaft of Tomb II had been emptied from below resulting in considerable disturbance of the stratification in the shaft. Montet attributed the presence of Roman glass in Tomb II, as well as bricks belonging to the Roman baths, to the disturbance of the levels. Part of the baths once covered the tomb of Ahiram unknown to the Romans at that period. In addition, the two plain sarcophagi in the burial chamber of Ahiram belong to an earlier period, making the problem of dating more complex.

Another group of scholars date the sarcophagus to the thirteenth or twelfth century B.C. basing their conclusion primarily on artistic evidence. The features and the dress of the figures on the sarcophagus resemble drawings of Asiatics seen in Egypt in Eighteenth Dynasty tombs. The "lotus-and-bud" motif is of Egyptian origin. The sarcophagus is borne by lions which is a characteristic of Syro-Hittite sculpture. Phoenician art was a composite art directly influenced by political trends in the Near East. The thirteenth century B.C. was a period when Egyptian and Hittite influences were at a height in this area. Emir Maurice Chehab, Director General of Antiquities of Lebanon, has expressed the following point of view.[26] Both Egyptian and Hittite influences are seen on the sculptured reliefs of the sarcophagus. The presence in Ahiram's tomb of vase fragments with the inscription of Rameses II and an ivory fragment of Mycenaean origin is evidence, in addition to other reasons, which support this view. Emir Maurice Chehab will publish a full study on the date of the sarcophagus in the near future.

Opinion still remains divided on the date of the sarcophagus of Ahiram. Perhaps further excavations at Byblos and at other sites will throw more light on this particularly difficult problem.

[26] Private communication, March 15, 1968.

33

Tombs VI, VII, VIII and IX had been robbed in antiquity because the burial chambers were dug entirely in the clay stratum underneath the rock, hence were accessible to thieves. Fragments of alabaster vases, faience cups and pottery were found though there were no objects of Egyptian origin in this group of tombs. Although they are of a later date than the first group of tombs (I, II, III and IV of the Middle Bronze Age) they are earlier than the tomb of Ahiram. Less care had been taken in the construction of the burial chambers and shafts. Robbers had managed to reach Tomb VIII from Tomb V passing through Tomb IX, through cavities between the rock and the underlying clay stratum. In Tomb IX the cover of a blue faience vase, conical in shape, bore the inscription of Abi, prince of Byblos; another fragment was found with the name Abishemu.[27]

Montet has published four new hieroglyphic inscriptions from Byblos which throw light on this period.[28] The first stele has an inscription of nine horizontal lines and refers to a prince of Byblos called Akäy. This prince had made repairs to the temple of Nut and had built a door of limestone and pine wood. Montet believes this was a continuation of work done on the temple by the father of Akäy. The stele also lists the different foodstuffs which were part of the funerary repast — bread, beer, beef and fowl in addition to funerary offerings of vases and vestments. This is the first time that the name Akäy appears at Byblos. The second stele has an inscription of six vertical lines and is fragmentary. Nonetheless the name of a new prince of Byblos is seen, 'Akery, son of Abishemu. According to Montet, the stele contains threats against unknown persons and promises of offerings. This prince also invokes the name of the Egyptian goddess Nut. The third inscription on limestone is very fragmentary and practically illegible. It refers to the rebuilding of the temple of Hathor, Lady of Byblos. As Byblos is referred to as *Kbn* in a manner similar to inscriptions of the Old Kingdom, Montet believes this fragment should be dated to that period. The last inscription, which Montet places in the period of the Middle Kingdom, refers to Ibshemuabi, son of Abishemu, prince of Byblos. Montet is tempted to connect this new prince of Byblos with Ibshemuabi, son of Abishemu of Tombs I and II of the royal necropolis. The name of Abishemu has appeared several times in Byblos on the following: the scimitar *(harpé)* found in

[27] *Byblos et l'Egypte,* p. 212, Nos. 852 and 853.

[28] Pierre Montet, "Quatre nouvelles inscriptions hiéroglyphiques trouvées à Byblos", *Kemi* XVII, 1964, pp. 61-68.

[29] *Byblos et l'Egypte*, p. 174, No. 653.

[30] P. Montet, *Kemi* XVI, 1962, pp. 89-90.

[31] *Fouilles de Byblos* II, Part 1, pp. 174-175, No. 8161.

[32] *Byblos et l'Egypte*, p. 212, No. 853.

Tomb II of the royal necropolis;[29] the inscribed obelisk found in the Temple of the Obelisks;[30] a fragment of a plaque;[31] a fragment of a blue faience vase.[32]

Some tombs which Montet termed as "archaic" were discovered during the excavations of the royal necropolis. These consisted of shallow, shapeless pits of two to three meters in diameter, the entrances to which were covered by several big flagstones. North of Tomb I of the royal necropolis, the first of these archaic tombs was found almost complete, although it had been broken into by stone masons in antiquity who had cut a subterranean passage leading from the shaft of Tomb II to the burial chamber of Tomb I. In the second "archaic" tomb nothing was found but pottery of crude ware with a large number of flint grits. A big jar with six handles was broken in such a way that the bones it originally contained were lying scattered around. Montet here had reached the Chalcolithic level that came to full light in Dunand's later campaigns. This illustrates one of the problems facing the excavators of Byblos. This burial of the Chalcolithic period is very surprising indeed so close to the Middle Bronze Age royal necropolis.

Other tombs of individuals of ancient Byblos came to light during Montet's last excavation season in 1924. Two of these tombs of individuals contained Middle Bronze Age fenestrated axes of the elongated variety and potsherds of Middle Bronze Age black polished ware. They are perhaps contemporary with some of the royal tombs of Byblos and illustrate how an inhabitant of the city, a rich merchant for example, was buried during the Middle Bronze Age.

The Temple of the Obelisks

The excavation by Maurice Dunand of the Middle Bronze Age temple, commonly called the Temple of the Obelisks, revealed valuable information on Byblos for the period covering the nineteenth to sixteenth centuries B.C. *(Fig. 63)*. This temple had been erected over the ruins of the Early Bronze Age temple which has been discussed in Chapter III above, pp. 20-21. It was built probably during the period of peace which followed the Amorite invasions and the destruction by fire of the city. It covered a much smaller

area than the extensive site occupied by the earlier temple. The Temple of the Obelisks was built over the Early Bronze Age sanctuary and surrounding court and followed closely the old outlines of the sacred court. It is possible that the walls were not covered yet by debris at the time of the building of the Temple of the Obelisks and therefore were incorporated into the later building. It is possible also that the walls came to light when the builders of the Temple of the Obelisks dug for the foundations of their building. Nevertheless the fact that the foundations and part of the superstructure withstood the destructive forces of centuries and were re-used in a building of a later period is proof of the superior workmanship and construction of the Early Bronze Age building. Dunand was obliged to rebuild the Temple of the Obelisks a short distance away in order to proceed with the excavations of the older temple.

The sanctuary of the Temple of the Obelisks stands in the center of the court. It is erected upon a *podium* (platform) as in later temples especially Roman. The *cella* (sanctuary) and *pro-cella* (courtyard) are the result of the division of the *cella* into halves by a wall with a large entrance in its center. The threshold is made of an obelisk and other obelisks appear elsewhere in the building re-used in the pavement and walls. The origin of these re-used obelisks is unknown.[33]

The main element in the *cella* is a stone pedestal standing on a substructure of masonry. This pedestal may have been intended for a monumental cult object. The *pro-cella* is subdivided into three parts: a central flagstone pathway leading up to the *adytum* (holy of holies) and two tiny irregular antechambers to the right and left of this passage. Under the floors of the antechambers a large number of highly valuable ex-voto offerings, many of them made of precious metal, were buried. One deposit was placed underneath a flat obelisk lying on its side and forming part of the foundations of the room. This deposit contained among other things, objects of faience and bronze figurines of human beings and animals — hippopotami, crocodiles, monkeys and cats *(Figs. 84-91)*. The pottery associated with these deposits dates to the Middle Bronze Age.

The court of the Temple of the Obelisks surrounds the sanctuary on three sides. Within this court a large number of obelisks of

[33] *Fouilles de Byblos* II, Part 2, pp. 644-654 for the description of the temple. The re-used obelisks may represent an older stage of the temple, elements of which were incorporated as construction materials during repairs.

[34] P. Montet, "Herichef à Byblos", *Kemi* XVI, 1962, pp. 89-90.

various sizes were discovered. The most important was the central one of a group of three set up against the north wall of the *cella* on which a relatively clear hieroglyphic inscription is preserved *(Fig. 68)* :[34]

BELOVED OF HERISHEF-RĒ ABISHEMU, PRINCE OF BYBLOS, RENEWED OF LIFE, HIS ROYAL SEAL-BEARER, KOUKOU, SON OF ROUTATA, JUST OF VOICE.

The worship of the Egyptian god Herishef (Harsaphes) was centered at Nen-nesou, capital of the Twentieth Nome of Upper Egypt. Montet makes a comparison with the inscription of Obelisk 15 from Tanis on which the name of Harsaphes is found. This inscription dates to the Fourteenth Dynasty during the reign of King Néhesy. According to Montet, the identification of the deity to whom the Temple of the Obelisks is dedicated is still unknown. Could there be a connection between the Abishemu of Tomb IX and the Abishemu of the inscribed obelisk?

The largest group of obelisks was erected in the south-western part of the court. Twenty-six obelisks of sandstone or limestone stood on rectangular or square bases in an irregular line. In some cases a stone "table" was placed in front or in back forming an offering table at the base of the obelisk. Other groups of obelisks were found fallen or standing in other parts of the court. Some contained niches in which ex-voto offerings were kept for a time, then collected to be buried by the priests of the temple. Several small shrines were discovered. One on the west side of the court is protected by two large limestone slabs. It is a tiny imitation of a "house of the god" in which a votive statue was probably housed. It has three stairs leading to it and the small holes on one side of the entrance possibly held the hinges of a wooden door *(Fig. 70)*.

Behind the rear wall of the *cella* is a well 1.70 meters deep. The side walls of the well are of masonry and are plastered with crushed limestone and painted red. A large cylindrical clay jar of the hydra-type fitted exactly into it. A stone table coated with crushed limestone plaster was found next to it. Against the southeast wall of the entrance court a place of sacrifice was discovered *(Fig. 69)*. This consists of a clay jar with a capacity of 675 liters. It is made of red clay and buried in the ground just to the right of a high rectangular basin. This basin rests on a substructure which

has been joined to the wall. The sacrificial animal was probably washed in the stone basin and sacrificed there or nearby. The polluted water ran through a small channel into a well plastered with crushed limestone.

Part of one building of the Early Bronze Age temple had been incorporated into the Temple of the Obelisks. The original north-eastern room of the earlier building had been retained and turned into a "jewelers' workshop" during the Middle Bronze Age. A cylindrical stone nearby may have been used as the work table *(Fig. 64)*. Many bronze objects, figurines and pommels of daggers were scattered about. This was the craft shop of the artists employed in the service of the temple.

Eight deposits of votive offerings were uncovered in the Temple of the Obelisks, totalling 1306 objects. It is believed that these ex-votos, having been exposed for a time, were buried for lack of space and became part of the treasures of the temple. Among the objects found by Dunand were gold fenestrated axes, human figurines of bronze covered with gold leaf, animal figurines of bulls, solar discs of precious metal and small models of cult ships *(Fig. 73-80)*. The offerings suggest Mesopotamian, Egyptian and Anatolian influences .

If a comparison is to be made between the Early Bronze Age temple complex and the Temple of the Obelisks it seems that the former temple was better built and better designed with vast rooms meant for special purposes. It was constructed at the height of flourishing trade relations. After the Amorite invasions and destruction of the temple by a vast conflagration, a new temple was built over the ruins utilizing masonry of the Early Bronze Age temple. Structurally, the new building was inferior. The walls were irregular and poorly built. The only spacious rooms were those incorporated from the earlier building, all other sections being built in a confused and irregular manner. It may be assumed that the basic need for a sanctuary following the burning of the city required rebuilding a temple while Byblos was still recovering from a heavy blow. Resumption of trade relations placed Byblos again at the center of commercial activity in the Eastern Mediterranean world. The city was rebuilt and her ships again sailed in search of new markets. Three stone anchors found in the court of the Temple of the Obelisks were perhaps placed there as ex-voto offerings. With the

revival of trade and industry a special quarter for artisans, metal workers, and potters appeared in the temple area. Many of the objects produced in these workshops were sold as votive offerings to pilgrims to the Temple of the Obelisks. Soon the temple became too small to hold all these offerings and they had to be buried. More than once the floors of the temple were covered over with crushed limestone until the temple was abandoned. Thus the deposits of offerings, all indicative of the high artistic level reached by local craftsmen of Byblos, were miraculously preserved until today.

Texts and Inscriptions

The Si-nuhe chronicle illustrates the love of home-land which characterized the Egyptian of the Middle Kingdom.[35] It tells us of the close relationship which existed between Egypt and Byblos at this period. Most of the story takes place in "Upper Retenu", a geographical term used by the Egyptians for the highland country of northern Palestine and southern and central Syria. The story gives us a picture of daily life in this area during the Middle Bronze Age.

An Egyptian official, called Si-nuhe, went into voluntary exile at the beginning of the reign of Sen-usert I (ca. 1971-1928 B.C.). It could have been that these were difficult times for an official at court. His flight corresponds to the interval between the death of Amenemhat I (founder of the Twelfth Dynasty) and the accession to the throne of his son, Sen-usert I. In this tale, Si-nuhe says that he had been in the service of Nefru, the daughter of Amenemhat I. For unknown reasons at the death of this king, Si-nuhe took flight and travelled south-east to avoid the peopled stretches of the Delta. He set off for Byblos and approached Qedem.[36] He placed himself under the protection of Ammi-enshi, ruler of Upper Retenu, who gave his daughter to Si-nuhe in marriage. For a time he enjoyed a life of plenty in this abundant agricultural community. The land which he calls Yaa, had figs, grapes, wine, milk, honey and olives.[37] During his exile Si-nuhe had the opportunity to meet a few Egyptians whom he entertained. His children grew to be men and Si-nuhe became counselor and military commander under Ammi-enshi. At long last Sen-usert I sent messages to Si-nuhe inviting him to return to the Egyptian court. The benevolent pharaoh reminded

[35] *ANET*, pp. 18-21. This account has been taken from John A. Wilson's translation of "Myths, Epics and Legends". On these letters see now Hans Goedicke, "Sinuhe's Reply to the King's Letter", *JEA* LI, 1965, pp. 29-47.

[36] *ANET*, p. 19. Qedem is a Semitic term for the "East" generally.

[37] *ANET*, p. 19. As Si-nuhe apparently went east from Byblos it is possible that he lived in the valley between the Lebanon and Anti-Lebanon ranges.

Si-nuhe that he was growing old and it was only proper to return to his country where an appropriate burial could be arranged. In a foreign country he would be placed in a sheepskin and put under the ground. Si-nuhe was overjoyed to receive the royal messages and replied that he would like to return escorted by three Asiatics. Si-nuhe surrendered his property and wealth to his eldest son and returned to Egypt with his Asiatic escorts. The pharaoh arranged that Si-nuhe be accompanied to the palace where he was greeted by the royal children and the queen. The pharaoh announced that Si-nuhe would be given the rank of courtier. The new rank demanded a change of dress. He was clothed in royal linen and settled in a house with a garden which had belonged to a former courtier. Meals were served to him three or four times a day and he received gifts from the royal children. A stone pyramid was erected by royal order and mortuary priests assigned to him. Preparations made for his proper burial included a statue overlaid with gold.

The tale of Si-nuhe gives us an interesting insight into the highland country east of Byblos and the life of the tribal community where he lived. This was a contrast to the more sophisticated life of the Egyptian court of the Middle Kingdom. Si-nuhe set off for Byblos, a city which he must have known well as an official in the court of the pharaohs. He chose to travel inland and settle in an agricultural community to make a complete break with Egypt. It is unlikely that a fugitive from the court of pharaoh could remain long in Byblos undetected.

Byblos also appears in the Execration Texts which are imprecations inscribed on terra cotta figurines and bowls. These were deliberately broken in the hope by sympathetic magic the person against whom the curses were directed would be similarly destroyed. In these texts the city of Byblos is mentioned, but not the name of the king of Byblos, as an enemy to be destroyed:[38]

> ALL THE ASIATICS — OF BYBLOS, OF ULLAZA, OF IY-ANAQ,
> OF SHUTU, OF IYMU'ARU, OF QEHERMY, OF REHOB,
> OF YARIMUTA...

The Execration Texts give additional evidence of the interest shown by pharaohs of the Middle Kingdom in the cities on the Syro-Palestinian coast and the hinterland. The pharaohs maintained detailed lists of cities and kings, making note of changes in rulers.

[38] *ANET*, p. 329, "The Execration of Asiatic Princes."

40

This would indicate that there were close relations between Egypt and these cities resulting in the presence of many Egyptians in Asia and Asiatics in Egypt. The magic formulae of the Execration Texts are only secondary to their full significance. Egyptian scribes of the Middle Kingdom were in possession of detailed information on neighboring cities no doubt obtained from official sources in the courts of the pharaohs.[39]

After the death of Amenemhat IV, last pharaoh of the prosperous Twelfth Dynasty, Egypt was divided into two kingdoms ruled by two dynasties. The Thirteenth Dynasty established its capital at Thebes in Upper Egypt and the Fourteenth Dynasty established its capital at Xois in the Delta. Confusion reigned in Egypt as there was no central authority. At Byblos this period likewise is obscure for lack of sufficient archaeological material. Dunand found a fragment of bas-relief with an inscription in hieroglyphic which reads:[40]

THE COUNT OF BYBLOS, INTEN, WHO REPEATS LIFE,
SON OF THE COUNT REYEN, THE TRIUMPHANT.

This inscription gives the name of the king of Byblos in hieroglyphs. In the column to the right of the inscription is the end of the name of Neferhotep I, one of the last pharaohs of the Thirteenth Dynasty. It is the earliest text which gives a chronological synchronism between a king of Byblos and a pharaoh. It is one of two inscribed monuments, the other being a scarab of *Waḥ-ib-Rê,* which have been found at Byblos dating to the period from the close of the Twelfth Dynasty to the beginning of the Eighteenth Dynasty.[41] The name of Inten also appears at Mari. A passage from a cuneiform inventory tablet found in the ruins of the royal palace of Zimri-Lim, king of Mari (1730-1700 B.C.) refers to a certain Yantin-ḫamu, king of Byblos, who had sent Zimri-Lim a gold vase weighing two thirds of a *mina.* Yantin-ḫamu (the Canaanite form of the name) is probably identical with the Byblian king whose name appears in Egyptian hieroglyphs as Inten at Byblos. The existence of Prince Inten of Byblos is known from two scarabs clearly inscribed: "Prince of Byblos, Inten" dated to the period immediately following the Twelfth Dynasty.[42] An indirect synchronism is seen involving three rulers, Neferhotep I of Egypt, Inten of Byblos and Zimri-Lim of Mari.

[39] G. Posener, *Princes et pays d'Asie et de Nubie,* Bruxelles, Fondation Égyptologue Reine Elizabeth, 1940, pp. 39-45.

[40] *ANET,* p. 229. See also *Fouilles de Byblos* I, pp. 197-198, No. 3065.

[41] *Fouilles de Byblos* II, Part 1, p. 24, No. 6923. This pharaoh is of the Thirteenth Dynasty.

[42] W.F. Albright, "An Indirect Synchronism between Egypt and Mesopotamia ca. 1730 B.C.", *BASOR* No. 99, 1945, pp. 9-17. The scarabs purchased by Newberry in 1924 were published in *JEA* XIV, 1928, p. 109 and are believed to be from Byblos. See also K.A. Kitchen, "Byblos, Egypt and Mari in the Early Second Millenium B.C.", *Orientalia* XXXVI, 1967, Part 1, pp. 39-54.

Monumental doorway of Rameses II at Byblos
(Beirut National Museum)

5   The Late Bronze Age
(1600-1200 B.C.)

Byblos and the Egyptian Eighteenth Dynasty

After the end of the Twelfth Dynasty and as a result of unrest in Syria, Asiatics filtered into the Delta and soon established themselves as local rulers. About a generation after Neferhotep I, shortly after 1700 B.C. the records show that Asiatics called "Hyksos" ruled all Egypt. Our major literary source is Manetho, an Egyptian priest and annalist (third century B.C.) who wrote a history of Egypt in Greek and compiled tables of dynasties and kings with lengths of their reigns. Manetho was hostile to the Hyksos whom he calls the "shepherd kings". He tells us that their rule was harsh. The Egyptian term "Hyksos" means "rulers of foreign countries".[1] Recent studies indicate that the Hyksos were only a small group of foreign dynasts rather than a numerous people with a particular civilization. Manetho's version also implies that Hyksos rule only meant a change of political leaders in Egypt and not a mass invasion of a numerically important ethnic element. Hyksos names can be recognized by their foreign etymology. Most of the Hyksos names are pure Semitic. The Fifteenth and Sixteenth Dynasties in Egypt were formed of Hyksos kings who established their capital at Avaris in the Delta. Their monuments and scarabs have been found throughout Lower and Upper Egypt as well as in Nubia. Scarabs of this period have been found at Byblos and in the tombs of Kafer-Jarra near Sidon. Towards the end of their rule in Egypt they introduced a number of improvements in military techniques in an attempt to uphold their rule against growing Egyptian opposition. The horse-drawn chariot, new types of daggers and arms

[1] T. Säve-Söderbergh, "The Hyksos Rule in Egypt", *JEA* XXXVII, 1951, pp. 53-71 for a full discussion of the Hyksos.

were imported from Asia. Khiyan, the most powerful Hyksos king reigned over Upper and Lower Egypt. His successors were content to reign in Lower Egypt and allowed a new dynasty of semi-independent kings at Thebes to be established in Upper Egypt. It was these kings of Thebes of the Seventeenth Dynasty who began the struggle for independence.

The founder of the Eighteenth Dynasty (1567-1320 B.C.) was Ahmes I.[2] He drove the Hyksos from Egypt and pursued them to Palestine where for three years he besieged Sharuhen. This appears to have been the limit of his campaign in the Palestinian direction as he had to return to Egypt to re-organize his kingdom and overcome factious opposition at home. His successor Amenhotep I extended the southern frontier to the Third Cataract. After a period of settled rule uninterrupted by revolt, the government was centralized in the hands of the pharaohs and Egypt became essentially a military state. The successor of Amenhotep I, Thut-mose I, invaded Palestine and Syria and marched as far as the Euphrates. He was succeeded by his son Thut-mose II. The principal queen of Thut-mose II, Hatchesput (Hashepsowe) usurped the kingship and took precedence over Thut-mose III, the son of Thut-mose II by a concubine. Hatchesput was more interested in internal affairs of Egypt than she was in acquiring Asiatic possessions. A militant party in the palace led by Thut-mose III overthrew her and seized power.

The enormous vigor of Thut-mose III brought to Egypt an Asiatic Empire. He undertook seventeen campaigns against Syria and Palestine and extended his dominion to the Euphrates and the Taurus mountains. He built a temple at Karnak dedicated to the god, Amon-Rē, on the walls of which he gave a graphic account of his campaigns. Some of these involved serious fighting while others were parades of strength. The conqueror recorded that during his eighth campaign he gave orders to have cedar trees cut in the vicinity of Byblos:[3]

WHEN MY MAJESTY CROSSED OVER TO THE MARSHES OF ASIA, I HAD MANY SHIPS OF CEDAR BUILT ON THE MOUNTAINS OF GOD'S LAND NEAR THE LADY OF BYBLOS. THEY WERE PLACED IN CHARIOTS, WITH CATTLE DRAWING (THEM). THEY JOURNEYED IN (FRONT OF) MY MAJESTY, IN ORDER TO CROSS THAT

[2] Alan Gardiner, *Egypt of the Pharaohs*, Oxford, Clarendon Press, 1961, pp. 172-210 for a history of Eighteenth Dynasty pharaohs Ahmes I (Amōsis I) to Amenhotep III (Amenōphis III). See also Étienne Drioton and Jacques Vandier, *L'Egypte*, Paris, Les Presses Universitaires de France, 1962, 4th ed., pp. 334 ff.

[3] *ANET*, p. 240 and n. 21.

GREAT RIVER WHICH LIES BETWEEN THIS FOREIGN COUNTRY AND NAHARIN.

"God's Land" was the east in general. The goddess of Byblos stands here for the city. This inscription refers to the forested area near Byblos where cedar wood could be easily procured. The Barkal stele gives further details of timber cutting for construction purposes:[4]

> EVERY YEAR THERE IS HEWED (FOR ME IN DJA)HI GENUINE CEDAR OF LEBANON, WHICH IS BROUGHT TO THE COURT — LIFE, PROSPERITY, HEALTH! TIMBER COMES TO EGYPT FOR ME ADVANCING . . . NEW (WOOD) OF NEGAU (IS BROUGHT), THE CHOICEST OF GOD'S LAND . . . TO REACH THE RESIDENCE CITY, WITHOUT PASSING OVER THE SEASONS THEREOF, EACH AND EVERY YEAR. WHEN MY ARMY WHICH IS THE GARRISON IN ULLAZA COMES, (THEY BRING TRIBUTE), WHICH IS THE CEDAR OF THE VICTORIES OF MY MAJESTY, THROUGH THE PLANS OF MY FATHER (AMON-RĒ), WHO ENTRUSTED TO ME ALL FOREIGN COUNTRIES. I HAVE NOT GIVEN (ANY) OF IT TO THE ASIATICS, (FOR) IT IS A WOOD WHICH HE LOVES.

During the ninth campaign of Thut-mose III, the following inscription tells us how timber was shipped to Egypt:[5]

> NOW EVERY PORT TOWN OF HIS MAJESTY WAS SUPPLIED WITH EVERY GOOD THING WHICH (HIS) MAJESTY RECEIVED (IN THE COUNTRY OF DJA)HI, WITH KEFTIU, BYBLOS, AND SEKTU SHIPS OF CEDAR, LOADED WITH COLUMNS AND BEAMS, AS WELL AS LARGE TIMBERS FOR THE (MAJOR WOOD) WORKING OF HIS MAJESTY.

Of interest in this context is the account of an official of Thut-mose III. He relates how he undertook a mission to secure cedar from Lebanon. This inscription, badly damaged, was found in the tomb of the Chief-Treasurer, Sen-nefer, at Thebes:[6]

> I ENTERED THE FOREST (PRESERVE) . . . I CAUSED THAT THERE BE PRESENTED TO HER OFFERINGS OF MILLIONS OF THINGS ON BEHALF OF (THE LIFE, PROSPERITY AND HEALTH OF THY MAJESTY) . . . IN BYBLOS, THAT I MIGHT GIVE THEM TO HER LORD FOR HER HEART'S SATISFACTION . . . GAVE . . . OF THE

[4] *ANET,* p. 240 and n. 27. Negau was probably a Lebanese or Phoenician area.

[5] *ANET,* p. 241 and n. 39. According to John A. Wilson *Keftiu* was Crete or the Eastern Mediterranean coast generally. The names of the three vessels indicate the commercial carriers of the time within the Eastern Mediterranean.

[6] *ANET,* p. 243 and n. 1. The term *khenti-she* here translated "forest preserve" was used in Egypt for royal domains according to John A. Wilson.

CHOICEST THEREOF. I BROUGHT AWAY (TIMBERS OF) 60 CUBITS
IN (THEIR) LENGTH . . . THEY WERE SHARPER THAN THE
BEARD OF GRAIN, THE MIDDLE THEREOF AS THICK . . . I
(BROUGHT) THEM (DOWN) FROM THE HIGHLAND OF GOD'S
LAND. THEY REACHED AS FAR AS THE FOREST PRESERVE . . .
(I SAILED ON THE) GREAT (GREEN) SEA WITH A FAVORABLE
BREEZE, LAND(ING IN EGYPT) . . .

Thus we see how timber was shipped to Egypt from Byblos during the Empire. Whether payment was made for the cedar wood during this period is not known. The inscriptions infer that either timber was exacted as tribute or the pharaohs maintained forest preserves or royal domains near Byblos. During the eleventh century B.C. we know from the Wen-Amon papyrus that kings of Byblos received payment for shipments of cedar wood. Scrolls from the palace archives were shown to Wen-Amon as evidence that previous transactions of timber shipments had been paid for by Egypt and had been recorded by the kings' scribes.

During the excavations of Montet a fragment of bas-relief with the cartouche of Thut-mose III was found. Dunand found six scarabs with the inscription of Thut-mose III. They are the first royal Egyptian inscriptions to be found at Byblos after a break of several   centuries.

At the death of Thut-mose III his son, Amenhotep II, came to the throne. His accession was met with a revolt in Syria but this was soon put down. At Byblos one scarab in white enamel paste with the cartouche of Amenhotep II on the reverse was unearthed. No inscriptions of his successor, Thut-mose IV, were found. On the other hand, there are five scarabs of his successor, Amenhotep III. During the reigns of Amenhotep III and his son Amenhotep IV (known as Akh-en-Aton) the relationship between Egypt and Byblos is well documented by the Tell-el-Amarna tablets.[7]

The Tell-el-Amarna Tablets

The Tell-el-Amarna tablets were discovered about one hundred and ninety miles south of Cairo in the ruins of the city of Akhetaton. The transfer of the capital from Thebes in Upper Egypt to its new site in Middle Egypt was prompted by religious dispute.

[7] J.A. Knudtzon, *Die El-Amarna Tafeln*, Vorderasiatische Bibliothek, Leipzig, 1907-1915, gives the transcription and translation of the tablets. A translation in English is found in Samuel B. Mercer (ed.), *The Tell-el-Amarna Tablets* I & II, Toronto, MacMillan Company of Canada, Ltd., 1939.

Amenhotep IV brooded upon religious matters and finally came to a vague monotheistic concept which offended the powerful priest-class at court. He held the solar disc in special veneration as a symbol of the supreme god. In the sixth year of his accession he declared that the Egyptian god Amon and all gods were fiction and that the one true deity manifested to man through Aton, the sun disc of Rē. The sun disc was the sign through which the unknown lord of the universe shed radiance on earth. This heresy was so displeasing to the wealthy priesthood of Amon-Rē that Amenhotep IV changed his name to Akh-en-Aton and moved his court from Thebes to Akhetaton (modern Tell-el-Amarna), bringing about an open conflict with the priesthood.

In 1887 a peasant woman digging on the site of the ruins of Akhetaton came across a large number of cuneiform tablets. The news of this discovery spread and the tablets were snatched up by dealers in antiquities; some tablets were sold to European museums and private dealers. Fortunately more tablets were found during subsequent excavations and the total collection now consists of 377 letters. The tablets come from the royal archives of Amenhotep III and his son, Akh-en-Aton. They consist primarily of correspondence between the Egyptian pharaohs and their vassals in Syria-Palestine, though some were written by the kings of Babylonia, Assyria, Mitanni and Hatti (Hittites). Most of these letters were written by Canaanite scribes in a conventional vulgar Akkadian full of "canaanitisms" in grammar and vocabulary.[8] The Akkadian language was the "diplomatic" language of the period. Cuneiform script was internationally used in writing not only Akkadian but other languages as well. Correspondence from Syria and Palestine include letters to the Egyptian court from Rib-Addi, king of Byblos (Gubla).[9] Rib-Addi was a contemporary of both Amenhotep III and Akh-en-Aton. He was an independent ruler, loyal to Egypt, functioning under the loose system of provincial government Egypt had established in Syria and Palestine. In his letters, Byblos appears to be the leader of a group of cities comprising Sigata (Zghorta?), Beruna (Batroun) and Bit-arha.

Egypt had risen as the dominant power in the Eastern Mediterranean as a result of the campaigns of Thut-mose III. While Amenhotep III lived, Egypt was able to retain authority in Asia as far north as the Euphrates. At his death Akh-en-Aton came to

[8] *ANET*, p. 483.

[9] *Die El-Amarna Tafeln*, Letters 1-54 are to Amenhotep III and Akh-en-Aton; Rib-Addi also wrote 6 letters to Amanappa; 2 letters to a high Egyptian official; 1 letter to Ḫaia; and 1 letter to Ianḫamu, agents of pharaoh.

the throne and the situation quickly deteriorated. Due to his religious pre-occupations Akh-en-Aton was indifferent to military affairs in spite of the growing power of the Hittites and the incursions of the Ḥapiru people. In the Amarna correspondence the Ḥapiru seem to be enemies of Egypt allied with Abdi-Ashirta and besieging Byblos and other loyal cities. Throughout the second millenium B.C., the Ḥapiru spread through the Near East. In times of disorganization and weak central authority local Ḥapiru played a large role in the petty warfare between towns and local rulers. The Ḥapiru were an element of the settled rather than that of the desert or nomadic population. They were considered as outlaws by Egypt.[10] They appear as auxiliaries in the army of the rebellious Abdi-Ashirta.

The correspondence between Rib-Addi and the pharaohs gives a vivid picture of the political situation in Canaan in general, and in Byblos in particular, during the fourteenth century B.C. The Hittite king, Shubiluliuma (ca. 1385 B.C.), to avoid a direct clash with Egypt sought to make territorial gains by instigating vassals of Egypt to break away from the empire. Abdi-Ashirta and later his son Aziru, Amorite princes of Lebanon and Syria, conspired with the Hittite king and openly attacked Canaanite cities which were loyal to Egypt. At the same time they themselves pretended to be loyal to the Egyptian court. There are fifty-four letters from Rib-Addi to the pharaohs Amenhotep III and Akh-en-Aton. In the early part of the correspondence the letters are addressed to Amenhotep III and are intended as warnings against the incursions of Abdi-Ashirta and the Ḥapiru on the coast. Byblos is in danger of being besieged by Abdi-Ashirta. The letters contain complaints that the pharaoh has neglected to maintain defenses against the Ḥapiru. In the latter part of the correspondence, after the death of Abdi-Ashirta, the situation becomes desperate because Byblos is besieged by Aziru. In his letters Rib-Addi entreats Akh-en-Aton for assistance and military support. In addition to the letters sent by Rib-Addi to Egypt there are two letters written by Ilirabiḫ of Byblos to Akh-en-Aton which are a final appeal for help against the enemy. These letters refer to the time when Byblos was in the hands of a hostile brother of Rib-Addi following the latter's flight to Beruta (Beirut). This brings to an end the correspondence between Byblos and Egypt. The remaining tablets of the Byblos

[10] M. Greenberg, *The Hab/piru*, American Oriental Series Volume 39, American Oriental Society, New Haven, 1955, pp. 85-91. It is now accepted that the SA GAZ and Ḥapiru are identical.

[11] *ANET,* p. 483. This translation is by W.F. Albright and George F. Mendenhall.

[12] *Die El-Amarna Tafeln,* "Rib-Addi to a high Egyptian official." For English translation see *The Tell-el-Amarna Tablets* I, pp. 263-265.

correspondence are letters from Rib-Addi to representatives of pharaoh in Egypt and the provinces.

The letters follow a standard form. After the usual salutation Rib-Addi invokes the blessing of Baalat of Gubla on the pharaoh. The letters contain the phrase "beneath the feet of the king, my lord, seven times and seven times I fall" and Byblos is referred to as the "true handmaid of the king".[11] Byblos remains loyal to Egypt during the entire period covered by the tablets. Likewise Tyre remains loyal but Sidon openly sides with Abdi-Ashirta and the Ḫapiru. Within Byblos, however, an opposing faction manifested itself in defiance of Rib-Addi's pro-Egyptian policy. An insurrection takes place against him within the city. In stating that "his gates have taken copper", Rib-Addi infers that certain officials had been bribed.[12] His situation is precarious. Rib-Addi requests troops from pharaoh stating that their presence would convince all the cities of the land of Amurru (Amorites) to join with the Egyptians and their vassals. Rib-Addi writes also to an Egyptian deputy of pharaoh, Ḫaia of Amurru, to request help against Abdi-Ashirta. In this letter Rib-Addi specifically asks for fifty pairs of horses and two hundred troops in order to hold Sigata.

As no reply was forthcoming from his appeals to pharaoh Rib-Addi writes to Amanappa, a high Egyptian official and general who knew Abdi-Ashirta, begging for his intervention and help. In a second letter to Amanappa, Rib-Addi states that in reply to the former's request, Rib-Addi has no copper and axes left to send him for he had already sent copper to the king of Tyre. Rib-Addi states that he fears the peasants will slay him.

As the situation deteriorates only two cities are left to Rib-Addi: Byblos and Beruna. All the other cities have deserted the Egyptian cause to side with Abdi-Ashirta and the Ḫapiru. Byblos is under siege and Rib-Addi has been wounded in an attempt to kill him. Rib-Addi again writes to pharaoh that he will be obliged to desert Byblos to save himself. He complains that pharaoh does not seem concerned about his plight; nor does the powerful agent of pharaoh, Ianḫamu, who resides in Syria at Iarimuta. Zimrida, king of Sidon, has made a treaty with Abdi-Ashirta and so has Iapa-Addi, a regent of pharaoh. Rib-Addi realizes that Abdi-Ashirta was professing allegiance to Egypt while in fact he was intriguing against her. In the face of Egyptian indifference several coastal cities

put their own interest first. For instance, the city of Sumur remained loyal to pharaoh as long as Abdi-Ashirta was loyal. When Abdi-Ashirta intrigued against Egypt Byblos replaced Sumur as the last "Egyptian" stronghold on the coast.

It can be seen from the correspondence that in addition to being besieged Byblos was in danger of famine. Rib-Addi states that for two years he has been rationing grain. He writes to Amanappa for the fourth time to inform him that although Ianḫamu, the Egyptian agent of pharaoh at Iarimuta, said that he had sent grain to Byblos it is not true. Rib-Addi knows that grain had been sent to Sumur therefore why has not grain been sent to Byblos also? Rib-Addi infers that his messenger had returned empty handed from Amanappa as well. In a fifth letter to Amanappa Rib-Addi warns that the Ḥapiru are now stationed near Byblos. Beruna had deserted to Abdi-Ashirta. It is imperative for Amanappa to persuade pharaoh to send chariots and troops at once.

As the situation becomes desperate Rib-Addi complains that although he has repeatedly written there has been no assistance from pharaoh. Abdi-Ashirta and his forces are now encamped before Byblos and unless help is forthcoming Byblos and the rest of Syria will fall to him and the Ḥapiru. Tyre threatens to desert the Egyptian cause and a revolution in Tyre has resulted in the murder of the pro-Egyptian party. Rib-Addi's sister and her children, who were sent to Tyre when Abdi-Ashirta lay siege to Byblos, have also been killed. Rib-Addi seems helpless.

In utter desperation Rib-Addi again writes to pharaoh to inform him that only Byblos remains loyal. Abdi-Ashirta, having realized that Egypt had not responded to Rib-Addi's repeated requests for aid, is now preparing to attack the city. He writes again to Amanappa requesting him to intervene and to ask pharaoh to send troops to hold back Abdi-Ashirta.

We learn from the letters that some time during the siege of Byblos Abdi-Ashirta met his death. In a letter to a provincial representative of pharaoh, Rib-Addi requests troops at once and at the same time informs him that Abdi-Ashirta was sick and dying. It appears indirectly in this letter that the Mi-lim people, an independent island or sea-faring people, and the people of Arvad (Aradus, an island off the coast of Syria) were responsible for the death of Abdi-Ashirta.

Whatever the cause, following the death of Abdi-Ashirta, his sons Aziru and Pubaḫla continue to attack the coastal cities. Only Sumur and Irqata are able to withstand the attacks. Sumur is besieged by land and by sea. Pubaḫla enters Ullaza and its people flee to Byblos. Rib-Addi reports that he has no food for them nor can he get any. Sumur is hard-pressed and pharaoh's deputy there is dead. Rib-Addi requests that Ianḫamu be sent as deputy to Sumur with troops. Apparently this was not done because in another letter Rib-Addi reports that Sumur has fallen. All his cities have united with the Ḫapiru and the peasants have gone over to the sons of Abdi-Ashirta. He begs pharaoh to send troops to retake the cities which have fallen to the enemy and thus restore stability in the area. Although he does not have sufficient troops to defend himself, Rib-Addi promises to remain loyal to pharaoh as long as he lives even though Aziru has taken all his cities except Byblos.

At this point the correspondence suggests that a reply has been received from pharaoh but instead of sending troops he is asking for timber. It is a request by pharaoh for boxwood. Rib-Addi replies that he is unable to furnish wood because his ships cannot sail to Zalḫi and Ugarit on account of Aziru. The only recorded response from Akh-en-Aton is a request for wood in reply to Rib-Addi's frantic appeals for military help and grain to prevent famine! Rib-Addi informs pharaoh that now the Hittites are also threatening Byblos. He states that the money sent from Egypt to the Mi-lim people has found its way into the hands of the sons of Abdi-Ashirta and other enemies. In desperation Rib-Addi suggests that Akh-en-Aton send ships to take him and Baalat of Gubla away to safety. Byblos is surrounded by Aziru and the Ḫapiru; Rib-Addi warns pharaoh once more against the king of the Hittites.

In a final attempt to draw the attention of Akh-en-Aton to the critical situation of the city, Rib-Addi writes that he has been advised to make peace with Aziru. He states that the people of Byblos, his courtiers and his wife have told him to defect to the son of Abdi-Ashirta and to make peace with him. This he refuses to do. As a last resort he has allied himself with Ammunira, king of Beruta (Beirut). Upon his return to Byblos he found the gates of the city closed and was refused admission to the city. He begs pharaoh for help, informing him further that he has lost two sons and women of his household who were obliged to surrender to Aziru.[13] It would

[13] *Die El-Amarna Tafeln,* No. 52. For English translation see *The Tell-el-Amarna Tablets* II, p. 449. This letter was written from Beirut. It is similar in script and clay to the letters of Ammunira of Beruta to the Egyptian court, Nos. 141-143.

appear that at the time Rib-Addi had been seeking assistance from Ammunira in Beruta his brother turned Byblos over to the sons of Abdi-Ashirta. Rib-Addi writes:[14]

[14] *Die El-Amarna Tafeln,* No. 53. For English translation see *ANET,* pp. 483-484.

> BEHOLD, MANY ARE THE PEOPLE WHO LOVE ME IN THE CITY; FEW ARE THE REBELS IN IT. WHEN AN ARMY OF ARCHERS GOES OUT AND THEY HEAR ABOUT THE DAY OF ITS ARRIVAL, THEN THE CITY WILL RETURN TO THE KING, MY LORD. LET MY LORD KNOW THAT I WOULD DIE FOR HIM. WHEN I AM IN THE CITY, I WILL PROTECT IT FOR MY LORD, AND MY HEART IS FIXED ON THE KING, MY LORD; I WILL NOT GIVE THE CITY TO THE SONS OF 'ABDU-ASHIRTA. SO MY BROTHER HAS ESTRANGED THE CITY IN ORDER TO GIVE IT TO THE SONS OF 'ABDU-ASHIRTA. LET THE KING, MY LORD, NOT HOLD BACK FROM THE CITY. VERILY, THERE IS MUCH SILVER AND GOLD WITHIN IT; IN ITS TEMPLE THERE IS MUCH WEALTH.

Rib-Addi's last letter to Akh-en-Aton contains a frantic appeal. He writes that his enemies are attempting to persuade Ammunira of Beruta to hand him over to Aziru. He also pleads for reinforcements to allow the city of Beruta to defend itself against Aziru and his troops. He states that the people of Byblos, believing he is dead, wish to turn the city over to Aziru. His last pitiful appeal to Akh-en-Aton is "Why does my lord hold himself back from me?"[15] With this question, the frantic pleas for help come to an end and Rib-Addi disappears from history.

[15] *Die El-Amarna Tafeln,* No. 54. For English translation see *The Tell-el-Amarna Tablets* II, pp. 457-465.

Two final letters, bringing the Byblos correspondence to a close, can be considered the epilogue to the tragedy of Rib-Addi, the faithful ally of pharaoh. Ilirabiḫ, a leading citizen of Byblos, reports to pharaoh that Aziru has committed shameful deeds. He has killed the kings of Ammia (identified with modern Enfé near Tripoli), Eldata, Irqata and Byblos. Ilirabiḫ and the city of Byblos protest that pharaoh's trust in Aziru is not justified. In his last letter Ilirabiḫ requests a garrison for Byblos and states that Aziru should be considered as the enemy of Egypt.

The Tell-el-Amarna correspondence in general and the Byblos letters in particular illustrate vividly the position of rulers who relied on pharaoh and remained loyal during this period. Letter after letter was sent to the Egyptian court appealing for help. The tone of the letters became one of despair in which flight appeared

as the only resource left for adherents to the Egyptian cause. Throughout the Tell-el-Amarna period, Abdi-Ashirta and his son Aziru openly professed their allegiance to Egypt although their actions proved the contrary. Toward the end of the Amarna age, the Hittites considered submission to Egypt treacherous and came to consider Aziru as their vassal. Shubululiuma, the crafty king of the Hittites, obliged Aziru to swear allegiance to him and thus annexed the Amorite kingdom of Syria and Lebanon as well as north Canaan to the Hittite Empire without striking a blow.

Byblos and Egypt after the Amarna Age

The Atenist heresy which had characterized the Amarna age barely survived the reign of Akh-en-Aton. His son-in-law, Tutankhamon, was forced to return to Thebes and make concessions to the powerful priesthood of Amon. On a stele erected in the Temple of Amon at Karnak (Thebes) Tutankhamon recorded his pious acts of restoration after the heresy. He had cedar brought from Lebanon, monuments made for the gods and doubled temple properties in gold and silver:[16]

[16] *ANET*, p. 252.

> HIS MAJESTY — LIFE, PROSPERITY, HEALTH! — HAS BUILT THEIR BARQUES UPON THE RIVER OF NEW CEDAR FROM THE TERRACES, OF THE CHOICEST (WOOD) OF NEGAU, WORKED WITH GOLD FROM THE HIGHLANDS. THEY MAKE THE RIVER SHINE.

Horemheb, the last ruler of the Eighteenth Dynasty, began the reconquest of Palestine to regain the empire. After the short reign of Rameses I (founder of the Nineteenth Dynasty 1303-1302 B.C.) his son and successor Seti I (1302-1290 B.C.) made a bold attempt to restore the empire of Thut-mose III. In a battle with the Hittite army led by Mursil II the Egyptians were victorious and Egyptian rule was re-established in Palestine, Canaan and south Syria. There is a scene on the walls of the Temple of Karnak of Asiatics cutting down trees for Seti I. The descriptive legend runs "...Lebanon. Cutting down (cedar for) the great barque upon the river, (Amon-U(zer-h)et, as well as for the great flagpoles of Amon..."[17] This is the first representation in art of cedars being cut.

[17] *ANET*, p. 254.

53

Upon his succession, Rameses II (1290-1224 B.C.), the son of Seti I, was faced by a revolt instigated by the Hittites. Rameses II was ambitious to repeat his father's successes in northern Syria. His first campaign took place during the fourth year of his reign. Rameses II led his troops along the coast of Palestine as far north as the Nahr-el-Kelb. In the spring of the fifth year of his reign Rameses II at the head of a large army marched into Canaan and Syria and met the Hittites at the Battle of Kadesh. The battle was not decisive but established the boundaries in Asia between Egypt and Hatti. An alliance was concluded between Rameses II and the Hittite king, Khattusilis. This treaty came to light in separate copies found both in the Egyptian capital of Thebes and the Hittite capital of Boghazköy, cities one thousand miles apart on opposite sides of the Mediterranean. The Egyptian version, written in hieroglyphic, can be read on a stele standing upright against a wall in the Temple of Karnak. The Hittite version is given on two clay tablets inscribed in Babylonian cuneiform. Neither king was to encroach upon the territory of the other and each pledged to render assistance in the case of attack from any other quarter. The friendship between the two great powers was cemented by a marriage alliance between Rameses II and the daughter of Khattusilis.

At the mouth of the Dog River (Nahr-el-Kelb) there can be seen today three stelae of Rameses II carved on the rock cliffs.[18] That Rameses II came to Byblos seems certain as parts of a large doorway bearing his cartouche have been found. This would indicate that apart from the erection of stelae at Nahr-el-Kelb the passage of Rameses II through Byblos was also commemorated.[19]

In addition to the doorway, there are several fragments from Byblos bearing inscriptions of Rameses II. Montet found two fragments of a stele: the first has part of a scene representing the pharaoh in front of a divinity and the second has two cartouches in which the names and titles of Rameses II are given.[20] Also discovered in the debris at the bottom of the shaft of Ahiram's tomb was a fragment of alabaster with the name of Rameses II. In the Ahiram burial chamber another alabaster fragment with his cartouche was found.[21] The sarcophagus of Ahiram has been dated to the Late Bronze Age (thirteenth to twelfth centuries B.C.) in view of this evidence. It is the opinion of some scholars that Ahiram and Rameses II were contemporary kings. Dunand has published a series of inscriptions

[18] F.H. Weissbach, *Die Denkmäler und Inschriften an Der Mündung Des Nahr El Kelb*, Berlin, Vereinigung Wissenschftlicher Verleger Walter de Gruyter & Co., 1922, pp. 22-23.

[19] *Fouilles de Byblos* I, p. 92, No. 1354.

[20] *Byblos et l'Egypte*, p. 48, Nos. 24 and 25.

[21] *Byblos et l'Egypte*, p. 225, No. 883; p. 227, No. 890.

[22] *Fouilles de Byblos* I, p. 53, No. 1315; p. 54, No. 1317; p. 56, No. 1320; p. 93, No. 1360; p. 339, No. 6031.

bearing the name of Rameses II found in different levels at Byblos.[22] The reign of Rameses II was a period of great prosperity. The presence of numerous inscriptions of this pharaoh here is evidence that close relations existed once again between Byblos and Egypt. With stability restored in the Near East, Byblos resumed her commercial activities.

Sandstone bust of Osorkon I
(924-889 B.C.),
a pharaoh of the
Twenty-Second Dynasty,
with a dedication
in Phoenician letters
to Baalat-Gebal by Elibaal,
king of Byblos

(Musée du Louvre)

6   The Early Iron Age

(1200-900 B.C.)

The Absence of Iron Age Levels at Byblos

The results of the excavations at Byblos have shown a curious fact which has been a source of discussion among scholars. In the excavated area at Byblos there is a complete absence of stratified levels of the Iron Age, that is, for the period 1200-600 B.C. In the area of the temples, immediately underneath the flagstones of the Roman temple (called *Bâtiments* I and II by Dunand) the archaeological levels belonging to the period of the Middle Kingdom in Egypt appeared (Middle Bronze Age 1900-1600 B.C.). In describing the Roman levels Dunand states: "At Byblos the Hellenistic and Roman levels are often directly superimposed on those of the Middle Kingdom."[1] Elsewhere on the site the excavators were unable to perceive any stratification of the Iron Age, a period which must have been one of prosperity and intense commercial activity. Large foundation stones of a building of the Persian period (550-330 B.C.) were unearthed to the east of the site. Apart from the tenth century royal inscriptions there are only a few fragments from Byblos to cover the Early and Middle Iron Ages. Any attempt to explain this lack of material must take into consideration that the site of Byblos has been occupied and exploited continuously by the inhabitants of the city. Barely had a building fallen down when a new building would arise making use of the materials and architectural elements of the older construction.[2] This process has continued from antiquity to modern times. A further disturbance of the site was caused by the modern houses which were built over the ancient city. These houses had reservoirs and wells, the digging of which brought to

[1] *Fouilles de Byblos* I, pp. 64 and 79.

[2] *Fouilles de Byblos* I, p. 53. In the wall of a building of the Byzantine level, a fragment with the inscription of Rameses II was found.

57

the surface objects from deeper levels.[3] Furthermore, the archaeo-logical levels down to the Roman period were badly disturbed by the construction of the Crusader castle. The Crusaders dug down into the Byzantine and Roman levels in their search for large building stones.[4] Finally, construction during the Hellenistic and Roman periods required deep foundations. The complete lack of Iron Age levels at Byblos has been attributed to similar foundations which could have been the cause for the obliteration of the stratified levels of this period.

In attempting to explain the absence of Iron Age levels at Byblos reference has been made to the testimonies of three classical authors who describe the arrival of Alexander the Great in Phoenicia.[5] There is evidence that Alexander destroyed Tyre but all three authors agree that Byblos surrendered willingly. In the opinion of some scholars Alexander razed Byblos in order to rebuild it on the Greek city pattern. In this process the Iron Age levels of the city were completely destroyed.

Dunand in his discussion of the city walls of Byblos says:[6]

> The city walls which had been built at the beginning of the Old Kingdom were no longer in use at the beginning of the Iron Age. At this period due to the elevation of the city within the ancient city walls, the city spread outwards over the walls, thus obliterating them.

The Iron Age was for all Phoenicia a period of maritime and commercial expansion. As a center for the timber trade the city of Byblos enjoyed a flourishing period of independence and prosperity. There was a continuous process of building and rebuilding within the city walls. At the beginning of the Iron Age ground level had reached the height of the ancient city walls and spread outwardly over them. Is it not possible that the Iron Age levels of Byblos at the height of its prosperity may be found outside the presently standing ancient city walls, that is to say under the buildings of the medieval town? Harden believes that the main Iron Age city is situated to the north of the site under the modern town.[7] There are several buildings which are mentioned in texts or appear on coins which have not yet been discovered at Byblos. The palace of Zakar-Baal, for instance, has not been found, yet we know from the report of Wen-Amon that it existed on a site close to the sea. The

[3] *Fouilles de Byblos* I, p. 13.

[4] *Fouilles de Byblos* I, p. 6.

[5] Arrian 2.15.6; Diodorus 17.40.2; Quintus Curtius 4.1.15-16.

[6] *Fouilles de Byblos* I, p. 6.

[7] D. Harden, *The Phoenicians*, London, Thames and Hudson, 1962, p. 28.

coin of the Emperor Macrinus (end of the second century of our era) has engraved on it the likeness of a temple of Byblos of the Roman period *(Fig. 121)*. This temple, according to Dunand, also has not been found.[8] This question must remain unanswered until further excavations are undertaken outside the presently excavated areas.

[8] *Fouilles de Byblos* I, pp. 74-79. See also G. Contenau, *La civilisation phénicienne*, pp. 128-129.

Wen-Amon and Tiglath-Pileser I in Byblos

During the twelfth century B.C. the entire political structure of the Eastern Mediterranean world underwent a change. The Dorian invasions of Greece displaced the Mycenaeans and kindred tribes who had inhabited Greece during the Late Bronze Age. The Dorians drove these tribes from their homes, pursuing them so that they took to the sea. Masses of homeless peoples moved across the sea and its coastlands displacing or merging with the older populations. This extensive migration of peoples in the Mediterranean was responsible for bringing an end to many older empires of the ancient world. For the Dorians, although uncivilized, possessed iron weapons and tools. The brilliant Bronze Age civilization of Mycenae was destroyed by the advent of the Iron Age.

A northern wave of tribes destroyed the Hittite Empire and descending along the coast overran Alalakh and Ugarit. Both cities were abandoned forever. They spread southwards along the Eastern Mediterranean coast probably as far south as Byblos. Another wave sailed towards Egypt. Called the "Sea Peoples" in the annals of Rameses III, they attacked Egypt but were repelled at the Battle of Pelusium in 1149 B.C.[9] Although the Egyptians were able to push them back into the sea they were unable to prevent some tribes from settling on the southern coast of Canaan where they were known as the Philistines.

[9] *ANET*, p. 262. The following is a list of the "Sea Peoples" taken from the records of Rameses III. "Their confederation was the Philistines (Peleset), Tjeker, Shekelesh, Denye(n) and Weshesh, lands united."

No doubt the arrival of the "Sea Peoples" in the Near East and their assimilation with the inhabitants of the coastal cities of Canaan gave an impetus to navigation and was responsible for the emergence of the maritime people called the Phoenicians. During the Golden Age of Mycenae, the Mycenaeans were the dominant sea-power in the east Mediterranean. After the destruction of Mycenae no single power controlled the seas. Phoenician ships

gradually gained ascendancy in the Mediterranean and sailed in search of trade and the establishment of trading-posts.

Egypt, no longer a dominant power in the Near East, was entering a period of political and economic decline. In Mesopotamia, the struggle for supremacy between Assyria and Babylonia during the thirteenth and twelfth centuries B.C. resulted in the emergence of Assyria as the dominant power. With the accession to the throne of Tiglath-Pileser I (ca. 1114-1076 B.C.), the Assyrians began to look westward and an expedition was undertaken to the Mediterranean Sea.

No longer politically or economically dependent upon Egypt Byblos during the eleventh century B.C. enjoyed a period of prosperity. It was at this time that Wen-Amon, the envoy of Herihor, the High Priest of Amon at Thebes (modern Luxor), undertook his mission to Byblos to procure cedar wood for the ceremonial barge of Amon.

The Wen-Amon papyrus, the last sizable Egyptian document mentioning Byblos, forms a suitable introduction to the city's history during the first millenium B.C. This document, now in the Moscow Museum, was found at El-Hibeh in Middle Egypt. It was written in the early Twenty-first Dynasty (eleventh century B.C.) shortly after the period it describes.[10] The events described are probably real, possibly exaggerated. There seems no reason to doubt that social and political conditions are faithfully portrayed. The document claims to be a report by Wen-Amon of his mission to Byblos to buy cedar wood for the barge of Amon. The year was either that of the last of the Ramessids or of the kingless period following the Twentieth Dynasty. Nesubanebded who ruled the Delta and Herihor who ruled in Upper Egypt are treated as effective rulers but are not given royal titles. Nesubanebded later became the first pharaoh of the Twenty-first Dynasty. The main value of this document is the picture it gives of the position of Egypt, now forced to beg and give a price for the timber of Lebanon which in the past had been exacted as tribute. Although Egypt was still attempting to assert herself as the predominant power in the Mediterranean area, former vassal cities were beginning to express independence of their great neighbor. Egypt was no longer able to exercise political control outside her own borders.

Herihor could only give Wen-Amon a small sum in gold and silver. He also entrusted him with a certain divine image called

[10] *ANET*, pp. 25-29. Reference has been made to John A. Wilson's translation of the papyrus. See also James Henry Breasted, *Ancient Records of Egypt* IV, Chicago, The University of Chicago Press, 1906, § 557.

[11] *ANET*, p. 26 and n. 12. Rameses II at the Battle of Kadesh marched at the head of four divisions, each under the standard of one of the great gods, Amon, Rē, Sutekh and Ptah.

[12] *ANET*, p. 26 and n. 5.

"Amon-of-the-Way". In the past images of gods had led the Egyptian armies into battle; in this case Wen-Amon had a "travelling Amon" to ensure the success of his mission.[11]

Wen-Amon left Thebes and, presenting his credentials to Nesubanebded at Tanis in the Delta, was well received. This ruler and his queen Tentamon arranged for a Syrian sea captain to take Wen-Amon to Dor. Formerly, when on official business, Egyptian envoys had travelled in great pomp with a large retinue. Wen-Amon arrived unaccompanied at Dor which he called "a city of the Tjeker". The Tjeker were one of the "Sea Peoples" associated with the Philistines in the great movements of the twelfth century B.C.[12] The Tjeker king, Beder, sent Wen-Amon fifty loaves of bread, one jug of wine and one leg of beef, indicating that he considered it still necessary to show honor to an emissary of Egypt.

On the ship at Dor a man stole a total of 5 *deben* of gold and 31 *deben* of silver from Wen-Amon. This amount, about 450 grams of gold and 2.8 kilograms of silver, was to pay for the Byblian timber. Wen-Amon complained to the king of Dor who took no initiative in apprehending the thief, claiming that the thief was not a Tjeker. After waiting nine days for reparations Wen-Amon left for Byblos by way of Tyre. The account of his voyage from Dor to Tyre is lost but on the way from Tyre to Byblos he states that he somehow recovered 30 *deben* of silver from a Tjeker as security for his loss at Dor.

Wen-Amon arrived at Byblos four months and twelve days after he left Thebes. Since he arrived on a foreign ship with no gifts and unaccompanied Zakar-Baal, king of Byblos, refused to receive him. He spent twenty-nine days in the harbor of Byblos and Zakar-Baal sent him messages every day telling him to get out of his harbor. In desperation Wen-Amon sent word to the king requesting a ship to sail back to Egypt. By a fortunate coincidence for Wen-Amon one of the noble youths in attendance upon Zakar-Baal was seized by divine frenzy and in prophetic ecstasy demanded that Wen-Amon and his image of Amon be summoned and honorably received. This secured for Wen-Amon an interview with the king.

Wen-Amon recorded: "I found him sitting (in) his upper room, with his back turned to a window, so that the waves of the great Syrian sea broke against the back of his head."[13] It would

[13] *ANET*, p. 26.

61

appear that the royal palace was built close to the sea from this figurative description.[14] Wen-Amon's polite salutation was in direct contrast to Zakar-Baal's cool, reserved greeting. The king of Byblos appeared annoyed that Wen-Amon had no credentials and had sailed on a non-Egyptian ship. This may have been a factor accounting for the hostile treatment that the Egyptian envoy received. Zakar-Baal being crafty and business-like doubted the validity of Wen-Amon's mission. The religious claims of the god Amon on Lebanon put forth by the Egyptian envoy did not impress the king. One must admit that Wen-Amon arrived at Byblos under dubious circumstances.

Wen-Amon told the king:[15]

> I have come after the woodwork for the great and august barque of Amon-Rē, King of Gods. Your father did (it), your grandfather did (it), and you will do it too!

Zakar-Baal replied:[16]

> To be sure, they did it! And if you give me (something) for doing it, I will do it! Why, when my people carried out this commission, Pharaoh — life, prosperity, health! — sent six ships loaded with Egyptian goods, and they unloaded them into their storehouses! You — what is it that you're bringing me — also?

Zakar-Baal had scrolls recording previous transactions brought out and had them read in Wen-Amon's presence. There were sums of one thousand *deben* mentioned in the records, proving that Egypt had paid for past shipments of timber. This is significant in that it shows that the kings of Byblos had been recording their business transactions for several generations. Zakar-Baal further stated that he felt no obligation to Egypt, either political or economic. He did admit, however, the debt of culture which his land owed Egypt as a source of civilization:[17]

> Now Amon has founded all lands. He has founded them, but he founded first the land of Egypt, from which you come; for skill came out of it, to reach the place where I am.

[14] *Byblos, son histoire, ses ruines, ses légendes*, p. 62. Dunand did not find the remains of a palace of the Iron Age at Byblos though he did find the foundations of the storehouses of a palace of the Middle Bronze Age (1900-1600 B.C.). This structure is situated close to the sea.

[15] *ANET*, p. 27.

[16] *ANET*, p. 27.

[17] *ANET*, p. 27. Zakar-Baal's statement has been corroborated by the excavations at Byblos. Art and sculpture have been subjected to strong Egyptian influence. During the Middle Bronze Age the kings of Byblos used hieroglyphic inscriptions showing that they bore titles conferred by pharaoh. See *ibid.*, p. 229.

Zakar-Baal refused to recognize political responsibility to the ruler of Egypt whom he did not refer to as pharaoh. He used the term "pharaoh" in referring to a former sovereign only.

Wen-Amon mentioned the religious ties existing between his country and Byblos, but this had no effect on Zakar-Baal. Wen-Amon was obliged to send a messenger to Nesubanebded and Tentamon to request further payment for the shipment of cedar wood. Zakar-Baal made arrangements to ship some timber while waiting for the additional payment as a sign of good will towards Egypt. When the logs were dragged down to the sea Zakar-Baal stated that he had acquitted himself of his part of the business transaction. He said:[18]

> See, the commission which my fathers carried out formerly, I have carried it out (also), even though you have not done for me what your fathers would have done for me, and you too (should have done)! Do as I wish, and come to load it in — for aren't they going to give it to you? Don't come to look at the terror of the sea! If you look at the terror of the sea, you will see my own (too)! Why I have not done to you what was done to the messengers of Kha-em-Waset when they spent seventeen years in this land — they died (where) they were.

Zakar-Baal said to his attendant: "Take him and show him their tomb in which they are lying." Wen-Amon said in fright: "Don't show it to me."[19] In an effort to intimidate Wen-Amon, Zakar-Baal referred to Egyptian envoys he kept in Byblos indefinitely until they died without completing the mission that had brought them to the city.

As further payment Nesubanebded sent to the king:[20]

     4 jars and 1 kak-men of gold
     5 jars of silver
    10 pieces of clothing in royal linen
    10 kherd of good Upper Egyptian linen
   500 (rolls of) finished papyrus
   500 cowhides
   500 ropes
    20 sacks of lentils
    30 baskets of fish

[18] *ANET,* p. 28 and n. 33.

[19] *ANET,* p. 28.

[20] *ANET,* p. 28.

63

In addition to these items Tentamon sent Wen-Amon the following for his personal use:[21]

21 *ANET*, p. 28.

5 pieces of clothing in good Upper Egypt linen
5 kherd of good Upper Egyptian linen
1 sack of lentils
5 baskets of fish

Zakar-Baal gave the order to have more timber felled. Three hundred men cut the trees and three hundred oxen dragged the logs to the shore of the sea. During this period the slopes above Byblos were heavily wooded. The area had not been exploited as in later periods, that is, from the tenth century B.C. on. Zakar-Baal still was not satisfied with the payment and Wen-Amon was obliged to promise further remuneration for the timber upon his arrival at Thebes.

Wen-Amon went to the sea shore to the place where the timber was lying. Seeing eleven ships belonging to the Tjeker, he sat down and wept through fear. Upon hearing of Wen-Amon's new troubles, Zakar-Baal sent him food and an Egyptian singer, instructing her to entertain him. The king recommended that Wen-Amon should eat and drink until a solution could be reached with the Tjeker. When morning came he had his assembly summoned. Standing in their midst he said to the Tjeker: "What have you come (for)?" They replied: "We have come after the blasted ships which you are sending to Egypt with our opponents." The king replied: "I cannot arrest the messenger of Amon inside my land. Let me send him away and you go after him to arrest him."[22] As Wen-Amon had appropriated 30 *deben* against his loss at Dor, possibly from a Tjeker on his journey between Tyre and Byblos, this could be a reason for Zakar-Baal's abandoning Wen-Amon to his enemies. Wen-Amon was able to escape from the Tjeker pirates but was cast by a storm on the shores of Alashiya (Cyprus). At this point his report breaks off and the conclusion is lost.

22 *ANET*, pp. 28-29 and n. 42.

Wen-Amon's report reveals the complete collapse of Egyptian prestige abroad and shows with what rapidity the most powerful empire of the Mediterranean area had declined under the weak successors of Rameses III. Since the story deals at close range with actual individuals and situations, even though possibly exaggerated, it does represent the situation ca. 1000 B.C. in Byblos.

The city was independent and prosperous. In Zakar-Baal's boast to Wen-Amon of independent power he states: "If I cry out to the Lebanon, the heavens open up and the logs are here lying (on) the shore of the sea."[23] Egypt no longer had political control in Phoenicia; only a fiction of traditional sovereignty in Palestine could be maintained at the Egyptian court.

When Tiglath-Pileser I of Assyria (1114-1076 B.C.) appeared on the Mediterranean coast, a pharaoh, probably Nesubanebded, feeling his exposed position on the Delta, believed it prudent to send the Assyrian king a crocodile.[24] In an inscription commemorating the rebuilding of the Anu-Adad temple in Ashur, Tiglath-Pileser I records:[25]

> I WENT TO THE LEBANON. I CUT (THERE) TIMBER OF CEDARS FOR THE TEMPLE OF ANU AND ADAD, THE GREAT GODS, MY LORDS, AND CARRIED (THEM TO ASHUR). I CONTINUED (MY MARCH) TOWARDS THE COUNTRY OF AMURRU. I CONQUERED THE ENTIRE COUNTRY OF AMURRU. I RECEIVED TRIBUTE FROM BYBLOS (GU-BAL). SIDON (SI-DU-NI), AND ARVAD (AR-MA-DA). I CROSSED OVER IN SHIPS (BELONGING) TO ARVAD, FROM ARVAD WHICH IS ON THE SEASHORE, TO THE TOWN SAMURI WHICH (LIES) IN AMURRU (A DISTANCE OF) 3 DOUBLE-MILES OVERLAND. I KILLED A NARWHAL WHICH THEY CALL "SEA HORSE" ON HIGH SEA.

It is not possible to ascertain whether Wen-Amon visited Byblos before the arrival of Tiglath-Pileser I in Phoenicia. If we are to take Albright's date for Zakar-Baal as ca. 1076 B.C. and assume that Tiglath-Pileser marched to Phoenicia towards the end of his reign, it would appear that both Assyrian king and Egyptian envoy visited Byblos within a short time of each other.[26]

Papyrus trade in the West: Byblos and Melos

Among the items sent by Nesubanebded to Zakar-Baal as payment for timber is the significant appearance of five hundred rolls of papyrus. Here is evidence that at this time the hieroglyphic and pseudo-hieroglyphic scripts, previously used to write on stone and metal, had been displaced by another type of writing at Byblos. Zakar-Baal had scrolls brought from the palace archives — which

[23] *ANET*, p. 27.

[24] David Daniel Luckenbill, *Ancient Records of Assyria and Babylonia* I, Chicago, University of Chicago Press, 1926, § 385. Luckenbill believes this is a stele of Tiglath-Pileser I re-used by Adad-Nirari II. There is no evidence that Adad-Nirari II visited the Mediterranean coast.

[25] *ANET*, p. 275.

[26] W.F. Albright, *JAOS* LXVII, p. 160.

assumes a cursive form of script—to show Wen-Amon that previous transactions of timber shipments had been recorded. This plus the evidence of the local inscriptions of the period found on the site of Byblos show that Phoenician scribes had discarded the numerous signs of the hieroglyphic scripts and developed their own alphabetic script of twenty-two letters.

There are five hundred coils of rope also mentioned as part of the payment for the cedar logs. This is evidence that, in addition to papyrus rolls, papyrus rope was an important item of export from Egypt. The *Odyssey* 21.390-391 refers to "a ship's cable made of papyrus". The Greeks therefore first used papyrus in the form of rope for sailing purposes at a period slightly earlier than Wen-Amon's visit to Byblos. Rope was also vital to the Phoenicians for the hauling and binding of cedar logs for shipment. Zakar-Baal said to Wen-Amon at the time timber was being prepared for him: "Give me the ropes (which) you have brought (to lash the cedar) logs which I am to cut down to make you..."[27]

During the eleventh century B.C. it would appear that a flourishing trade in papyrus rope and papyrus rolls existed between Egypt and Byblos. Herodotus (1.1) gives evidence of the extent of the commercial activities of the Phoenicians: "Among other places to which they (the Phoenicians) carried Egyptian and Assyrian merchandise, they came to Argos, which was about that time preeminent in every way among the people of what is now called Hellas." The Greeks associated papyrus, an article of Egyptian origin, with the city of Byblos. The Greek word for papyrus and the Greek name for the city are the same, indicating that Byblos was known as the center from which papyrus could be obtained. Herodotus further tells us, basing himself on early tradition, that the Phoenicians who came with Cadmus and settled in Greece introduced writing. Although writing existed in Greece during the Late Bronze Age, the memory of this was lost by the time of Herodotus. The forms of the early Greek letters are so similar in details to the Phoenician and Semitic alphabets of the ninth and eighth centuries B.C. that they must have been derived from North Semitic writing. A comparison of the letter-forms and of the names of the letters, meaningless in Greek but descriptive in Semitic languages, leaves no doubt of the truth of this tradition. Herodotus (5.58) in stating that the Greeks refer to their letters as Φοινικήια γράμματα

27 *ANET*, p. 27. For ropes made of papyrus in Egypt see Alfred Lucas, *Ancient Egyptian Materials and Industries*, 3rd ed., London, 1948, pp. 160-161.

(*phoinikia grammata*) "Phoenician characters" uses the linguistic point, the oldest name of the alphabet, as proof of its Phoenician origin. In addition to using papyrus rope for sailing purposes, it is probable that the Greeks also used papyrus for writing from ca. 800 B.C. onward, at the time the alphabet was adopted.

A reference to colonization in the Aegean can be found in a text of Stephanus of Byzantium written in the fifth century A.D. He relates that the inhabitants of Byblos were responsible for the colonization of the island of Melos. "The Phoenicians were its first settlers, whence it was called *Byblis* from the Phoenicians of Byblos."[28] The old name of Melos is Mimblis. The names *Mimblis* and *Mimallis*, with their variants, could plausibly be interpreted as successive corruptions of *Byblos*.[29] In the absence of archaeological or other corroboratory evidence it is difficult to know what weight to assign to this testimony.

During the Iron Age in the Mediterranean basin civilization was diffused by the plantation of Greek colonies. The new cities were overseas settlements of emigrant farmers looking for new lands to cultivate and for whom there was no room in the narrow valleys of Greece. Likewise the Phoenicians in an effort to find new markets were establishing trading centers and ports for their ships. The references to papyrus in the *Odyssey* and to the founding of Melos by the inhabitants of Byblos are two texts that point to overseas trade and colonization during the eleventh century B.C.

Tenth Century Royal Inscriptions of Byblos

The major written sources for the tenth century B.C. are passages from the Old Testament and the royal inscriptions of the kings of Byblos.[30] To gain a better understanding of this century a brief historical survey of the political and economic situation in the Near East is in order.

Following the death of Tiglath-Pileser I in 1075 B.C., a succession of weak kings ruled Assyria. Tributary states shook off whatever control Tiglath-Pileser I had imposed and Assyria was reduced to a small state contained within the upper valley of the Tigris and Euphrates. The history of the country from his death to the end of the tenth century is obscure.

[28] Stephanus of Byzantium, *Ethnica* s.v. *Melos,* p. 450, ed. A. Meineke (Berlin, 1849; reprinted Graz 1958).

[29] Pliny, *Natural History* 4.12.70. "Melos, with the town of that name, called by Aristides Mimblis, by Aristotle Zephyria, by Callimachus Mimallis."

[30] 1 Chronicles 14.1; 1 Kings 5.1-18; 1 Kings 9.10-14; Albright, *JAOS* LXVII, 1947, pp. 153-160.

Political events in Egypt had resulted in disunity and internal weakness. Under Rameses XI (ca. 1114-1087 B.C.) a local dynast of Tanis called Nesubanebded assumed political control of the Delta. At the death of Rameses XI, Nesubanebded of Tanis became king of Lower Egypt. At Thebes Herihor, the high priest of Amon became king of Upper Egypt. Manetho chronicled Nesubanebded and his Tanite successors alone as kings of the Twenty-first Dynasty.[31] Unity was restored between the two kingdoms by Sheshonk I (945-924 B.C.), the Libyan warrior prince of Bubastis in the Delta who seized the throne and became the founder of the Twenty-second Dynasty. Sheshonk I is the Shishak of the Old Testament (1 Kings 11.40).

The Philistines over whom Egypt had maintained some control since Rameses III repelled the "Sea Peoples" at Pelusium, established a confederacy of five city-states: Gaza, Ekron, Ashdod, Gath and Ashkelon each ruled by its own king. These cities attempted to expand even attacking southern Phoenicia.[32] During the early part of the tenth century the Israelites and the Philistines engaged in wars. David, who had risen to power after defeating the Philistines, was made king of the Hebrews.

In an effort to extend the boundaries of his newly founded kingdom David overthrew Hadad, king of Edom, who took refuge in the Egyptian city of Tanis and married the sister of Tahpenes, the wife of the pharaoh.[33] The Egyptian court had become the refuge of dispossessed princes and Egyptian royal ladies were given in marriage to foreign kings and chiefs. Israel's monarchs avoided challenging Egypt directly and desired marriage alliances which would give prestige to their new royalty. Solomon, the son of David, made a marriage alliance with pharaoh and brought his daughter to Jerusalem.[34]

During his reign Solomon engaged in a vast building program. Jeroboam became his most dangerous political opponent and fled to Egypt where he sought refuge in the court of Sheshonk I until Solomon's death.[35] Heavy taxation imposed upon the people of Israel to finance the building program and political dissatisfaction under Solomon's son and heir, Rehoboam resulted in the secession under Jeroboam of the northern part of the Hebrew kingdom. Sheshonk I profited from this division and ca. 930 B.C. marched against Jerusalem. He returned to Egypt with the spoils of the

[31] Gardiner, *Egypt of the Pharaohs*, p. 316.

[32] Justin, *Abrégé des histoires philippiques de Trogue Pompée* I, Paris, Librairie Garnier Frères, 18.3.5.

[33] 1 Kings 11.18-19.

[34] 1 Kings 3.1.

[35] 1 Kings 11.40.

[36] 1 Kings 14.25-26.

[37] *ANET*, p. 264 and n. 3. Sheshonk's presence on Asiatic soil is also confirmed by a fragment of a monumental stele with his name found at Meggido.

temple built by Solomon, the golden shields and the treasures of the palace.[36] At Byblos a statue-base of Sheshonk I was found on which are his cartouche and three incomplete lines of Phoenician letters, a dedication of Abibaal, king of Byblos.[37]

Sheshonk I did not attempt to enforce his authority over Israel and Judah, this being too expensive a course, but wisely left the two kingdoms to their mutual rivalries. The empire of Solomon had been broken up in the interest of Egypt and Sheshonk I had secured the prestige and succession of his dynasty. Egypt, except for a temporary increase of wealth under these kings, was no stronger and decline soon set in again. Sheshonk I died in 924 B.C. and was succeeded by his son Osorkon I (924-889 B.C.).

[38] R. Dussaud has published the inscriptions in *Syria* V, 1924 and *Syria* VI, 1926. W.F. Albright republished the inscriptions in *JAOS* LXVII, 1947. To these inscriptions Albright adds the one of Ahiram, placing it at the beginning of the tenth century B.C.

A series of Phoenician royal inscriptions of this tenth century period have been found.[38] An inscription engraved on a stele of King Yehimilk (ca. 950 B.C.) was found by Dunand during his first campaign. The stele was buried in five meters of debris in the area between the Crusader castle and the colonnade at a point directly above the Roman levels. The Temple of Baalat-Gebal is found in this general area and the restoration which Yehimilk undertook is probably connected with it:[39]

[39] *JAOS* LXVII, p. 156. Diringer places the Yehimilk inscription in the eleventh century B.C. See *Writing*, p. 114.

> THE TEMPLE WHICH YEHIMILK, KING OF BYBLOS, BUILT —
> IT WAS HE WHO RESTORED THE RUINS OF THESE TEMPLES.
> MAY BAAL-SHAMEN AND BAAL-(ATH)-GEBAL AND THE ASSEMBLY OF THE HOLY GODS OF BYBLOS PROLONG THE DAYS OF
> YEHIMILK AND HIS YEARS OVER BYBLOS AS A RIGHTFUL KING
> AND A TRUE KING BEFORE THE H(OLY) GODS OF BYBLOS!

A royal inscription is found on a fragment of the base of a seated Egyptian figure. The inscription consists of the cartouche of Sheshonk I (founder of the Twenty-second Dynasty ca. 945-924 B.C.) and a dedication by Abibaal, king of Byblos (ca. 925 B.C.). The latter is made up of three incomplete lines of Phoenician letters. The text must have been inscribed on the base of the statue during the lifetime of Sheshonk I or immediately after his death:[40]

[40] *JAOS* LXVII, pp. 157-158.

> (THE STATUE (?) WHICH) ABIBAAL, KING OF (BYBLOS, SON OF
> YEHIMILK(?), KING) OF BYBLOS, (BR)OUGHT FROM EGYPT FOR
> BAAL(ATH-GEBAL, HIS LADY. MAY BALAATH-GEBAL PROLONG
> THE DAYS OF ABIBAAL AND HIS YEARS) OVER BYBLOS!

An important inscription is found on the bust of a statue in reddish sandstone of Osorkon I (924-889 B.C.) the son and successor of Sheshonk I. The statue, at present in the Louvre, was for many years in the hands of private collectors. It has been agreed that this statue comes from Byblos and was set up in the Temple of Baalat-Gebal by King Elibaal (ca. 915 B.C.). The inscription is:[41]

[41] *JAOS* LXVII, p. 158. Elibaal may have been the brother of Abibaal.

> THE STATUE WHICH ELIBAAL, KING OF BYBLOS, SON OF YEHI(MILK, KING OF BYBLOS), MADE (FOR BA)ALATH-GEBAL, HIS LADY. MAY BAALATH(-GEBAL) PROLONG (THE DAYS OF E)LIBAAL AND HIS YEARS OVER (BYBLOS)!

Dunand found two other fragments: the upper arm of a statue bearing the cartouche of Osorkon I with four Phoenician letters above the cartouche, and a fragment of an elbow.[42] These were found in the surface debris during the excavation campaigns in 1926. Montet has also published three fragments which he has attributed to Osorkon I. One of these fragments bears part of a royal cartouche which he believes should be read as Osorkon.[43] Whereas Abibaal's text can be dated by the form of its letters, the inscription of Elibaal is evidence that the latter was contemporary to Osorkon I. Either Osorkon I presented the statue to Elibaal, or Elibaal ordered the statue of pharaoh from Egypt. In any case the reddish sandstone is from the quarry at Mokattem near Cairo.

[42] *Fouilles de Byblos* I, p. 18, No. 1048.

[43] *Byblos et l'Egypte*, pp. 49-54, Nos. 26-30.

The last royal inscription of the tenth century B.C. is of the utmost importance because if provides the key to the genealogy of the kings of Byblos during this century. The inscription refers to a wall which was built for the Temple of Baalat-Gebal by King Shipit-Baal:[44]

[44] *JAOS* LXVII, p. 158.

> THE WALL WHICH SHIPIT-BAAL, KING OF BYBLOS, SON OF ELIBAAL, KING OF BYBLOS, SON OF YEHIMILK, KING OF BYBLOS, BUILT FOR BAALATH-GEBAL, HIS LADY. MAY BAALATH-GEBAL PROLONG THE DAYS OF SHIPIT-BAAL AND HIS YEARS OVER BYBLOS!

The inscriptions of Abibaal and Elibaal are evidence that the kings of Byblos towards the end of the tenth century wished to heal the break with Egypt. Relations between the kings of Byblos and the pharaohs of the Twenty-first Dynasty during the eleventh century were strictly commercial as seen in the Wen-Amon papyrus. The

military expedition of Sheshonk I which once again brought Egyptian forces into Palestine contributed to this change in attitude. As in the past the city of Byblos made no resistance to the invader. From the time of Egyptian domination in Phoenicia Byblos followed a policy of cooperation. Instead of attempting to gain a fuller degree of independence, Byblos sided with the Egyptians to whom she remained faithful under all circumstances. Yet the city was never a province of Egypt nor was she administered by Egyptians. In a true merchant spirit Byblos preferred the advantages resulting from an alliance with a big empire in which the city held a privileged position to complete independence with its attendant danger.

Towards the end of the tenth century the kings of Byblos looked east with apprehension as Assyria under Adad-Nirari II (912-890 B.C.) was becoming a military threat. In the previous century Tiglath-Pileser I had reached the shores of the Mediterranean but, after collecting tribute, had returned to Ashur. Would a new conqueror from Assyria do the same? The kings of Byblos, after a period of indifferent relations with Egypt, hastened to strengthen their ties with the vigorous Egyptian dynasty founded by Sheshonk I which had already shown signs of its imperialism. In the past a stable dynasty in Egypt had furthered the commercial activities of Byblos. Perhaps such conditions would now exist again.

Trade with the Kingdom of Israel

During the reign of Solomon (974-937 B.C.) commercial ties were established between the Phoenician city-states and Israel. Solomon and King Hiram of Tyre agreed to commercial exchanges which lasted over a period of twenty years. Tyre was the most enterprising of the Phoenician city-states in respect to trade. In 1 Kings 5.6-18 Hiram is also referred to as the king of the Sidonians. This reference can be correlated with Homeric passages where the term *Sidonian* is identified with the Phoenicians in general (cf. Iliad 23.740). Although Hiram seemed to have some authority over the "men of Gebal" (Byblos), there is no evidence that Tyre had political authority over the city. Byblos during the tenth century was ruled by independent kings whose names are known from the royal inscriptions. It is possible that Tyre acted as middleman in

commercial transactions of importance, with Sidon and Byblos acting as suppliers of raw materials and skilled workmen.

The transactions between Solomon and Hiram are described in detail in various books of the Old Testament. Not long after David's capture of the Jebusite stronghold on Mount Zion, Hiram sent messengers to him in Jerusalem. 1 Chronicles 14.1 relates: "And Hiram, king of Tyre, sent messengers to David, and cedar trees, also masons and carpenters to build a house for him." David accepted their services and a palace was built for him. 2 Samuel 7.2 states: "The king said to Nathan the prophet, 'See now, I dwell in a house of cedar but the ark of God dwells in a tent'." This pre-supposes the building of a temple which was done on such a grand scale during the reign of Solomon. 1 Chronicles 22.2-5 relates how David made the preparations for the construction of the temple, feeling his son Solomon was too young and inexperienced for such an undertaking. He provided the materials for the construction before his death including "cedar timbers without number; for the Sidonians and Tyrians brought great quantities of cedar to David" (1 Chronicles 22.4).

The agreement between Hiram and Solomon was that Tyre should furnish cedar and cypress timber in return for agricultural products (1 Kings 5.10). The narrow coastal plains of Phoenicia were inadequate for growing wheat and importation was necessary for a growing population.[45] According to 1 Kings 5.11, twenty thousand *kors* of wheat and twenty thousand *kors* of beaten oil (oil pressed from olives — one *kor* equals 365 liters) were allocated to Hiram on a yearly basis.

A large number of workmen were employed on the project of cutting timber. Carpenters and workmen from Phoenicia went to Israel to prepare, trim and process the timber as the Israelites were not trained for this type of work. Thus, important phases in the construction of both temple and palace were done by the Phoenicians. 1 Kings 5.18 states: "So Solomon's builders and Hiram's builders and men of Gebal did the hewing and prepared the timber and stone to build the house."

At the completion of both the temple and palace after twenty years a further payment was made by Solomon, this time not in agricultural products but in land. Twenty cities in the land of Galilee were given to Hiram. It is possible that the cities proved

[45] Centuries later, during the Roman period, the people of Tyre and Sidon came to Herod in a delegation. Acts 12.20 states that the delegation asked for peace because their country depended on Herod's country for food.

46 1 Kings 9.11-14.

inadequate payment for the cedar, cypress timber and gold sent to Solomon by the city-states of Phoenicia. When Hiram came from Tyre to see the cities he said: "What kind of cities are these which you have given me, my brother?"[46] Hiram was under the obligation to pay Sidon and Byblos for their part in the procurement, processing and shipment of timber and for the work furnished as trained specialists in Jerusalem.

The completion of the temple and palace of Solomon terminated the important commercial transactions between Hiram and Solomon. For Israel, the palace gave prestige to the monarchy, the temple satisfied the religious needs of the people. For the Phoenician city-states wheat and oil were assured for local consumption for a period of twenty years and a new outlet was secured for the export of timber. During the tenth and ninth centuries B.C. Israel was exposed to the cultural influence of Phoenicia. Phoenician techniques in art and architecture were imitated and adapted by the Hebrews. Although Phoenicia and Israel comprised a single cultural area, the Phoenicians due to their geographical position on the coast were more exposed to various influences from other countries. They borrowed and adapted and passed on these cultural influences to their neighbors through trade.

The Dog River Stelae. Inscriptions of the ancient kings of Egypt, Assyria and Babylonia.
Keepsake, *Album de la Syrie et de l'Egypte*, Paris, Abel Le Doux, 1843

7   The Middle Iron Age
(900-550 B.C.)

Byblos and the Assyrian Empire

The major sources for this period are the Assyrian royal inscriptions and passages from the Old Testament. The archaeological material from Byblos is meagre and no texts have been found on the site to throw light on this period.

The first direct contact with the Assyrian Empire occurred at the time of the expedition of Tiglath-Pileser I (1114-1076 B.C.). The coastal city-states of Phoenicia paid the customary tribute following which the king withdrew his armies to Ashur. However, it was not until the early ninth century that Assyria presented a real threat. In 877 B.C. Ashurnasirpal II led an expedition to Carchemish and Phoenicia. Upon his approach the principal cities of Phoenicia made haste to submit. Embassies laden with tribute were sent to meet the Assyrian monarch in the hope of paving the way for a nominal subjection. Ashurnasirpal II tells us that after cleansing his weapons in the Mediterranean Sea he performed sheep-offerings to the gods:[1]

[1] *ANET,* pp. 275-276. The Assyrian and Babylonian historical texts are translated by A. Leo Oppenheim.

> THE TRIBUTE OF THE SEACOAST — FROM THE INHABITANTS OF TYRE, SIDON, BYBLOS, MAHALLATA, MAIZA, KAIZA, AMURRU, AND (OF) ARVAD WHICH IS (AN ISLAND) IN THE SEA, (CONSISTING OF): GOLD, SILVER, TIN, COPPER CONTAINERS, LINEN GARMENTS WITH MULTICOLORED TRIMMINGS, LARGE AND SMALL MONKEYS, EBONY, BOXWOOD, IVORY FROM WALRUS TUSK — (THUS IVORY) A PRODUCT OF THE SEA — (THIS) THEIR TRIBUTE I RECEIVED AND THEY EMBRACED MY FEET.

There is a reference to cedar in the palace of Ashurnasirpal II which infers that the Assyrian king returned to his capital with this precious timber.[2]

There are no records extant referring to the remaining years of the reign of Ashurnasirpal II to indicate any further military expeditions. Apart from nominal subjection Byblos and the other Phoenician city-states were not oppressed by Assyria. Shalmaneser III (858-824 B.C.), the son and successor of Ashurnasirpal II, fearing an uprising reversed his father's policy and undertook a series of military campaigns against the Aramean kingdoms of north Syria. From the sixth to the twenty-first year of his reign Shalmaneser III carried out almost continuous war against his chief adversaries, the kings of Damascus, Hamath (modern Hama) and what he termed "the twelve kings beside the sea, above and below".[3] At some time during these campaigns Shalmaneser III set up sculptured stelae of himself as testimony to his greatness. He refers to one in the region of the Amanus mountains. He also refers to a stele he had engraved by the sea. He states that after receiving tribute from "the kings of the seashore" he marched down the coast and "fashioned a stele with an image of myself as overlord in order to make my name/fame lasting forever and e(rected it) near the sea".[4]

At the Dog River (Nahr-el-Kelb) between Beirut and Byblos the mountains of Lebanon plunge down to the sea. Here can be seen several sculptured stelae of ancient conquerors. Side by side with the three Egyptian monuments of Rameses II there are several Assyrian inscriptions. Weissbach identifies the sixth, the text of which is partly legible, with Esarhaddon. He states that the others are too mutilated to enable them to be identified.[5] Rouvier however claimed that he could identify the stelae of the following kings: Rameses II, Tiglath-Pileser I, Ashurnasirpal II, Shalmaneser III, Sennacherib, Esarhaddon and Nebuchadnezzar.[6] According to Weissbach, identification of these stelae must remain insoluble due to the erosion, mutilation and lack of supporting evidence.

By far the most important battle Shalmaneser III fought against the Aramean coalition was the Battle of Qarqar in 853 B.C. Ben-Adad I (Adad-'idri in the inscriptions), king of Damascus, had been forming alliances with his neighbors, political manoeuvres presenting a threat to Shalmaneser III. The first step the Assyrian

[2] Jorgon Laessoe, *People of Ancient Assyria,* London, Routledge and Kegan Paul, 1963, pp. 103-104.

[3] *ANET,* p. 279.

[4] *ANET,* pp. 277-278.

[5] F. H. Weissbach, *Die Denkmäler und Inschriften an der Mündung Des Nahr el Kelb,* pp. 22-23.

[6] Jules Rouvier, *Gebal-Byblos, son histoire dans l'antiquité et sa nécropole phénicienne,* 1899, p. 12. See also Herodotus 2.106. In a passage describing the military exploits of "Sesostris" who some scholars believe is Rameses II, Herodotus states that he saw the stelae of this pharaoh when he visited Syria.

monarch took was to defeat Irhuleni, king of Hamath (Hama). Irhuleni and Ahab, king of Israel (considered a vassal by Ben-Adad), had come to the king of Damascus' aid. Shalmaneser III records the number of soldiers who took part in the Battle of Qarqar and the type of military equipment his enemies used. It is interesting to see that none of the Phoenician city-states, except Arvad, is mentioned by name as having taken part in the battle. This may be due to the fact that the geographic position of Arvad rendered it more subject to involvement in Aramean internal politics since it was the most northern Phoenician city-state. It is probable that under pressure the city was obliged to make a token contribution of two hundred soldiers as recorded by Shalmaneser III.[7]

In spite of the boasts of Shalmaneser III the Battle of Qarqar was indecisive. Nevertheless, the king of Damascus was weakened and Ahab of Israel found it opportune to revolt against his overlord. The revolt was unsuccessful and Ahab was slain in battle. Judah and Moab, the vassals of Israel, made use of this opportunity to revolt against Israel. Celebrating the liberation, Mesha, king of Moab, set up the well-known stele at Diban called the Moabite stone. The script resembles the Phoenician alphabetic inscription found on the lid of the sarcophagus of Ahiram at Byblos.[8] In the eighteenth year of his reign (ca. 840 B.C.) Shalmaneser III continued the struggle against Hazael, the son of Ben-Adad.[9] In the twenty-first year of his reign (ca. 837 B.C.) Shalmaneser III marched against Hazael:[10]

> IN MY TWENTY-FIRST YEAR, I CROSSED THE EUPHRATES FOR THE TWENTY-FIRST TIME. I MARCHED AGAINST THE TOWNS OF HAZAEL OF DAMASCUS. FOUR OF HIS LARGER URBAN SETTLEMENTS I CONQUERED. I RECEIVED TRIBUTE FROM THE COUNTRIES OF THE INHABITANTS OF TYRE, SIDON AND BYBLOS.

It is clear that the inhabitants of Byblos made haste to offer tribute to appease the Assyrian monarch. Shalmaneser III recorded additional tribute sent on ships by the inhabitants of Tyre and Sidon.[11]

A final campaign against Damascus was waged and Shalmaneser III ravaged the kingdom but spared the city. Before his death in 824 B.C., civil war broke out and for two years his sons fought for the succession. Damascus, Hamath, Israel and Babylon revolted.

[7] *ANET*, p. 279.

[8] W. F Albright, *JAOS* LXVII, 1947, p. 159.

[9] *ANET*, p. 280.

[10] *ANET*, p. 280.

[11] *ANET*, p. 281.

The son accepted by Shalmaneser was Shamsi-Adad V (824-811 B.C.). There are no inscriptions extant describing events during his reign as it relates to the Mediterranean coast. It would appear that he restricted his military campaigning to the subjugation of Babylon and wars against the northern highlands and the Medes. Adad-Nirari III (810-783 B.C.) undertook an expedition to regain the kingdoms which had revolted from Assyria. He marched on Damascus and led an expedition to Palestine imposing tribute on Tyre, Sidon, Israel, Edom and Palestine.[12]

Although Byblos is not specifically mentioned in this text it is probable that tribute was collected on this occasion. At this period most of the Phoenician city-states followed a common policy. The cities retained their kings and their laws. Apart from paying fixed tribute to Assyria the trade of the Phoenician cities prospered. During this period Assyria had under her control the important trade routes across Asia. The hinterland of the Aramean kingdoms in central Syria, the Hittite principalities in northern Syria and the kingdom of Israel were all under Assyrian control. Assyria could have cut off the land trade routes of the Phoenician city-states had she wanted to. Being tributary to Assyria, Tyre, Sidon and Byblos were safeguarded by a power on which they were dependent. Tyre can be taken as an example of the flourishing conditions under which the Phoenician city-states prospered during the first period of Assyrian domination. The prophet Isaiah (23.2-8) has given a general description of the extent of the commercial expansion and prosperity at Tyre. This can also apply to the other Phoenician city-states of the period.

Adad-Nirari III died in 783 B.C. Though the records are not clear concerning his successor Shalmaneser IV (782-772 B.C.) there is evidence that during the reign of Assur-Nirari V (753-746 B.C.) campaigns were undertaken against Arpad and Damascus. Urartian advances along the northern frontier of Assyria deprived Assyria of the control of the trade routes, control of the metal trade of Asia Minor and the supply of horses. Economic distress in Assyria led to a number of revolts. Assur-Nirari V was murdered with the whole of the royal family.[13]

In 744 B.C. Tiglath-Pileser III (cf. 2 Kings 15.29) came to the throne. He reversed Assyrian foreign policy in the Middle East and set about energetically to the consolidation and unification of

[12] *ANET*, p. 281.

[13] H. W. F. Saggs, *The Greatness that was Babylon*, London, Sidgwick & Jackson, 1962, pp. 103-104. See L.H. Grollenberg, *Atlas of the Bible*, trans. and ed. Joyce M.H. Reid, London, Thomas Nelson & Sons, Ltd., 1957, p. 143. Arpad is modern Tell Erfâd north of Aleppo.

[14] *ANET*, p. 282.

an empire. At first he restricted himself to the collection of tribute. In the tribute lists of Tiglath-Pileser III the names of the kings of two Phoenician city-states are given:[14]

> (I RECEIVED) THE TRIBUTE OF KUSHTASHPI OF COMMAGENE, URIK OF QU'E, SIBITTI-BE'L OF BYBLOS . . . (MA)TAN-BE'L OF ARVAD...

[15] W.F. Albright, *JAOS* LXVII, p. 160.

Sibitti-be'l is called Shipit-Baal II by Albright and reigned at Byblos ca. 740 B.C.[15] The tribute mentioned in the list comprises gold, silver, tin, iron, antimony, linen garments with multicolored trimmings and "garments of their native (industries) (being made of) dark purple wool".[16] In another inscription Tiglath-Pileser III recorded tribute and gives the names of two kings of the Phoenician city-states, Byblos and Tyre:[17]

[16] *ANET*, p. 282.

[17] *ANET*, p. 283.

> I RECEIVED TRIBUTE FROM KUSHTASHPI OF COMMAGENE, REZON OF DAMASCUS, MENAHEM OF SAMARIA, HIRAM OF TYRE, SIBITTI-BI'LI OF BYBLOS, URIKKI OF QU'E . . . GOLD, SILVER, TIN, IRON, ELEPHANT HIDES, IVORY, LINEN GARMENTS WITH MULTICOLORED TRIMMINGS, BLUE-DYED WOOL, PURPLE-DYED WOOL, EBONY-WOOD, BOXWOOD-WOOD, WHATEVER WAS PRECIOUS (ENOUGH FOR A) ROYAL TREASURE; ALSO LAMBS WHOSE STRETCHED HIDES WERE DYED PURPLE, (AND) WILD BIRDS WHOSE SPREAD-OUT WINGS WERE DYED BLUE, (FURTHERMORE) HORSES, MULES, LARGE AND SMALL CATTLE, (MALE) CAMELS, FEMALE CAMELS WITH THEIR FOALS.

[18] On the question of the Phoenician dye industry, see now Frans Bruin, "Royal Purple and the Dye Industries of the Mycenaeans and Phoenicians", in *American University of Beirut Festival Book* (Festschrift) Centennial Publications, Beirut 1967, pp. 295-325, with extensive bibliography.

This unique reference mentions stuffed and decorated animals. The use of purple dye in coloring wool and lambs' hides is evidence that the Phoenician city-states were known for their skill in the textile industry. Tyre in particular was famed for the purple dye industry. It may have been the technique used in the extraction of the dye from the murex — a snail-like shellfish — that caused the purple of Tyre to be held in such esteem. It has been roughly estimated that the value of one gram of pure purple-dye was equivalent to ten to twenty grams of gold.[18] Whether Byblos possessed purple dye factories is not known. On the other hand Byblian coins of the fourth century display the murex shell which may indicate that it was of particular importance to the city (see obverse of coin of King Adramelek, p. 90).

Tiglath-Pileser III began to tighten his control over the tributary states leaving them no vestige of the independence which they had enjoyed under Egypt. His policy was to re-arrange the populations in the cities and to carry out deportations of peoples from one area to another. The main reason for transporting people away from their homeland was to prevent the possibility of revolt. Dispersion broke down ethnic and religious groups. Such a community cut off from its own homeland and separated from the main group was less likely to revolt. The Assyrians and later the Babylonians forcibly transported whole communities from one end of their empires to the other. Incidentally this effected a very thorough pooling of talent and experience making their cities quite cosmopolitan. Tiglath-Pileser III also appointed Assyrian governors over the cities responsible directly to himself.[19] In this manner he brought about complete centralization of his government.

From a fragmentary annalistic text of Tiglath-Pileser III it is clear that the Phoenician coastal states, although not subject to deportation measures, had Assyrian governors over them:[20]

> . . . THE TOWN HATARIKKA AS FAR AS THE MOUNTAIN SAUA, (. . . THE TOWNS:) BYB(LOS), . . . SIMIRRA, ARQA, ZIMARRA, . . . UZNU, (SIANNU), RI'RABA, RI'SISU, . . . THE TOWNS . . . OF THE UPPER SEA, I BROUGHT UNDER MY RULE. SIX OFFICERS OF MINE I INSTALLED AS GOVERNORS OVER THEM . . .

Byblos and the other Phoenician city-states were spared the mass exodus forced upon Israel. Tiglath-Pileser III states at the end of the inscription: "Israel . . . all its inhabitants (and) their possessions I led to Assyria. They overthrew their king Pekah and I placed Hoshea as king over them."[21] This was direct intervention in the internal affairs of a neighboring kingdom and the Phoenician city-states naturally became alarmed at the extreme measures taken by Tiglath-Pileser III.

Sargon II (721-705 B.C.) ascended the throne of Assyria in 721 B.C.[22] An inscription from Khorsabad (Dur-Sharrukin), Sargon's new capital, gives evidence that the Phoenician city-state Simirra participated in a revolt together with Arpad, Hama, Damascus and Samaria against Sargon II.[23] The king states that after putting down the rebellion he killed the rebels in their cities. For the first time severe punitive measures by Assyria were taken against a Phoenician

[19] *ANET*, p. 283.

[20] *ANET*, p. 283.

[21] *ANET*, p. 284; 2 Kings 15.29-31.

[22] D. Luckenbill, *Ancient Records of Assyria and Babylon* I, § 829 has published directly after texts of Tiglath-Pileser III, a fragmentary text of Shalmaneser V; the only text extant of Tiglath-Pileser's successor.

[23] *ANET*, p. 285.

[24] *ANET*, p. 285.

city-state. The revolt failed and Simirra is heard of no more in the records.[24]

The harsh treatment by Sargon II could have been a factor in the revolt of Elulaeus, king of Sidon (Luli in the Assyrian inscriptions) during the reign of Sennacherib (704-681 B.C.). Sennacherib undertook a military campaign against Elulaeus, capturing Sidon and its dependent cities. Elulaleus fled and Sennacherib installed Ethbaal upon the throne of Sidon, forcing him to pay tribute. The kings of the Phoenician city-states made haste to send tribute to the Assyrian monarch:[25]

[25] *ANET*, p. 287.

> AS TO ALL THE KINGS OF AMURRU-MENAHEM FROM SAMSI-MURUNA, TUBALU FROM SIDON, ABDILITI FROM ARVAD, URUMILKI FROM BYBLOS, MITINTI FROM ASHDOD, BUDUILI FROM BETH-AMMON, KAMMUSUNABDI FROM MOAB (AND) AIARAMMU FROM EDOM, THEY BROUGHT SUMPTUOUS GIFTS . . . AND KISSED MY FEET . . .

The rest of the inscription deals with the siege and fall of Jerusalem.

Once again Byblos found it expedient not to get involved in Assyrian military operations in Phoenicia. After Sennacherib captured Sidon and her dependencies the kings of Byblos and Arvad sent the customary tribute to the Assyrian conqueror. Byblos followed a policy of non-alignment which was to prove wise. She was unable to stand off an invader from a military and strategic point of view. The city had not the advantage of Tyre and Arvad which could easily become island fortresses.

Upon accession to the throne of Assyria Esarhaddon (680-669 B.C.) states that a certain Abdimilkutte of Sidon revolted against him. Esarhaddon destroyed Sidon and executed Abdimilkutte.[26] He forcibly transported the inhabitants of Sidon to Assyria to do forced labor in the building of his palace. This harsh treatment and especially the deportation measures made the other Phoenician city-states fear retaliation if they did not submit to the Assyrian king. The king of Byblos hurried to comply with the Assyrian monarch's demands:[27]

[26] *ANET*, p. 290. This event took place during Esarhaddon's Syro-Palestinian campaign.

[27] *ANET*, p. 291.

> I CALLED UP THE KINGS OF THE COUNTRY HATTI AND (OF THE REGION) ON THE OTHER SIDE OF THE RIVER (EUPHRATES) (TO WIT): BA'LU, KING OF TYRE, MANASSEH, KING OF JUDAH,

QAUSHGABRI, KING OF EDOM, MUSURI, KING OF MOAB, SIL-
BEL, KING OF GAZA, METINTI, KING OF ASHKELON, IKAUSU,
KING OF EKRON, MILKIASHAPA, KING OF BYBLOS, MATANBAʻAL,
KING OF ARVAD, ABIBAʻAL, KING OF SAMSIMURUNA, PUDUIL,
KING OF BETH-AMMON, AHIMILKI, KING OF ASHDOD —
12 KINGS FROM THE SEACOAST.

The kings whom Esarhaddon called the "12 kings from the
seacoast" along with ten kings from Cyprus were forced to transport
to Nineveh the building materials for his royal palace:[28]

> ALL THESE I SENT OUT AND MADE THEM TRANSPORT UNDER
> TERRIBLE DIFFICULTIES, TO NINEVEH, THE TOWN (WHERE
> I EXERCISE) MY RULERSHIP, AS BUILDING MATERIAL FOR MY
> PALACE: BIG LOGS, LONG BEAMS (AND) THIN BOARDS FROM
> CEDAR AND PINE TREES, PRODUCTS OF THE SIRARA AND
> LEBANON MOUNTAINS, WHICH HAD GROWN FOR A LONG
> TIME INTO TALL AND STRONG TIMBER, (ALSO) FROM THEIR
> QUARRIES (LIT: PLACE OF CREATION) IN THE MOUNTAINS,
> STATUES OF PROTECTIVE DEITIES MADE OF ASNAN-STONE,
> STATUES OF (FEMALE) ABZAZTU, THRESHOLDS, SLABS OF
> LIMESTONE, OF ASNAN-STONE, OF LARGE-AND SMALL-
> GRAINED BRECCIA . . .

Esarhaddon must have installed or tolerated a certain Balu
(Baal) as king of Tyre for his name henceforth appears in the inscrip-
tions describing the campaigns against the coastal cities and Egypt.[29]
During his tenth campaign Esarhaddon laid siege to Tyre because
Balu of Tyre had conspired with Taharqa, king of Egypt. No
mention is made of Byblos and Arvad so it can be assumed that
both remained out of the conflict. Esarhaddon then proceeded to
Memphis. Among the Nahr-el-Kelb stelae noted above is one of
Esarhaddon. The Assyrian king tells in this inscription of his entry
into Memphis and mentions the articles he took to Assyria from
the royal palace. He made members of the royal family accompany
him, also physicians, divination experts, goldsmiths and cabinet
makers.[30]

Although Esarhaddon succeeded in effecting the conquest of
Egypt ca. 670 B.C., within a year Taharqa was re-instated. His successor, Ashurbanipal (668-633 B.C.), prepared an expedition to regain

[28] *ANET*, p. 291. On this
occasion an important
amount of cedar wood must
have been taken from the
forests of Lebanon.

[29] *ANET*, p. 291.

[30] *ANET*, p. 293.

[31] *ANET*, p. 294.

Egypt. In one inscription he states that the "kings of the seashore" brought him gifts and that he forced them to supply ships and forces to accompany him to Egypt.[31]

Ashurbanipal's second campaign was also directed against Egypt, but in his third campaign he marched against Tyre. He blockaded Tyre by land and sea until the city faced starvation and was forced to surrender. No mention is made of Byblos. The king says Arvad aroused his displeasure and he forced the city to submit. Iakinlu, king of Arvad, brought his daughter with a large dowry to Nineveh.[32]

[32] *ANET*, pp. 295-296.

These inscriptions indicate that although Tyre and Arvad were able to put up some resistance, Byblos was unwilling because of political expediency to defy the Assyrian king. The remainder of the inscriptions concerning Ashurbanipal's reign deal with his campaigns against the Arabs.[33] All these texts prove, however, that if Assyria had been mild in her treatment of the subject Phoenician states in earlier times, the Assyrian kings gradually became tyrannical and cruel. The inscriptions show that they exacted costly tribute, in some cases on an annual basis. With the reign of Tiglath-Pileser III and the succeeding period mass executions took place. Populations were deported throughout the Middle East and Assyrian governors were appointed who were directly responsible to the Assyrian king. During the reign of Ashurbanipal Byblos followed a different policy from that of Arvad and Tyre. Both of the latter cities opposed Ashurbanipal openly. Byblos followed the prudent course, that is, to submit to the demands of the conqueror, to yield before being forced to yield. In a tribute list from Palestine which dates to a period between Sargon II and Esarhaddon we find:[34]

[33] *ANET*, pp. 297-300.

[34] *ANET*, p. 301.

> TWO MINAS OF GOLD FROM THE INHABITANTS OF BIT-AMMON;
> ONE MINA OF GOLD FROM THE INHABITANTS OF MOAB;
> TEN MINAS OF SILVER FROM THE INHABITANTS OF JUDAH;
> (. . . MI)NAS OF SILVER FROM THE INHABITANTS OF (EDOM)
> . . . THE INHABITANTS OF BYBLOS, THE DISTRICT OFFICERS
> OF THE KING, MY LORD, HAVE BROUGHT . . .

The nature of the tribute Byblos paid on this occasion is not clear due to the fragmentary condition of the text. The inscription is significant however in that it shows Byblos was consistent in her policy of non-alignment with her sister Phoenician city-states when

it involved opposition to the Assyrian Empire. Ever ready to pay tribute when required, Byblos was spared the harsh treatment received by Tyre, Sidon and Arvad.

Byblos and the Babylonian Empire

The Assyrian Empire was beset by troubles shortly after Ashurbanipal's reign which led to its dissolution and the fall of Nineveh in 612 B.C. The arrival in southwestern Asia of hordes of Scythians greatly weakened Assyria.[35] Assyria appeared to be the only bulwark against this tide of barbarism. The Phoenician city-states, without any actual revolt, regained their independence by default. The combined attack of Medes and Babylonians on Assyria was to lead to the final collapse of the Assyrian Empire.

The Phoenician city-states soon found their newly gained independence precarious. On the one hand, Babylon might lay claim to the territory previously held by Assyria. On the other, Egypt was showing signs of renewed designs on Phoenicia. Herodotus records that Egypt under Psammetichus had imperialistic designs on Syria. He relates: "The reign of Psammetichus lasted for fifty-four years, during twenty-nine of which he was engaged in the siege of Azotus (Ashdod), a large town in Syria until he finally took it."[36] Although this appears to be an exaggeration by Herodotus it could indicate that faced with this double danger the Phoenician city-states had no alternative but to cooperate.

For the first time there can be seen some effort toward a confederation of the Phoenician states headed by Tyre. Rivalry and petty jealousies were forgotten in an effort to unite to ward off foreign intervention. Whether this cooperation was military or commercial is open to conjecture. No matter what interpretation is given, Ezekiel in his prophecy against Tyre shows the conditions under which the cooperation took place. The prophecy is of further interest because it gives a description of the materials with which a Phoenician ship of this period was built, as well as the technical terms of Phoenician navigation. Ezekiel curses Tyre and predicts the destruction of the city at the hand of Nebuchadnezzar:[37]

> The word of the Lord came to me: "Now you, son of man, raise a lamentation over Tyre, and say to Tyre, who

[35] Herodotus, *The Histories* 4.1; Strabo, *The Geography of Strabo* 11.8, § 4 and Ezekiel 38.2-16. See also *The Greatness that was Babylon*, pp. 136-139.

[36] Herodotus 2.157. Psamtik I was founder of the Twenty-Sixth Dynasty, called the Saite Dynasty. Ashdod is located on the Palestinian coast.

[37] Ezekiel 27.1-9 R.S.V. The place name Zemer is conjectural as published by the R.S.V. replacing the original "Tyre".

dwells at the entrance to the sea, merchant of the peoples on many coastlands, thus says the Lord God: 'O Tyre, you have said, I am perfect in beauty.' Your borders are in the heart of the seas; your builders made perfect your beauty. They made all your planks of fir trees from Senir; they took a cedar from Lebanon to make a mast for you. Of oaks of Bashan they made your oars; they made your deck of pines from the coasts of Cyprus, inlaid with ivory. Of fine embroidered linen from Egypt was your sail, serving as your ensign; blue and purple from the coasts of Eli'shah was your awning. The inhabitants of Sidon and Arvad were your rowers; skilled men of Zemer were in you, they were your pilots. The elders of Gebal and her skilled men were in you, caulking your seams; all the ships of the sea with their mariners were in you, to barter for your wares.''

Before the arrival of the Babylonians the Phoenician city-states enjoyed great wealth and commercial expansion. They maintained friendly relations with Egypt. Herodotus reports that during the reign of Necho, the successor of Psammetichus, the circumnavigation of Africa was accomplished. This daring exploit by a fleet manned by a Phoenician crew was an extraordinary feat. Herodotus says that the Phoenicians in the course of the third year returned to Egypt. They reported that as they sailed on a westerly course around the southern end of Libya (Africa) they had the sun to their right, that is to the north.[38]

[38] Herodotus 4.42. This probably is a legendary account.

Herodotus' testimony infers that the Phoenician city-states were independent and wealthy as they sailed the seas in search of new trading posts. This happy state of affairs was not to last. In 605 B.C. Nebuchadnezzar, son of Nabopolassar, the king of Babylon who was now aged and sickly, led the armies of Babylon against Egypt. The army of Necho stood before Carchemish. The Egyptians were routed and Nebuchadnezzar pursued Necho to the frontiers of Egypt. The hasty flight of the Egyptian forces left the whole country open to the invading army. Nebuchadnezzar would have continued his march into Egypt had not news reached him that Nabopolassar had died. He quickly returned to Babylon in order to avoid a disputed succession. Thus matters in Egypt, Syria and Palestine were left in a confused and unsettled state.

This first experience with the forces of Babylon gave evidence of their strength and cruelty. It was a factor in the development of close ties between Egypt and the Phoenician city-states. Egypt appeared now as the only protection against Babylon. Encouraged by their alliance with Egypt, in the course of a few years Judaea and Phoenicia, under the leadership of Ithobaal, king of Tyre revolted against Nebuchadnezzar and declared themselves independent.[39] Ezekiel's prophecy was to prove correct.[40] Nebuchadnezzar marched against the king of Tyre. He besieged Tyre, Sidon and Jerusalem. Jerusalem submitted and Sidon capitulated as the city was suffering from pestilence.[41] Tyre continued to resist for a period of thirteen years but ultimately was captured by the king of Babylon. No mention is made of Byblos in this punitive expedition. It is possible that Byblos during this period was not considered important in a political or military sense.

Weissbach has published an inscription of Nebuchadnezzar found at Wadi Brisa near the source of the Orontes River in north Lebanon concerning his campaigns in Phoenicia. It describes the extensive logging operations undertaken by the king in the cedar forests of Lebanon. The Wadi Brisa inscription states in part:[42]

AT THAT TIME, THE LEBANON, THE (CEDAR) MOUNTAIN, THE LUXURIOUS FOREST OF MARDUK, THE SMELL OF WHICH IS SWEET, THE HI(GH) CEDARS OF WHICH, (ITS) PRO(DUCT), ANOTHER GOD (HAS NOT DESIRED, WHICH) NO OTHER KING HAS FE(LLED) . . . MY NABU MARDUK (HAD DESIRED) AS A FITTING ADORNMENT FOR THE PALACE OF THE RULER OF HEAVEN AND EARTH, (THIS LEBANON) OVER WHICH A FOREIGN ENEMY WAS RULING AND ROBBING (IT OF) ITS RICHES — ITS PEOPLE WERE SCATTERED, HAD FLED TO A FAR (AWAY REGION). (TRUSTING) IN THE POWER OF MY LORDS NEBO AND MARDUK, I ORGANIZED (MY ARMY) FOR A(N EXPEDITION) TO THE LEBANON. I MADE THAT COUNTRY HAPPY BY ERADICATING ITS ENEMY EVERYWHERE (LIT.: BELOW AND ABOVE). ALL ITS SCATTERED INHABITANTS I LED BACK TO THEIR SETTLEMENTS (LIT.: COLLECTED AND REINSTALLED). WHAT NO FORMER KING HAD DONE (I ACHIEVED): I CUT THROUGH STEEP MOUNTAINS, I SPLIT ROCKS, OPENED PASSAGES AND (THUS) I CONSTRUCTED A STRAIGHT ROAD FOR THE (TRANSPORT OF THE) CEDARS.

[39] Josephus, *Against Apion*, 1.21.

[40] Ezekiel 28.2-11.

[41] 2 Kings 24.10-16 for fall of Jerusalem; Ezekiel 28.22-23 for the fall of Sidon.

[42] *ANET*, p. 307. This translation has been taken from F.H. Weissbach, *Die Inschriften Nebukadnezars II im Wadi Brisa und am Nahr El-Kelb*, Leipzig, J.C. Hinrichs'sche Buchandlung, 1906, pp. 13-35.

I MADE THE ARAHTU FLO(AT) (DOWN) AND CARRY TO MARDUK, MY KING, MIGHTY CEDARS, HIGH AND STRONG, OF PRECIOUS BEAUTY AND OF EXCELLENT DARK QUALITY, THE ABUNDANT YIELD OF THE LEBANON, AS (IF THEY BE) REED STALKS (CARRIED BY) THE RIVER. WITHIN BABYLON (I STORED) MULBERRY WOOD. I MADE THE INHABITANTS OF THE LEBANON LIVE IN SAFETY TOGETHER AND LET NOBODY DISTURB THEM. IN ORDER THAT NOBODY MIGHT DO ANY HARM (TO THEM) I ERE(CTED) THERE A STELE (SHOWING) ME (AS) EVERLASTING KING (OF THIS REGION) AND BUILT . . . I, MYSELF, . . . ESTABLISHED . . .

Nebuchadnezzar states that he had a stele set up during his expedition to Lebanon. Although the king claimed that he did this to protect the inhabitants of Lebanon from harm, it stands to reason that this stele was set up at the Dog River (Nahr-el-Kelb) to serve as a reminder to the coastal city-states that their overlord was Nebuchadnezzar, the mighty king of Babylon. The Dog River stele is fragmentary and has also been published by Weissbach. Part of the inscription reads:[43]

FROM THE SHORE OF THE EUPHRATES ABOVE THE CITY
TO THE SHORE OF THE EUPHRATES BELOW THE CITY,
I HAD A STRONG WALL BUILT EASTWARD AROUND BABYLON.
I DUG ITS MOAT, THE SLOPE OF WHICH I FIRMED UP
WITH BITUMEN AND BRICK.
I BUILT A HIGH, STRONG WALL OF BITUMEN AND BRICK
ALONG ITS EDGE. ITS GATEWAYS I BUILT STRONGLY;
I INSTALLED DOORS OF CEDAR-WOOD COVERED WITH BRONZE...

For further information on this period reference is made to a prism, presently in Istanbul, which was found in Babylon. Here are listed the names and duties of members of the court of Nebuchadnezzar. Among them are the names of the master of ceremonies, the chief of engineers, the overseers of the slave girls and the cup-bearer. There is mention of a Phoenician "Hanunu", the chief of the royal merchants.[44] On another side of this prism seven kings are mentioned as receiving pensions from the royal Babylonian household: the king of Tyre, the king of Gaza, the king of Sidon, the king of Arvad, the king of Ashdod, the king of Mir(. . .), the king of . . ."[45] As the inscription is fragmentary it is not clear whether the king of Byblos was included in this list.

[43] F.H. Weissbach, *op. cit.*, pp. 35-37.

[44] *ANET*, p. 308.

[45] *ANET*, p. 308 (v).

Administrative documents found in Babylon shed further light on the relation between Babylon and Byblos. It is clear that craftsmen of Byblos held a privileged position during the Babylonian period. The tablets on which the inscriptions are found list deliveries of oil for the subsistence of persons who were either prisoners of war or otherwise dependent upon the royal household of Babylon. The two tablets published mention allotments of oil to Judaeans, Medians, Lydians and Greeks, as well as allotments to persons from Ashkelon, Tyre, Byblos, Arvad and Egypt:[46]

[46] *ANET*, p. 308.

> 1 1/2 SILA (OIL) FOR 3 CARPENTERS FROM ARVAD, 1/2 SILA EACH
>
> 11 1/2 SILA FOR 8 DITTO FROM BYBLOS, 1 SILA EACH . . .
>
> 3 1/2 SILA FOR 7 DITTO GREEKS, 1/2 SILA EACH
>
> 1/2 SILA TO NABU-ETIR THE CARPENTER
>
> 10 (SILA) TO IA-KU-U-KI-NU, THE SON OF THE KING OF IA-KU-DU (I.E. JUDAH)
>
> 2 1/2 SILA FOR THE 5 SONS OF THE KING OF JUDAH THROUGH QANA'A (. . .)

The point of pertinent interest is that Byblian craftsmen are found as far away as Babylon. The position of carpenter was a privileged one; there are eight from Byblos in contrast to three from Arvad, none from Tyre and Sidon. The larger amount of oil allotted to each of the carpenters from Byblos is interesting. Could it be indicative of the superior position of Byblian carpenters in the Babylonian administration? Confirmation of this may come from the Wadi Brisa inscription of Nebuchadnezzar which gives a description of the amount and type of wood cut down from the mountains of Lebanon.[47] The inscription gives evidence that to facilitate the transportation of so many cedar logs, a slip-way was cut into the rock. Special roads had to be built through the mountains for this operation. The logs were hauled overland, then tied together and floated down the Euphrates. This was an immense undertaking at that time. References of uses to which cedar wood were put in Babylon are seen in the Wadi Brisa stele. The inscription mentions roofing for a temple room made of cedar from "the forest and the mountains of Lebanon", the cedar being covered with red gold and encrusted with precious stones.[48] A mast for a ceremonial ship made of cedar covered with red gold is also mentioned.[49] The Nahr-

[47] *Die Inschriften Nebukadnezars II im Wadi Brisa und am Nahr El-Kelb*, pp. 13-35.

[48] F.H. Weissbach, *op. cit.*, p. 19.

[49] F.H. Weissbach, *op. cit.*, p. 21.

[50] F.H. Weissbach, *op. cit.*, pp. 35-37.

el-Kelb stele of Nebuchadnezzar tells us that gates of cedar wood covered with bronze were made for the great wall the king built in Babylon.[50] Carpenters of Byblos, with a tradition of thousands of years in timber processing and construction, travelled to Babylon to supervise the building of the temple and the king's palace.

At Byblos, according to the excavation reports so far published, there is no evidence of Babylonian occupation. However stratified archaeological levels belonging to this age have not been found. In the area within the city walls there are no inscribed monuments pertaining to this period.

Obverse of silver coin of Adramelek,
king of Byblos (ca. 340 B.C.)
Galley (eye-shaped hawse-hole);
prow terminating in lion's head
containing three hoplites
with crested helmets
and round shields;
zigzag line of waves

Below:
hippocamp and murex

Above:
hippocamp's tail
initials: ⊤𝗫

8   The Late Iron Age

(550-330 B.C.)

Byblos and the Persian Empire

In addition to the archaeological material and the hoard of silver coins found at Byblos the works of two classical authors shed light on this period. Herodotus, a Greek traveller and historian of the fifth century B.C., is our source for the Greek and Persian wars. Diodorus Sicilus (first century B.C.) wrote a history in which there are references to Byblos and Phoenicia during the period from the Graeco-Persian war of 480-479 B.C. to the successors of Alexander.

Byblos and the Phoenician city-states do not specifically appear in historical texts for the rest of the Babylonian period. The conquest of Babylon by Cyrus, king of Persia, made him heir to the Babylonian Empire but he did not immediately implement his claim. An inscription referring to the deeds of Cyrus mentions that all rulers paid hommage to him upon his taking Babylon. "All the kings of the entire world from the Upper Sea to the Lower Sea . . . brought their heavy tribute and kissed my feet in Babylon."[1] Cyrus was engaged in campaigns against the Massagetae which tied up the major part of his armed forces in the northeast thereby permitting Phoenicia to enjoy a period of autonomy. Evidence of Phoenician independence and control of the sea routes is seen in Herodotus. He states: "Among the Ionians . . . the islanders among them had nothing to fear, for the Phoenicians were not yet subjects of the Persians nor were the Persians themselves shipmen."[2]

An administrative decree of Cyrus allowed all displaced persons to return to their homelands. This included the leaders of the Jewish

[1] *ANET*, pp. 315-316.

[2] Herodotus 1.143.

91

nation in exile and permission was given to them to leave Babylon and proceed to Jerusalem.[3] This furnished another opportunity for the Phoenician city-states to renew commercial relations with their neighbors of the past. Ezra 3.7 states that cedar wood and Phoenician artisans made their way to Jerusalem to take part in the new rebuilding program of the city.

Upon the death of Cyrus and the accession of Cambyses in 529 B.C. direct intervention by Persia in the Eastern Mediterranean occurred. Cambyses made preparations for an attack on Egypt. This was deemed necessary because Egypt had regained power and some of her earlier greatness. Herodotus states that during the reign of Amasis (Ahmose II of the Twenty-sixth Dynasty) Phoenicia lost Cyprus to Egypt and the Cypriote fleet joined forces with Egypt.[4] Persian strategy demanded subjugation of Egypt if Persia was to dominate the Eastern Mediterranean world. To accomplish this conquest the Mediterranean seaboard must first be occupied and an understanding reached with the city-states of Phoenicia to furnish a fleet. An arrangement was made whereby the city-states placed their fleets at the disposal of the Persian monarch. In return Persia did not occupy the cities and allowed them to retain their native kings. All during the Persian period the kings of the Phoenician city-states commanded their naval contingents.[5] Herodotus emphasized the fact that Phoenician participation in the Persian fleet was made on a friendly basis. When Cambyses made plans for a campaign against Carthage the Phoenicians refused to sail because they considered the city a colony of Tyre. Herodotus states that the fleet without Phoenician sails was too weak to undertake the campaign. He further relates: "Cambyses did not think fit to bring pressure to bear because the Phoenicians had taken service under him of their free will and his whole naval power was dependent on them."[6]

Herodotus' testimony indicates that the Phoenician fleet was a very important factor in maintaining the power of the Persian state in the west. The Persians placed complete confidence in the Phoenician city-states and allowed them certain benefits. The cities were allowed to keep their native kings, municipal administration, national laws and religion. The kings of Byblos during the fourth century B.C. minted coinage with their names inscribed in Phoenician letters. On the stele of Yehawmilk, king of Byblos, the king is garbed in the Persian fashion.[7] His dress and headdress resemble that of

[3] *ANET*, p. 316; Ezra 1.1-11.

[4] Herodotus 2.182.

[5] Arrian, *Anabasi Alexandri* 2.20.1-2 gives an illustration of Phoenician independence. At the end of the Persian period "Gerostratus, king of Aradus, and Enylos, king of Byblos, learning that Alexander held their cities left Autophradates and his fleet and arrived with their contingents to side with Alexander."

[6] Herodotus 3.19-20.

[7] *Byblos et l'Egypte*, p. 5.

[8] *Fouilles de Byblos,* Atlas (1926-1932), Plate XCI, coins Nos. 6309 and 6310.

[9] Herodotus 3.91.

[10] Diodorus, *Diodorus Siculus* 16.41. See also Canticles 4.8. The love-garden is described as a *pardes* (Hebrew) which the LXX accurately transliterates as *paradeisos.* Both words are derived from an Iranian word meaning "enclosure" which in Avestan is *pairidaeza.*

[11] *Fouilles de Byblos* I, p. 72 for reference to column bases. M. Dunand announced the fortress in a paper presented at the Archaeological Symposium held at the American University of Beirut (March 7-10, 1967) on "The Role of the Phoenicians in the Interaction of Mediterranean Civilizations".

[12] Roland G. Kent, *Old Persian,* New Haven, American Oriental Society, 1953, p. 144.

the Persian king found on the coins of Sidon during the Persian period.[8]

The Persians instituted a vast administrative system incorporating all subject countries under Persian rule. Phoenicia was united in the fifth satrapy with Syria, Cyprus and Palestine and was taxed lightly compared to the other satrapies.[9]

The Persian king also maintained a park *(paradeisos)* and a royal residence in Sidon.[10] The Beirut National Museum displays the capital of a large column with the double protome of a bull which no doubt comes from the royal palace at Sidon. At Byblos two column bases have been found which belong to the Persian period. To the northeast of the ancient city of Byblos outside the Early Bronze Age city walls the remains of an impressive fortress of the Achaemenid period have recently been discovered.[11]

Under Persian rule the city-states of Phoenicia were encouraged to establish an internal organization. Tyre, Sidon and Aradus were united by federal bonds and had a common council which met at Tripolis. Diodorus (16.41) relates the founding of Tripolis in the fourth century B.C. with the participation of the city-states of Tyre, Sidon and Aradus.

The successor of Cambyses, Darius Hystaspis (ca. 521-486 B.C.) introduced a period of intense commercial activity. He united the most distant parts of the Persian empire by trade routes. Herodotus (4.52-58) gives a detailed description of the royal highway. He states that there were one hundred and eleven post-houses on the road from Sardis (Lydia) to Susa. Such facilities for travel enabled Greeks like Herodotus to visit distant Babylon. The commercial activities of the Phoenician city-states benefited by the extensive road-building program. It not only facilitated transportation but provided security of the roads. Yehawmilk at this time engaged in costly building operations in the temple of Baalat-Gebal. This is a reflection of the prosperity of the times.

A building inscription of Darius I states that cedar was transported to Persia for building purposes: "The cedar timber, this — a mountain by name Lebanon — and from there was brought."[12] Toward the end of the sixth century, Darius established a uniform coinage throughout the Persian empire modelled on the coinage of Lydia. The Greeks called the coins "darics". At first the coins were crudely made of gold. Obviously this was not convenient for

extensive circulation. Herodotus tells us that silver coinage was subsequently issued by a Persian satrap in Egypt who wished to compete with Darius.[13] How much weight can be attributed to this statement is not known but the term "daric" was extended to these coins also. The Phoenicians at this early period made no attempt to mint coins of their own. They felt little need for it since their trade with Greek lands, where coinage flourished, had practically ceased. The earliest Phoenician coinage was minted at Tyre about the middle of the fifth century B.C.[14] Sidon, Aradus and Byblos followed during the late fifth century or early fourth century. The introduction of this coinage probably indicates the growing weakness of the Persian empire and a rebirth of Phoenician trade with Greek lands.

The Ionian revolt against Persia interrupted the peace. This spread to Caria and the whole of Cyprus. At the request of the Persian king the Phoenician city-states provided a fleet. Ships were sent to the Cilician coast and transported troops to Cyprus. The fleet then anchored in the bay opposite Salamis, Cyprus, where the Ionian fleet was drawn up. The engagement that followed was the first encounter between the Phoenicians and the Greeks. The Phoenicians lost the battle at sea but the Persian land forces defeated the Cypriotes.[15] That hatred existed between the Phoenicians and the Greeks can be easily understood. It was based on commercial rivalry. The Greeks in the Aegean were challenging Phoenician dominance of the sea-lanes.

After the Ionian revolt was put down the Phoenician city-states enjoyed a period of peace. Darius, however, looked for fresh conquest in the west. According to Herodotus (3.135-138) he had already sent a spying mission of Persian nobles in Phoenician ships to the coast of Greece. He wished to add Greece to his vast empire. No doubt the Phoenicians did all they could to encourage Darius as their fear of Greek competition on the seas increased. The part played by the fleets of the Phoenician city-states is well described by Herodotus. There were great losses when the fleet under Mardonius was sunk off Mount Athos. In the expedition against Greece led by Xerxes the Phoenicians played a prominent role not only in the naval engagements but also in the field of engineering. The loss of the fleet off the rocky coast of Mount Athos convinced Xerxes of the need for digging a canal through the isthmus which

[13] Herodotus 4.168.

[14] George Francis Hill, *Catalogue of the Greek Coins of Phoenicia*, London, Longmans & Co., 1910, Introduction cxxvi.

[15] Herodotus 5.108 and 5.112.

[16] Herodotus 7.23.

joins Athos to the mainland. No sooner was the canal dug than the sides caved in. Herodotus tells us: "In the section of the canal allotted to the Phoenicians they took out a trench double the width prescribed for the actual finished canal and by digging at a slope gradually contracted it as they got further down until at the bottom their section was the same width as the rest."[16] It was due to the ingenuity and skill of the Phoenicians that the canal was successfully completed.

Another important engineering work was undertaken by Phoenicians and Egyptians at the Hellespont. Xerxes ordered the construction of a bridge over which his land forces could move. The Phoenicians using flax cables and the Egyptians using papyrus passed the cables from shore to shore supported by an almost continuous line of boats. Planks were then laid across the cables and covered with brushwood while a thick layer of earth was placed on top. A violent storm destroyed the bridge but another was quickly built.[17]

[17] Herodotus 7.34-36.

[18] Herodotus 7.89-95.

The fleet which Xerxes assembled to accompany the land army amounted to 1207 vessels.[18] The Phoenicians contributed 300 triremes; there were 200 ships from Egypt and 150 from Cyprus. Xerxes showed a marked preference for the Phoenician vessels. He always boarded a Sidonian vessel when he had need for a ship on special occasions.[19]

[19] Herodotus 7.128.

In the naval encounter at Salamis, Greece, the difficult fighting fell to the Phoenicians. They opened the battle and forced the Athenians to retreat. The Phoenicians however were ultimately overpowered and took to flight. The narrowness of the seas was a factor in this defeat as was the fact that the Athenians, Eginetans and the Corinthians were fighting in home waters. Xerxes from his silver footed throne on Mount Aegaleos surveyed the disaster and held the Phoenicians responsible for the rout. He laid the whole blame on the Phoenician contingent and when some of the captains appeared before him to furnish explanations he had them executed on the spot.[20] He threatened the other Phoenician commanders who were so alarmed that they deserted the fleet and sailed away.[21] Although the war between Persia and Greece was transferred to Asia there is no mention of Phoenician participation. The Phoenician ships retired from Samos on the approach of the Greek fleet under Leotychides.[22] Nor did the Phoenicians take part in the

[20] Herodotus 8.90.

[21] Diodorus 11.60, § 5-6.

[22] Herodotus 9.96.

Battle of Mycale. It was only in 465 B.C. when the war passed from the Aegean to the southern coast of Asia Minor and Cyprus was threatened that the Phoenician fleet appeared in support of the Persian king. Since many of the cities of Cyprus were Phoenician colonies it stands to reason that the Phoenician city-states would become involved. The Phoenician fleet continued to render service to the Persian king. From 465 to 390 B.C. they protected Cyprus from the Athenians and more than once fought them off.[23] They continued to serve Persia never showing the least inclination to revolt.

[23] Diodorus 14.79.8.

However the decline of Persia had set in. In 375 B.C. a Persian attempt to recover Egypt failed. In 366 B.C. the revolt of the satraps began and spread throughout Asia Minor. In 351 B.C. Sidon, humiliated by the conduct of the Persian authorities, revolted under Tennes and induced other Phoenician city-states to follow. The Sidonians expelled the Persian garrisons, devastated the royal park and burned the stores of grain for the Persian cavalry.[24] Tennes, leader of the revolt, treacherously handed over the city of Sidon when besieged by King Ochus (Artaxerxes). In spite of that he was executed by the Persian king. Ochus marched against Egypt and effected its reconquest.

[24] Diodorus 16.41, § 1 and 5.

There is evidence in Herodotus that during the Persian period Phoenicians exploited gold mines on the Greek island of Thasos. Herodotus claims to have seen these mines and tells us:[25]

[25] Herodotus 6.47.

> These Phoenician mines lie between Coenyra and a place called Aenyra, on the south-eastern side of Thasos, facing Samothrace. A whole mountain has been turned upside down in the search for gold.

Royal Inscriptions of Byblos

During the Persian period the Temple of Baalat-Gebal underwent important changes and additions. The stele of Yehawmilk, king of Byblos, gives an account of the reconstruction of the temple. This important inscription was found shortly after the Renan mission and is presently in the Louvre. At the top of the stele there is a representation of Baalat-Gebal and the king of Byblos. The goddess has on her head the solar disc between cow's horns like

[26] *Byblos et l'Egypte,* pp. 5 and 10.

[27] *Fouilles de Byblos* I, p. 56.

[28] *ANET,* p. 502. According to Rosenthal, the identity of the second of the three main objects Yehawmilk dedicates to the goddess is not clear. Instead of an "engraved object" it might have been a door.

the Egyptian Hathor-Isis and holds a staff with a lotus flower in her left hand like her Egyptian counterpart *(Fig. 104).*[26] The king is garbed in the Persian fashion. Although this ex-voto was discovered in 1869, a fragment completing most of its lower right hand corner was found sixty years later by Dunand in the Byzantine levels at Byblos.[27]

Yehawmilk states:[28]

I AM YEHAWMILK, KING OF BYBLOS, THE SON OF YEHARBA'L, THE GRANDSON OF URIMILK, KING OF BYBLOS, WHOM THE MISTRESS, THE LADY OF BYBLOS, MADE KING OVER BYBLOS. I HAVE BEEN CALLING MY MISTRESS, THE LADY OF BYBLOS, (AND SHE HEARD MY VOICE). THEREFORE I HAVE MADE FOR MY MISTRESS, THE LADY OF BYBLOS, THIS ALTAR OF BRONZE WHICH IS IN THIS (COURTYARD), AND THIS ENGRAVED OBJECT OF GOLD WHICH IS IN FRONT OF THIS INSCRIPTION OF MINE, WITH THE BIRD (?) OF GOLD THAT IS SET IN A (SEMIPRECIOUS) STONE, WHICH IS UPON THIS ENGRAVED OBJECT OF GOLD, AND THIS PORTICO WITH ITS COLUMNS AND THE (CAPITALS) WHICH ARE UPON THEM, AND ITS ROOF: I, YEHAWMILK, KING OF BYBLOS, HAVE MADE (THESE THINGS) FOR MY MISTRESS, THE LADY OF BYBLOS, AS I CALLED MY MISTRESS, THE LADY OF BYBLOS, AND SHE HEARD MY VOICE AND TREATED ME KINDLY. MAY THE LADY OF BYBLOS BLESS AND PRESERVE YEHAWMILK, KING OF BYBLOS, AND PROLONG HIS DAYS AND YEARS IN BYBLOS, FOR HE IS A RIGHTEOUS KING. AND MAY (THE MISTRESS) THE LADY OF BYBLOS, GIVE (HIM) FAVOR IN THE EYES OF THE GODS AND IN THE EYES OF THE PEOPLE OF THIS COUNTRY AND (THAT HE BE) PLEASED WITH THE PEOPLE OF THIS COUNTRY. (WHOEVER YOU ARE) RULER AND (ORDINARY) MAN, WHO MIGHT (CONTINUE) TO DO WORK ON THIS ALTAR AND THIS ENGRAVED WORK OF GOLD AND THIS PORTICO, MY NAME, YEHAWMILK, KING OF BYBLOS, (YOU SHOULD PUT WITH) YOURS UPON THAT WORK, AND IF YOU DO NOT PUT MY NAME WITH YOURS, OR IF YOU (REMOVE) THIS (WORK AND TRANSFER THIS WORK FROM ITS FOUNDATION) UPON THIS PLACE AND (. . . , MAY) THE MISTRESS, THE LADY OF BYBLOS, (DESTROY) THAT MAN AND HIS SEED BEFORE ALL THE GODS OF BYBLOS.

Another interesting inscription from the lid of a white marble sarcophagus was found by Dunand in the accumulated debris of the Crusader castle. This fragment has on it an inscription in Phoenician letters of Batno'am, mother of Ozbaal:[29]

[29] *Fouilles de Byblos* I, p. 31.

> IN THIS SARCOPHAGUS I, BATNO'AM MOTHER OF OZBAAL, KING OF BYBLOS, SON OF PILLET-BAAL, PRIEST OF BAALAT, DO LIE; GARBED IN A GOWN AND HEADDRESS WITH A GOLD PLATE COVERING MY MOUTH, IN THE SAME APPAREL AS ALL ROYAL PERSONS BEFORE ME.

Dunand believes that Batno'am was not a queen but by orders of her son, the king of Byblos, she was buried with royal honors. She very proudly had inscribed the articles of royal apparel with which she was to be adorned for burial. Ozbaal's reign is placed ca. 350 B.C.

Dunand found this sarcophagus lid under 1.5 meters of debris which came from the foundations of the Crusader castle. The Roman lamps, Byzantine lamps, Arabic inscription on a stele and Egyptian figurines found in this area prove the extent to which the stratification of Byblos was disturbed. An inscription on porous limestone was found in this debris. The name of the deceased is not known but apparently was the son of a king. He appears to be the son of Shipit-Baal III whom Albright has placed in the Persian period.[30] As in the case of Batno'am the tomb of this unnamed son of Shipit-Baal was also disturbed in antiquity. The inscription consists of three fragments:[31]

[30] W.F. Albright, *JAOS* LXVII, 1947, p. 160.

[31] *Fouilles de Byblos* I, pp. 31-32.

Fragment A:

> "...SON OF SAFATBA'AL, KING OF BYBLOS, I HAVE MADE THIS TOMB...
> ...SARCOPHAGUS UPON SARCOPHAGUS. THAT IS WHY I HAVE...
> ...IN THIS TOMB WHERE I LIE IN PEACE — IN THIS PLACE...
> ...I HAVE GROWN UP AMONGST THE GREAT AND I HAVE GIVEN...
> ...IF YOU VIOLATE THIS TOMB TO DISTURB MY BONES. IF..."

Fragment B:

> ...NEAR THIS TOMB...
> ...THE TOMB THAT YOU...
> ...SARCOPHAGUS (?) UPON SARCOPHAGUS...
> ...AND BA'ALAT AND ALL THE GODS...

Fragment C:

...BAʿAL-SHAMIN (?) AND BAʿAL...
...BAʿALAT AND ALL THE GODS...

A grey pottery jar which had been buried upright in the ground, containing a large number of silver coins, was found at Byblos during the excavations of M. Dunand. The hoard consisted of coins minted by kings of Byblos who reigned during the Persian period. There were one hundred and twenty coins on which were inscribed in Phoenician letters the name of Ozbaal, king of Byblos who reigned ca. 350 B.C.; thirty-one coins with the inscription of Adramelek (ca. 340 B.C.) and thirty-five coins of Ayinel (ca. 333 B.C.).[32] Ayinel (Ainel) is generally identified with Enylos who was king of Byblos when Alexander the Great arrived in Phoenicia. Another coin of a fourth century Byblian king has been published by Hill — the quarter stater of Elpaal (before 362 B.C.).[33] This coin was no longer in circulation at the time the hoard was made. The coins of Ozbaal, Adramelek and Ayinel are shown in Figs. 101-103.

[32] *Fouilles de Byblos* I, p. 407.

[33] *Catalogue of the Greek Coins of Phoenicia*, p. 94 for the description of the El-Paal quarter-stater.

Head of deified Alexander the Great
wearing the horns of Ammon
(the head of Alexander the Great
appears on the obverse
of coins of Lysimachus,
king of Thrace 323-281 B.C.)

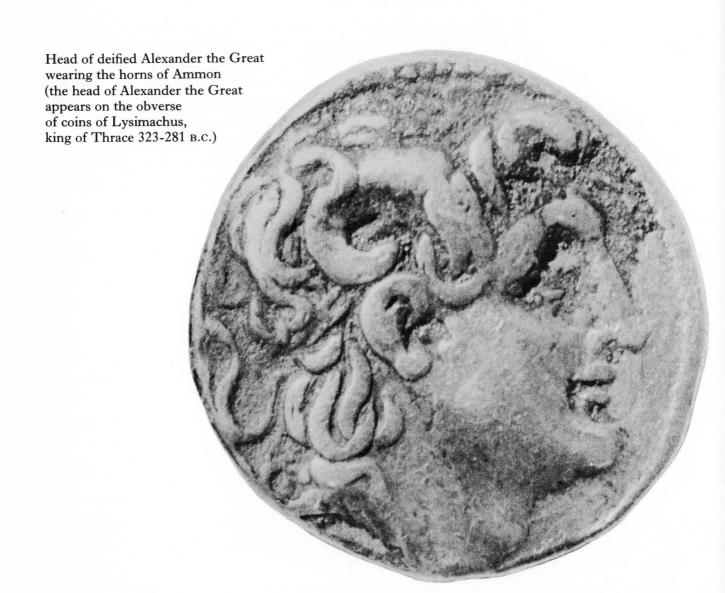

9

The Hellenistic Age
(330-64 B.C.)

Alexander the Great and his conquest of the Near East

The invasion of Asia by Alexander the Great began in 333 B.C. Since he was not in a position to contest the sovereignty of the seas with the naval power of Persia, he wisely crossed into Asia Minor, his goal being the conquest of the Eastern Mediterranean coast and ultimately Persia.[1] Three classical authors have written full accounts of Alexander's conquest of Phoenicia and Asia. Arrian, a Greek born in Nicomedia in A.D. 96 adheres to two main authorities: Ptolemnaeus and Aristobolus. Ptolemnaeus (Ptolemy) was Alexander's general and one of the dynasts who established the kingdom of the Lagids in Egypt after Alexander's death. Diodorus of Sicily (first century B.C.) recounts the history of Alexander and the ensuing period basing his account on Hieronymous of Cardia.[2] Quintus Curtius (date unknown) also wrote a history of Alexander covering his campaigns in Phoenicia and Asia. All three sources will be referred to in this chapter.

The defeat of Darius Codamannus at Issus and his withdrawal to the Euphrates left the entire Mediterranean coast unprotected before Alexander's advancing forces. The capture of the coastal bases from which the Persian fleet operated was of strategic importance to Alexander. Once he controlled these bases he could break up the fleet as they would have no place to make up crews and no base of operations. The important role that the Phoenician fleets played in the military and naval operations of this period cannot be underestimated and is emphasized in Alexander's speech before the siege of Tyre. The fear of revolt of the Greek states and the

[1] Arrian 1.11.3; Diodorus 1.22.5.

[2] William Tarn and G.T. Griffith, *Hellenistic Civilization,* London, Edward Arnold Ltd., 1959, p. 283.

possibility that the Persians would transfer the war to the Greek mainland made it imperative that Alexander control Phoenician seaports and the fleet.[3]

Alexander in person led his forces down the coast of Phoenicia. The city-states were in a difficult position. On the one hand if they resisted the Macedonian conqueror he might pillage their cities and punish them severely. On the other hand the Persian fleet was manned by Phoenicians and kings of the Phoenician city-states were sailing with the fleet at this time. Enylos, king of Byblos, according to Arrian was at sea when Alexander arrived at Byblos.[4]

Arrian tells us of the submission of the cities of Phoenicia:[5]

> He himself went towards Phoenicia. On his way Straton, son of Gerostratus, met him; he was king of the Aradians and those near Aradus; Gerostratus sailed with Autophradates, and the rest of the princes of Phoenicia and the kings of the Cyprians sailed with him too. But Straton meeting Alexander crowned him with a golden crown, yielding up to him the island of Aradus and Marathus which lay opposite it on the mainland, a great and prosperous city, with Sigon and Mariamne and all else under his sway.
>
> Alexander marched from Marathus and received the surrender of Byblos, Sidon, also, invited by the Sidonians themselves, who loathed Persia and Dareius.

It can be seen from the above testimony that Aradus gave Alexander a royal reception. In the absence of the king of Aradus, his son presented Alexander with a golden crown. Alexander received the surrender of Byblos probably from the elders of the city. The Sidonians officially invited Alexander into their city in view of the grievance they held against the Persians.

Diodorus treats these events more briefly but deals at great length with the siege of Tyre:[6]

> Then he marched on towards Egypt, and as he came into Phoenicia, received the submission of all the other cities, for their inhabitants accepted him willingly.

Quintus Curtius in the *History of Alexander* gives the following account:[7]

[3] Arrian 2.17.1-2. Several classical authors use the literary form of speeches as an analysis to express the political motives of the time. Arrian's analysis of the political situation can be seen in Alexander's speech before Tyre.

[4] Arrian 2.20.1.

[5] Arrian 2.13.7-8 and 2.15.6.

[6] Diodorus 17.40.2.

[7] Quintus Curtius, *History of Alexander* 4.1.15-16.

Then Alexander marched down into Phoenicia and received the town of Byblos in surrender. From there he came to Sidon, a city re-knowned for its antiquity and fame of its founders.

When Alexander announced that he intended to offer sacrifice in the Temple of Herakles (Melqart) at Tyre, the Tyrians refused him access to the city. Tyre consisted of the continental city and the island fortress situated in the sea some little distance from the mainland. For the siege of Tyre Alexander used land and naval forces. Gerostratus, king of Aradus and Enylos, king of Byblos deserted the Persian fleet and sailed with their ships and men to join Alexander against Tyre. According to Arrian:[8]

[8] Arrian 2.20.1-2.

> Meanwhile Gerostratus, king of Aradus and Enylos of Byblos, learning that Alexander held their cities, left Autophradates and his fleet and arrived with their own contingents, and with them the Sidonian triremes, so that a total force joined him (Alexander) of some eighty Phoenician sail. There arrived also at the same time triremes from Rhodes, nine, in addition to their state guardship, three from Soli and Mallos and ten from Lycia, and a fifty-oar from Macedon, its captain Proteus son of Adronicus. Soon also the kings of Cyprus put in at Sidon with about 120 sail, having learnt of Dareius' defeat on the Issus, and scared by Alexander's hold over all Phoenicia. To all these Alexander let bygones be bygones, supposing that it was rather from necessity than choice that they had joined naval forces with the Persians.

Why did Aradus, Byblos and Sidon turn against their sister city-state Tyre? The people of these cities knew that their survival depended upon their commercial activities. Each city-state depended upon its ability to sail the seas and sell its wares. If Tyre with its fortified position preferred to resist Alexander there was no reason whatsoever to follow the same policy. The Phoenician city-states required peace and stability for commercial intercourse with neighboring countries. Alliance to a strong empire as in the past would encourage prosperity. It was in the interest of the Phoenician city-states that their fleets join Alexander before Tyre. Quintus Curtius states that for the siege of Tyre Alexander had timber brought

down from the mountains of Lebanon. "A great amount of rocks was available, supplied by Old Tyre, timber was brought from Mount Libanus for making rafts and towers."[9] Diodorus relates that a powerful northwest gale blew up and damaged the mole being constructed in order that the land forces of Alexander could reach the island fortress. Alexander was about to give up the siege. Driven by ambition he sent to the mountains "and felling huge trees he brought them branches and all and placing them besides the mole broke the forces of the waves".[10]

Phoenicia and the Wars of the Successors of Alexander

After the death of Alexander and the division of his empire Phoenicia was given to Laomedon of Mitylene. Ptolemy of Egypt attacked Laomedon and annexed Phoenicia to his own satrapy.[11] In 315 B.C. attacked by Antigonus, Ptolemy relinquished his conquests. Antigonus had come to Phoenicia to organize a naval force. Ptolemy was holding all the ships from Phoenicia and their crews in Egypt and Antigonus had very few ships. Camping before continental Tyre he called together all the kings of Phoenicia and the viceroys of Syria demanding that they assist him in building ships. This important ship-building operation was carried out in the shipyards of Tripolis, Byblos and Sidon:[12]

> He (Antigonus) himself collected wood cutters, sawyers, and shipwrights from all sides, and carried wood to the sea from Lebanon. There were eight thousand men employed in cutting and sawing the timber and one thousand pair of draught animals in transporting it. This mountain range extends along the territory of Tripolis, Byblos and Sidon, and is covered with cedar and cypress trees of wonderful beauty and size. He established three shipyards in Phoenicia — at Tripolis, Byblos and Sidon — and a fourth in Cilicia, the timber for which was brought from Mount Taurus. There was also another in Rhodes, where the state agreed to make ships from imported timber.

This text is the only historical account of logging in Lebanon preserved by classical authors. It emphasizes the importance of Byblos as a center for the timber trade and also gives the reason

[9] Quintus Curtius 4.2.18-19.

[10] Diodorus 17.42.6.

[11] Diodorus 18.43.2.

[12] Diodorus 19.58.2-5.

for the deforestation of the mountains — the periodic mass cutting for naval needs. It also implies that Byblos and Sidon had territory outside the city proper belonging to the city.

With his newly acquired fleet Antigonus blockaded Tyre by sea and land, forcing the city to surrender. Ptolemy's garrison was allowed to leave and Antigonus established his own garrison at Tyre.[13] Demetrius, the son of Antigonus, ruled Phoenicia until 287 B.C. when it once again passed over to Ptolemy. It remained a dependency of the Ptolemies for nearly seventy years.

The Seleucids under Antiochus III made Phoenicia a battlefield in their wars against the Ptolemies. In 219 B.C. Antiochus III drove the Egyptians out of Seleucia, invaded Phoenicia and took Tyre and Accho (which was now called Ptolemais) and threatened Egypt.[14] During the following period the cities of Phoenicia passed back and forth between the two powers. In 198 B.C. Phoenicia and Coele-Syria passed into the possession of the Seleucid kings.[15] The Phoenicians welcomed this change because the establishment of Alexandria was a threat to their commerce. The Seleucid kings granted many new privileges to the Phoenicians. With the consent of their Seleucid overlords the Phoenician cities issued their own coins, bearing legends in both Greek and Phoenician with Greek or Phoenician emblems.[16] Byblos minted coins during this period. A Seleucid-Byblian coin has on the obverse the crowned head of Antiochus IV Epiphanus (175-164 B.C.). On the reverse a Phoenician Kronos is holding a scepter. He has six wings similar to the six-winged creature described by Philo of Byblos.[17]

The Hellenization of Byblos

Byblos at this time was rapidly Hellenized. Such a large number of Greeks settled in Syria and Phoenicia under the Seleucids that to be a Tyrian, Sidonian or Byblian in the Graeco-Roman age was no evidence that a man had Phoenician blood in his veins. The native learned men and authors of the time had Greek or Latin names, for example: Marinus, Paulus, Boethus, Diodotus, Philo and Hermippus. The language in which books were now written was Greek and only in rare cases is there reason to suppose that authors had any knowledge of Phoenician texts. Philo of Byblos claimed

[13] Diodorus 19.61.5. This is another instance where the Phoenician cities Byblos and Sidon took part in the blockade of Tyre.

[14] Polybius, *The Histories* 5.62.

[15] Polybius 16.18.

[16] *Fouilles de Byblos* I, pp. 409-411 for list of coins found at Byblos.

[17] Jules Rouvier, *Numismatique des villes de la Phénicie*, Beirut, 1900, pp. 42-44.

that he had access to works in Phoenician and he was responsible for recasting Phoenician mythology upon a Greek type.[18]

There are various inscriptions belonging to this period which prove that Byblos completely succumbed to Hellenization. In 1860 Renan found a vast number of fragmentary Greek inscriptions in the surface debris at Byblos and Dunand later came across fragments of statuary and many inscribed and stamped jar handles.[19] There is a Greek inscription published by Dunand which is of interest. It refers to one Dionysodoros and his son Aspasios who held the office of *gymnasiarchos* (director of the gymnasium) at Byblos.[20] The civic office of *gymnasiarchos* is characteristically Hellenistic. The *gymnasion* was one of the indispensable aspects of Greek education and was closely associated with the *ephebeia*. The *ephebeia* were young men of fourteen years or older who took their athletic exercise and probably a part of their education in the *gymnasion*.[21] The inscription clearly suggests that a gymnasium was maintained at Byblos during this period. The city had adopted one of the main features of Hellenized cities. The names Dionysodoros and Aspasios both are Greek names.

Several interesting Greek inscriptions were found by Renan. One was a small base which probably supported a statue of a goddess. On one side of the base there is a vase with two sphinxes and a few letters on either side. On the bottom of the base the remainder of the inscription is found: "Most beloved Eumene dedicated this statue of the Heavenly Goddess."[22]

Another inscription published by Renan was found in a sepulchre. It was inscribed on a large flagstone found in the middle of the chamber:[23]

LEARN THAT DIONYSIA MY VIRTUOUS WIFE LIES HERE, BENEATH ME IN THIS SEPULCHRE WHICH HER HUSBAND HAS ADORNED FOR HER, SO THAT IT BE HERE AN ADMONITION FOR THEY WHO PASS BY TO BEAR WITNESS TO THIS RESPECTABLE COUPLE. SUCH IS LIFE, DEAR PASSERBY, CONSISTING OF HOPES AMONG THE LIVING. THEREFORE REJOICE. MAY THE RAPIDITY OF THE FLIGHT OF TIME ESCAPE YOU NOT. THIS IS THE TOMB OF SERAPION, THE TEACHER OF THE EPHEBES.

This inscription provides further evidence that the institution of the *ephebeia* existed at Byblos. 2 Maccabees 4.12 states that Antiochus IV Epiphanes built a *gymnasion* at the foot of the acropolis

[18] F. Jacoby, *Die Fragmente der Griechischen Historiker,* Dritter Teil C, No. 790.

[19] The jar handles, many of which are Rhodian, are catalogued in both volumes of *Fouilles de Byblos.* They are too numerous to include in this chapter.

[20] *Fouilles de Byblos* II, Part 1, p. 60. This large block of stone was found in surface excavations in 1933.

[21] Pierre Jouguet, *Macedonian Imperialism and the Hellenization of the East,* London, Kegan Paul, Trench, Trubner and Co., Ltd., 1928, p. 322.

[22] *Mission de Phénicie,* p. 162.

[23] *Mission de Phénicie,* p. 184.

in Jerusalem. Imposition by force in Jerusalem of a feature so typical of the Greek way of life sparked the revolt of the Maccabees. There is no indication that the inhabitants of Byblos resented the imposition of Greek customs and culture. On the contrary they adapted themselves to the influences of Hellenization to such an extent that it is with difficulty that a distinction can be made between Greeks and native Phoenicians during this period.

A council of elders existed at Byblos during the Hellenistic age as shown by an inscription from the tomb of Domna, wife of Dionysodoros:[24]

[24] Père Jouis Jalabert, s.j., "Inscriptions grecques et latines de Syrie", *Mélanges de la Faculté Orientale de l'Université Saint-Joseph* I, 1906, p. 140.

> TOMB OF DOMNA, WIFE OF DIONYSODOROS, THE *Bouleutes* (CITY ELDER), SON OF DIONYSIOS AND GRANDSON OF DIOPHANTOS.

Dionysodoros was a member of the senior council and held the title of "elder". A passage in Ezekiel (27.9) mentions the elders of Gebal in the metaphorical ship which represents the city of Tyre. Two texts — one from the Babylonian period and the other from the Hellenistic age — refer to this civic office at Byblos.

The name of a funeral director, Abaskantos, on a sarcophagus of this period indicates that Greek names were common in Byblos. The grim humor of Abaskantos and pride in his ability as undertaker of Byblos is apparent from this inscription:[25]

[25] Louis Jalabert, "Inscriptions grecques et latines de Syrie", *Mélanges de la Faculté Orientale de l'Université St. Joseph* I, 1906, pp. 132-133.

> I, ABASKANTOS, WHO HAVE ADORNED (FOR DEATH) ALL THE DECEASED, IT IS ANOTHER WHO HAS PUT ON ME THIS ROBE AND LAID ME IN THE SEPULCHRE. IF I HAD BEEN AWARE OF MY FATE AND KNOWN BEFOREHAND THE HOUR OF MY DEATH, IT WOULD HAVE BEEN I, IN DYING, WHO WOULD HAVE CLOTHED MYSELF IN THIS MORTUARY ROBE.

Positive evidence that by the first century B.C. the city-states of Phoenicia had been completely Hellenized can be seen in Plutarch. In the *Life of Lucullus* there is a passage which states that the rule of Tigranes, king of Armenia, who controlled Phoenicia ca. 83-69 B.C. was "grievous to the Hellenes".[26] Plutarch in this context

[26] Plutarch, *Life of Lucullus* 21.3.

is referring to the inhabitants of the cities of Phoenicia and the Seleucid empire. By calling them "Hellenes" he is giving further evidence that the inhabitants of these cities had so completely accepted the Greek way of life that they were even referred to as "Hellenes".

Mosaic pavement of the bust of Bacchus
from the Roman theater at Byblos

(Beirut National Museum)

10   The Roman Period

(64 B.C.-A.D. 330)

Phoenicia and Syria under Roman Rule

The weakness of the Seleucid kings gradually brought about an end to their empire. Civil wars between aspirants to the throne caused instability and revolts. In 83 B.C. the states forming the Seleucid empire invited Tigranes, king of Armenia, to govern the country.[1] Phoenicia was ruled by him from around 83 to 69 B.C. at which time the Romans intervened actively in the Middle East. Tigranes was forced to retreat to Armenia and was succeeded by the last of the Seleucids, Antiochus XIII Asiaticus, 69-65 B.C. The Roman general Pompey revised the political divisions in the Near East and Phoenicia was included in the province called "Syria" by the Romans.[2]

Strabo in his *Geography* describes the arrival of Pompey at Byblos. Strabo, who lived during the time of Augustus, wrote a detailed description of the countries of the Near East including what he called Coele-Syria and Phoenicia. The text in Strabo concerning Pompey's subjection of the city of Byblos has given rise to various interpretations. The passage includes a description of the Bekaa valley (which Strabo calls the Massyas Plain):[3]

> After Macras one comes to the Massyas Plain, which contains also some mountainous parts, among which is Chalcis, the acropolis, as it were, of the Massyas. The beginning of this plain is the Laodiceia near Libanus. Now all the mountainous parts are held by Ituraeans and Arabians, all of whom are robbers, but the people in the plains are farmers; and when the latter are harassed by

[1] Strabo 11.14.15.

[2] M. Carey, *History of Rome* (2nd ed), London, MacMillan & Co., Ltd., 1960, p. 357.

[3] Strabo 16.2.18. Chalcis is identified with Anjar; Botrys with Batroun; Theuprosopon with Chekka. See René Dussaud, *Topographie historique de la Syrie antique et médiévale*, Paris, Librairie Orientaliste Paul Geuthner, 1927, pp. 81-83. Dussaud tends to identify Gigartus with Zghorta.

109

the robbers at different times they require different kinds of help. These robbers use strongholds as bases of operation; those, for example, who hold Libanus possess, high up on the mountain, Sinna and Borrama and other fortresses like them, and down below, Botrys and Gigartus and the caves by the sea and the castle that was erected on Theuprosopon. Pompey destroyed these places; and from them the robbers overran both Byblos and the city that comes after Byblos, I mean the city Berytus, which lie between Sidon and Theuprosopon. Now Byblos, the royal residence of Cinyras, is sacred to Adonis; but Pompey freed it from tyranny by beheading its tyrant with an axe; and it is situated on a height only a slight distance from the sea.

This text is evidence that in the time of Augustus there existed in the Bekaa an Arabic-speaking kingdom which Strabo called Ituraean. Its political capital was at Chalcis (Anjar) and its religious center at Heliopolis (Baalbeck). The Ituraeans had strongholds in the mountains as bases for raiding operations. Just above the seacoast they operated from caves and also held Botrys (Batroun) and Gigartus (Zghorta). The Ituraeans terrorized caravan trade and would descend from their strongholds to raid nearby cities and overran both Byblos and Beirut. Some modern editors of Strabo interpret the passage to mean that when Pompey came to Byblos somebody called Cinyras was tyrant and Pompey beheaded him. Frazer states: "The last king of Byblos bore the ancient name of Cinyras"; Hill refers to "a tyrant named Cinyras".[4] However there is an objection to this interpretation. Strabo refers to Homer all the time and presumed his readers were aware of the Cinyras in Homer and mythology.[5] Therefore the name Cinyras does not refer to the last king of Byblos but to the king of Cyprus in early legend who was also connected with the Adonis myth. The tyrant of Byblos therefore is nameless. He was no doubt an Ituraean Arab.

Perhaps this passage could be interpreted to mean that upon the expulsion from Phoenicia of Tigranes by Lucullus in 67 B.C. there was no strong government to restrain the incursions of the Ituraeans. For four years they held sway over Phoenicia and Coele-Syria occupying Byblos and Beirut and, as we shall see, Tripolis as well. After Pompey's arrival on the coast the Ituraeans were

[4] James George Frazer, *The Golden Bough, A Study in Magic and Religion*, 3rd ed., IV, Adonis Attis Osiris Vol. I, London, MacMillan & Co., Ltd., 1955, pp. 27-28. See Hill, *Catalogue of the Greek Coins of Phoenicia*, Introduction lxii.

[5] *Iliad* 11.20. Strabo has already discussed Cinyras in 1.2.32.

forced to withdraw to their mountain strongholds where they were ensconced in the time of Augustus when Strabo wrote his geography. This can be considered the first Arab occupation of Byblos and Beirut.

A passage in Josephus can be compared with Strabo's passage concerning Pompey's activities in Syria and Phoenicia.[6] Josephus describes the dispute between Aristobulus and his brother Hyrcanus for the succession to the throne of Judaea and their request for Pompey's mediation. Josephus states that Pompey told their envoys to inform Aristobulus and Hyrcanus to present themselves for his arbitration in Damascus. On his way to Damascus to settle the dispute Pompey passed through several localities:[7]

> And on the way he demolished the citadel at Apamea, which Antiochus Cyzicenus had built, and he also devastated the territory of Ptolemy, the son of Mennaeus, a worthless fellow, no less than was Dionysius of Tripolis, a relative of his by marriage, who was beheaded; but Ptolemy escaped punishment for his sins by paying a thousand talents, with which Pompey paid the wages of his soldiers. He also destroyed the fortress of Lysias, of which the Jew Silas was lord. And passing the cities of Heliopolis and Chalcis, he crossed the mountain that divides the region called Coele-Syria from the rest of Syria and came to Damascus.

Josephus states that the tyrant at Tripolis was a relative of Ptolemaeus, son of Mennaeus, king of Chalcis.[8] By correlating both passages there emerges concrete evidence that the tyrant of Tripolis was an Ituraean Arab who was beheaded by Pompey in his operations against the Ituraeans. The Josephus passage shows Pompey's parallel activity in Tripolis and the Bekaa as compared to Strabo's account of Pompey's operations against the Ituraeans in the mountain fortresses and the coastal cities of Botrys, Byblos and Berytus.

A final text which may concern Pompey and may refer to this period is found in the work of a chronicler of the Byzantine period called Malalas. This text reflects the belief in a garbled version of the refounding of Byblos by Pompey after he had expelled the Ituraeans from the city:[9]

[6] Josephus, *Jewish Antiquities* 14.38-40. 1 Chronicles 5.19 states that the trans-Jordan tribes Reuben and Gad at an undetermined date made war against four tribes including LXX Ἰτουραίων (Ituraean). 1 Chronicles shows them infiltrating north, a process which we can confirm in Jewish and classical sources.

[7] Josephus, *Jewish Antiquities* 14.38-40.

[8] Josephus, *Jewish Antiquities* 13.392.

[9] Ioannis Malalae, *Chronographia,* Corpus Scriptorum Historiae Byzantinae, Bonn, L. Dindorf, 1881, p. 211. The fact that Pompey put to death the tyrant of Byblos may account for the statement in Malalas that the city was founded in the time of Pompey.

> There was a certain powerful general called Byblos who
> founded a village on the seacoast of Phoenicia, walled it
> and made it a city. He called it Byblos after himself.

Roman domination proved to be advantageous to the Phoenician city-states. Rome kept strict control over the Mediterranean and in a sweeping operation Pompey was able to reduce the pirate fleets which made navigation dangerous. Byblos flourished under the *Pax Romana*. The excavations at Byblos prove that large temples were built. The theater, Roman baths, the basilica and extensive drainage are evidence that Byblos had become an important center at this time.

In *Jewish Antiquities* 15.95 Josephus states that Mark Anthony gave Cleopatra various cities of Phoenicia as a gift:

> He also gave her the cities between the Eleutherus River
> and Egypt, with the exception of Tyre and Sidon which
> he knew to have been free from the time of their ancestors
> although she earnestly pleaded that they be given to her.

It is implied that Byblos was included in the sweeping gift of Mark Anthony to the Egyptian queen.

Pliny gives a description in *Natural History* 5.17.78 of the Phoenician coastal cities and the names of the rivers:

> While on the coast, below Mt. Lebanon, are the river
> Magoras, the colony of Berytus called Julia Felix, Lion's
> town, the river Lycus, Palaebyblos, the river Adonis, the
> towns of Byblos, Botrys, Gigarta, Trieres, Calamos,
> Tripolis inhabited by people from Tyre, Sidon and Aradus.

Josephus describes in *Jewish Wars* 1.422 the various bounties made by Herod the Great to foreign cities, including public buildings to cities of Phoenicia:

> After founding all these places, he proceeded to display
> his generosity to numerous cities outside his realm. Thus
> he provided gymnasia for Tripolis, Damascus and Ptole-
> mais, a wall for Byblos, halls, porticoes, temples and
> market-places for Berytus and Tyre, theatres for Sidon
> and Damascus.

An inscription in Phoenician letters was discovered by Montet in 1923 at Byblos. It was carved on a small altar found in the temple

area and measured thirty-six centimeters in height. Although the letters can be clearly read the interpretation of the inscription has led to different views. The form of the letters suggests to Dussaud that this altar was dedicated about the beginning of the first century of our era. He reconstructed the inscription:[10]

[10] *Byblos et l'Egypte,* p. 258. See also René Dussaud, "Inscription phénicienne de Byblos de l'époque romaine", *Syria* VI, 1925, p. 271.

I HAVE MADE THIS ALTAR
I 'ABDESHMOUN, THE BUILDER
SON OF IS'A, FOR OUR LORD AND FOR THE STATUE
OF BA'AL. MAY HE BE BLESSED AND MAY HE HAVE LONG LIFE.

According to Dussaud the altar is not only dedicated to a divinity but also to the Emperor Augustus. Byblos felt the power of Rome soon after Pompey arrived in Syria and Phoenicia. Byblos minted coins in the Imperial period; the first coin published by both Rouvier and Hill is a coin on the obverse of which is the head of Augustus.[11] Dussaud believes that it is natural for an individual living during this period at Byblos to dedicate a religious monument to the Emperor.[12] The most probable interpretation according to Dussaud is that 'Abdeshmoun, the person dedicating the altar, is asking for the blessing of Baal (Jupiter) for himself and for long life for the Emperor.

[11] J. Rouvier, *Numismatique des villes de la Phénicie,* p. 48 (Gébal-Byblos coins). See also Hill, *Catalogue of the Greek Coins of Phoenicia,* p. 99.

[12] Dussaud, *Syria* VI, 1925, p. 272. Dussaud states that the inhabitants of Tarragone dedicated an altar to Augustus in 25 B.C. (Dio Cassius 53.25).

Buildings of the Roman Period at Byblos

The Roman buildings no longer exist on the site of Byblos as they were removed by Dunand to allow for further excavations. They consisted of two large temples, baths and a basilica, all of which originally stood directly above the Middle Bronze Age levels. The theater and the colonnade have been rebuilt on the site.

During the excavations in 1925 Dunand came to the conclusion that the two temples called by Montet the "Egyptian" and the "Syrian" temples were in fact parts of one important building complex of the Roman period. This large temple, called temporarily *Bâtiments* I and II, had been built over the foundations of successive architectural stages of the Temple of Baalat-Gebal.[13] Built during the Early Bronze Age (ca. 2800 B.C.) it was destroyed by fire during the Amorite invasions. It was rebuilt during successive periods by the kings of Byblos. At the time of building their temple at Byblos the Romans levelled off the ruins of the buildings and covered up

[13] *Fouilles de Byblos* I, pp. 66-79.

113

the floors with large flagstones. A brief description of the temple is in order. During his campaigns in 1921 and 1922 Montet discovered, to the southwest of the Crusader castle, the foundations of two buildings.[14] Part of the second building was located in the garden between the house of one Ibrahim Housamy and a cheikh.[15] Thus Montet was unable to come to a decision whether these ruins comprised one or two temples. In the so-called "Egyptian" temple there were three seated colossi facing west *(Fig. 110)*. He also unearthed a standing statue approximately two meters from the seated group. All four statues were made of local limestone and were badly mutilated.[16] In front of the statues there was a flagstone court. Behind the seated colossi Montet found two column bases and to the southeast he unearthed a stone basin. In this general area at a depth between three and four meters Montet found a fragment of bas-relief with two representations of a pharaoh kneeling before a deity.[17] When Montet removed the flagstones of the so-called "Syrian" temple he unearthed a large number of valuable objects spread over a wide area. These included fragments of stone vases of Old Kingdom pharaohs, beads, scarabs and a variety of statuettes of human figures and animals. In his second campaign Montet found a jar with a lid, which has been called the "Montet jar", buried upright against a foundation wall under the flagstones.[18] Nearly one thousand objects including jewelry, scarabs, bronze torques and toggle pins were found in this jar which suggest that accumulated treasures of earlier periods were gathered and placed in jars by priests of the temple in order to hide them and preserve them.

The Romans re-used the stone colossi and the two column bases, which have been dated to an earlier period, to embellish their temple.[19] A colossal limestone statue was found in a later excavation by Dunand lying on its side in the region of this temple *(Fig. 109)*. The colonnade bordered the street which led from the Temple of Baalat-Gebal to the north of the city *(Fig. 112)*.

Another large temple came to light in the Roman levels at Byblos.[20] The north-western section of this temple had been built over the Middle Bronze Age Temple of the Obelisks which, in its turn, lay superimposed on the Early Bronze Age temple complex (see Chaps. 3 and 4). From the Early Bronze Age through the Roman period it would appear that there were two principal temples continuously in use — the Temple of Baalat-Gebal and the temple

[14] *Byblos et l'Egypte*, p. 29.

[15] *Byblos et l'Egypte*, p. 29.

[16] *Byblos et l'Egypte*, pp. 29-30.

[17] *Byblos et l'Egypte*, pp. 35-38, No. 11.

[18] *Byblos et l'Egypte*, pp. 111-125.

[19] *Fouilles de Byblos* I, pp. 71-72.

[20] *Fouilles de Byblos* II, Part 1, pp. 26-41. See also *La civilisation phénicienne*, pp. 128-129. Several scholars believe that this temple may be the one that is seen on the coin of Emperor Macrinus (2nd century A.D.). The temple on the Macrinus coin can be seen in Fig. 121.

of a male deity. Like the Temple of Jupiter at Baalbeck, the latter has some features of a Semitic sanctuary. It was composed of a *peribolus* (entrance court), the *pro-cella* (courtyard) and the *cella* (sanctuary). The foundations of several columns were located in the *peribolus* of the temple. Porches could be identified on the outer walls. There was a highly developed system of drainage. Two small sanctuaries were found to the northeast and northwest. The foundations of four columns of the *prostyle in antis* type, that is, columns in front of the portico standing completely free from the front of the temple, stood at the façade of the building. No remains were found of the actual superstructure. No architectural elements were found *in situ* which permitted the re-arrangement of the columns. The Crusaders exploited this particular area as a "quarry" so thoroughly that it is possible the columns of this temple were incorporated in the castle. No inscriptions were found by which the temple could be dated with precision. If the temple went back as early as the Hellenistic age it had been re-used in Roman times.

When Dunand uncovered the Roman theater in the surface excavations he found it in a delapidated condition *(Fig. 113)*.[21] It was situated near the northeastern corner of the great temple and like the temple, had been used as a Crusader "quarry". All that was preserved were the first five steps, the *pulpitum* (stage) and the floor of the stage. It has the hemicycle and seven sectors of steps, both of which are characteristics of the Greek theater. The theater faced the setting sun. The floor of the stage was originally covered with white tessary with a black border. Facing the spectators was a mosaic pavement of a representation of the bust of the god Bacchus, presently in the Beirut National Museum. The *pulpitum* was decorated with ten small Corinthian type columns. Of the superstructure nothing remained except the thick wall built where the steps ended. A stone altar base was found facing the *pulpitum*. There are holes bored in the first tier of steps to support wooden poles set up to hold a protective awning for the audience. Coins found in the foundations of the theater date the construction to A.D. 218. A small road two meters wide led from the theater to the temple and to the baths. The baths, part of which were built over the shaft and tomb of Ahiram, have been called the "Baths of the Theater". In order to reach the Middle Bronze Age levels, Dunand removed the theater and rebuilt it by the sea *(Fig. 114)*.

[21] *Fouilles de Byblos* II, Part 1, pp. 41-46.

115

The building which contained the baths was also incomplete.[22] There were three hot rooms with their substructures of columns of round baked bricks. Two of these rooms contained their original floors of white mosaic. The remains of a rectangular basin in one room indicated that this room was the *frigidarium* (a room kept at low temperature used as a cooling room in a Roman bath).

Another important building of Byblos of the Roman period was a large basilica of rectangular plan.[23] The outer walls were built of sandstone and on some of these stones mason marks could be seen. The large size of the blocks was characteristic of certain constructions of the Flavian emperors though no inscriptions were found to date the building with precision. It had a nave consisting of two rows of five columns. Apparently this building was used at the same time as the theater because a flagstone road ran between the two constructions. The use to which the basilica was put is unclear. No object was found to indicate that a cult was practiced there. It would appear to be a civil basilica or an important public building of the Roman period.

The remains of a *nympheum* (a shrine sacred to the nymphs) were found during the excavations to the northeast of the Crusader castle outside the ancient city walls of Byblos.[24] This elegant structure had niches decorated with columns in which originally statues had been placed. There were basins into which water flowed and an area of flagstones in front of the *nympheum* to which several roads led coming from the north towards the city.

Texts Concerning Roman Byblos and its Inhabitants

A vague reference to a Byblian sophist of the Roman period named Aspasios states that he wrote an encomium in Greek for Hadrian. Could it be that Hadrian passed by Byblos? The encomium was possibly composed and presented to the Emperor as a fitting welcome to the city:[25]

> Aspasios of Byblos; sophist contemporary with Aristides and Hadrian. He wrote *On Byblos* . . . Encomium of the Emperor Hadrian and others.

Henri Seyrig has published an inscribed lead weight which he believes is from Byblos.[26] On one side of the weight there is an

[22] *Fouilles de Byblos* II, Part 1, p. 48.

[23] *Fouilles de Byblos* II, Part 1, pp. 49-51.

[24] *Byblos, son histoire, ses ruines, ses légendes*, pp. 72-73.

[25] F. Jacoby, *Die Fragmente der Griechischen Historiker*, Dritter Teil C, 792 Fr.1.

[26] Henri Seyrig, *Antiquités syriennes*, 55; "Le grand prêtre de Dionysos à Byblos", *Syria* XXXI, 1954, pp. 68-73.

inscription in Greek with the name of Aspasios who was market inspector, grandson of the high priest of Dionysos. On the other side there is engraved the solar disc between cow's horns characteristic of the headdress worn by Isis and Baalat-Gebal. Two factors have led Seyrig to conclude that the weight is originally from Roman Byblos. Isis' headdress figures on coins of Byblos but is not seen on coins from Syria;[27] and the name "Aspasios" is common at Byblos. The inscription is as follows:[28]

> DURING THE MARKET INSPECTION APPOINTMENT OF ASPASIOS, SON OF APOLLODOROS, SON OF ASPASIOS, HIGH PRIEST OF DIONYSOS.

Seyrig believes that the title of high priest of Dionysos is the Greek equivalent to the title of high priest of Adonis since there is no evidence that the cult of Dionysos was practiced at Byblos.

Several texts indicate that citizens of Byblos sought their fortunes in foreign places. A funeral stele in Greek states that a Byblian called Euphrosinos, the son of Hermes, died at Minoa on the Greek island of Amorgus. The stele was set up by his wife Rufa. The inscription ends with the phrase: "he (Euphrosinos) was excluded from his country by the three fates," implying that his residence in a foreign land had been decreed by divine will which also denied him burial at Byblos.[29] A woman from Byblos was buried at Beth She'arim in Palestine during the Roman period. In Catacomb 12, Room 1 in the right hand wall there is an arcosolium containing one grave only. On the two upper ends of the arch are inscriptions in red paint. The inscriptions which resemble each other in content but differ in formulation are in Greek:[30]

> BE COMFORTED, O MATRON CALLIOPE
> NO ONE IS IMMORTAL; SHE WAS FROM BYBLOS

The second inscription reads:

> APSE OF CALLIOPE OF BYBLOS, THE MATRON.

Finally an honorary decree from Delphi tells of a Byblian sophist named Aurelius who lived there during the second century A.D. Although this inscription is fragmentary it tells us that the sophist of Byblos was made a citizen of Delphi and was given the office of *Bouletes* (elder).[31] He was also granted *proedria,* the privilege to

[27] *Catalogue of the Greek Coins of Phoenicia*, p. 97, coin No. 14 (1st cent. B.C.).

[28] Seyrig, *Syria* XXXI, 1954, p. 68.

[29] *Inscriptiones Graecae*, Ed. Maior XII (Berolini Apvd Georgivm Reimervm MCMVIII), Fascicle 7, 305.

[30] M. Schwabe, "Greek Inscriptions Found at Beth She'arim in Fifth Excavation Season", *Israel Exploration Journal* IV, Jerusalem, Hadassah Apprentice School of Printing, 1954, p. 250.

[31] *Supplementum Epigraphicum Graecum* XVIII, Leiden, A.W. Sythoff, 1962, No. 191.

occupy the front row in the Greek theater and at public games and assemblies, as well as *promanteia*: priority in consulting the oracle. These honors were bestowed usually on distinguished foreigners.

Aelian (ca. A.D. 170-235) a Roman author and teacher of rhetoric wrote *Varia Historia* in Greek. This work, consisting mainly of anecdotes of men and customs, is valuable as it contains excerpts from earlier writers. Aelian makes a statement concerning Byblos:[32]

> A Byblian who finds something in the street will not pick it up unless he has left it there himself.

This is flattering testimony by a Roman author to the integrity of the inhabitants of Byblos.

From a comparison of various ancient texts there can be little doubt that wine from Byblos was considered a delicacy. Hesiod (eighth century B.C.) in *Works and Days* 589 mentions a mysterious beverage used for summer drinking which he calls βίβλινος οἶνος *(biblinos oinos)*, to be read wine from Byblos or wine made from papyrus. Since we have no evidence that wine can be made from any part of the papyrus plant this must refer to the place from which the wine came. Herodotus (2.92) states that the Egyptians ate the top of papyrus stalks, in fact papyrus was best enjoyed when baked in a red hot oven. He goes on to tell us that Egypt imported wine from Greece and Phoenicia:[33]

> I will now tell of a thing that but few of those who sail to Egypt have perceived. Earthen jars full of wine are brought into Egypt twice a year from all Greece and Phoenicia besides: yet one might safely say there is not a single empty wine jar anywhere in the country. Each governor of a district must gather in all the earthen pots from his own township and take them to Memphis and the people of Memphis must fill them with water and carry them to those waterless lands of Syria.

Theocritus, a Greek poet born in Syracuse (ca. 310-250 B.C.) in *Idyll 14* describes a drinking party in which "a hogshead of Bybline wine, fine and fragrant — four years in the cask" was consumed.[34]

Athenaeus, a native of Naucratis in Egypt who lived in Rome at the end of the second century A.D., wrote a text discussing the

[32] Aelian, *Varia Historia* 4.1.

[33] Herodotus 3.6.

[34] Theocritus, *Idyll 14* 10-20. *The Greek Bucolic Poets*, Cambridge, Harvard University Press, 1950.

118

[35] Athenaeus, *The Deipno-sophists* I, Cambridge, Harvard University Press, 1951. See Introduction viii.

[36] Athenaeus I, 29 <u>B</u>.

[37] *ANET*, p. 28.

[38] *ANET*, p. 282.

[39] *Geographi Graeci Minoris* II, ed. Muller, "Tautios Orbis Descripto", p. 518, Paris, 1861; reprinted Hildesheim, 1965.

[40] Names of kings of Byblos during the tenth century B.C. are: *Yehimilk, Abi-Baal, Eli-Baal* and *Shipit-Baal*. During the Roman period there is an inscription of *'Abdeshmoun*, the builder. See *Syria* VI, 1925, p. 271.

[41] Lucian, *De Dea Syria*, trans. Herbert A. Strong, London, Constable & Co., Ltd., 1913, p. 30.

gastronomic habits of his day.[35] He refers to the mock-epic gastronomic writer Archestratus of Syracuse (fourth century B.C.) who is the only ancient source to connect Bybline wine with Phoenicia. He states: "I praise too, Bybline wine from sacred Phoenicia," comparing it with Lesbian wine.[36] These texts illustrate the popular appeal of wine from Byblos over several centuries.

In addition to the papyrus trade and wine exports a comparison of ancient texts shows that Byblos was also a commercial center for linen. In the Wen-Amon papyrus (eleventh century B.C.) linen was listed among items received from Egypt in exchange for cedar wood.[37] During the eighth century B.C., in a tribute list of Tiglath-Pileser III, in addition to gold, silver, tin and copper, the kings of Byblos and Arvad sent as tribute linen garments with multicolored trimmings and garments of their native industries being made of dark purple wool.[38] This is evidence that textile industries existed in these cities. A passage from Ezekiel (27.7) can be considered proof that during the seventh century B.C. Egypt furnished the Phoenician city-states with fine linen. During the Roman period Byblos not only exported linen but was considered the commercial center of the linen trade.[39]

Cults of Byblos during the Roman Period

There can be no doubt that the Phoenicians were a people in whose minds religion occupied a prominent place. The temple was the center of activities where pious worshippers gave abundant and costly offerings. Both the kings of Byblos and their subjects bore names compounded with those of gods.[40] The Temple of Baalat-Gebal in particular received costly gifts from the pharaohs of Egypt and the kings of Byblos throughout successive periods in its history. A description of these cults in Roman times is given in the works of three classical authors of the period — Plutarch, Philo of Byblos and Lucian of Samosata. There is some reason to believe that Philo of Byblos lived during the second century A.D. at Byblos and there is evidence that Lucian travelled to Syria, Phoenicia and Egypt around A.D. 148.[41]

Plutarch (A.D. 46-120), a priest of the Pythian Apollo at Chaeronia, Boeotia, wrote a treatise called *On Isis and Osiris*. During the Roman period Byblos was associated with Egypt in myth and

ritual. This is seen in the myth of Isis and Osiris. The Byblian episodes of this myth appear nowhere in native Egyptian literature of any period and were obviously added to the myth in the Hellenistic age as part of the general syncretism of this age. In Plutarch's account the search by Isis for Osiris' body brought her to the shores of Byblos. Typhon (the name Plutarch has given to the Egyptian god Seth) had treacherously killed Osiris and placed his body in a wooden chest which he cast into the Nile. The chest was carried out to sea and floated from Egypt to Byblos where it was cast upon the shore. There it was enveloped in a clump of heather which grew around it and concealed it. The king of Byblos admiring the great size of the trunk used it as a pillar to support the roof of his house.[42]

Plutarch states that the name of the queen of Byblos at the time of Isis' search for Osiris was Astarte. Plutarch describes Isis' trip to Byblos:[43]

> Thereafter Isis, as they relate, learned that the chest had been cast up by the sea near the land of Byblos and that the waves had gently set it down in the midst of a clump of heather. The heather in a short time ran up into a very beautiful and massive stock, and enfolded and embraced the chest with its growth and concealed it within its trunk. The king of the country admired the great size of the plant, and cut off the portion that enfolded the chest (which was now hidden from sight), and used it as a pillar to support the roof of his house. These facts, they say, Isis ascertained by the divine inspiration of Rumour, and came to Byblos and sat down by a spring, all dejection and tears; she exchanged no word with anybody, save only that she welcomed the queen's maidservants and treated them with great amiability, plaiting their hair for them and imparting to their persons a wondrous fragrance from her own body. But when the queen observed her maidservants, a longing came upon her for the unknown woman and for such hairdressing and for a body fragrant with ambrosia. Thus it happened that Isis was sent for and became so intimate with the queen that the queen made her the nurse of her baby. They say that the king's name was Malcander; the queen's name some say was Astarte, others Saosis, and still others Nemanus, which the Greeks call Athenais.

[42] M. Dunand, *BMB* XVI, 1964, pp. 75-79. Early Bronze Age dwellings at Byblos had seven stone bases for wooden pillars to support the roof.

[43] *On Isis and Osiris* 357.15. The spring at Byblos where presumably Isis met the queen's maidservants is called today *Ayin-el-Malik* (the spring of the king) by the natives of Jebeil. See Fig. 115.

Isis did not breastfeed the baby but gave him her finger to suck. At night she burned the human form of the infant who was immediately transformed into a swallow which flew around the wooden pillar that enveloped the body of Osiris. The queen seeing her child in flames uttered a loud cry and thus her son lost his chance for immortality. Isis finally made known her identity and requested the pillar in the king's palace. She removed the chest in which the body of Osiris lay and then the wooden pillar was placed in the temple at Byblos where it became an object of veneration. Isis had the wooden chest containing the body of Osiris placed on a ship and then sailed away to Egypt. While passing the Fidar River to the south of Byblos a violent storm arose. With one angry look Isis dried up the bed of the river.

Plutarch's treatise is interesting for two reasons. In the first place it shows that during the Roman period Byblos was associated with Egypt in myth; secondly the treatise reflects connections between Byblos and Egypt in the remote past. These have been confirmed by the excavations.

There is no extant native religious literature from Phoenicia covering the first millenium B.C. except for extracts from Philo of Byblos. These have been preserved in Eusebius' *Praeparatio Evangelica*.[44] Philo claimed that he had access to the writings in Phoenician of Sanchuniathon, a priest born in Berytus (Beirut) in the eleventh century B.C. Philo's work illustrates early religious beliefs of the Phoenicians on the creation of the world. Some of the texts mention Byblos:[45]

> Among the Byblians (Agrotes) is especially called the greatest of the gods.
> In the time of these there is born a certain Elioun called the Highest and a female called Berout who lived in the vicinity of Byblos.

It is probable that the Elioun of this text is the Alyan-Baal of Ugaritic mythology and the Elyōn of the Old Testament:

> In the time of these (preceding gods) Kronos put a wall around his habitation and founded Byblos of Phoenicia, the first city.
> And in the time of these, Kronos gives Byblos the city to the goddess Baaltis who is also Dione.

[44] Jacoby, *op. cit.*, 790 Fr. 1-2.

[45] Jacoby, *op. cit.*, 790 F 2 § 12; F 2 § 15; F 2 § 19; F 2 § 35.

121

Philo is identifying the goddess Baaltis with the Greek goddess Dione. It would appear that this is a transcription by Philo from the original text in Phoenician and the goddess Baaltis is none other than Baalat-Gebal. Evidently Philo was in touch with good Phoenician tradition when he put Baalat-Gebal's name in Greek and associates her with a Greek counterpart.

The cult of Adonis was centered at Byblos and was similar to other cults in the Near East which had the same characteristic features centered on the rhythm of the seasons. Originally it was a nature cult inspired by the productivity of the soil. Aphrodite (Astarte) was the embodiment of generation and procreation in perpetuity, her consort Adonis assumed the role of the youthful male god personifying the transitory seasonal sequence of vegetation.[46] In describing Byblos Strabo during the first century A.D. wrote that "Byblos, the royal residence of Cinyras, is sacred to Adonis".[47] Annuals festivals were held in honor of Adonis at Byblos and elsewhere.

Lucian gives us an account of the secret rites of Adonis practiced at Byblos:[48]

> I saw at Byblos a large temple, sacred to the Byblian Aphrodite: this is the scene of the secret rites of Adonis: I mastered these. They assert that the legend about Adonis and the wild boar is true, and the facts occurred in their country, and in memory of this calamity they beat their breasts and wail every year, and perform their secret ritual amid signs of mourning through the whole countryside. When they have finished their mourning and wailing, they sacrifice in the first place to Adonis, as to one who has departed this life: after this they allege that he is alive again, and exhibit his effigy to the sky. They proceed to shave their heads, too, like the Egyptians on the loss of their Apis. The women who refuse to be shaved have to submit to the following penalty, to stand for the space of an entire day in readiness to expose their persons for hire. The place of hire is open to none but foreigners, and out of the proceeds of the traffic of these women a sacrifice to Aphrodite is paid.
> Some of the inhabitants of Byblos maintain that the Egyptian Osiris is buried in their town, and that the

[46] E.O. James, *The Ancient Gods*, New York, G.P. Putnam's Sons, 1960, pp. 97 and 105.

[47] Strabo 16.2.18.

[48] Lucian, *The Syrian Goddess*, trans. Herbert A. Strong, London, Constable & Co., Ltd., 1913, § 6-9.

public mourning and secret rites are performed in memory not of Adonis but of Osiris. I will tell you why this story seems to be worthy of credence. A human head comes every year from Egypt to Byblos, floating on its seven days' journey thence; the winds, by some divine instinct, waft it on its way: it never varies from its course but goes straight to Byblos. The whole occurrence is miraculous. It occurs every year, and it came to pass while I was myself in Byblos, and I saw the head in that city.

There is, too, another marvelous portent in the region of the Byblians. A river, flowing from Mount Libanus, discharges itself into the sea: this river bears the name of Adonis. Every year regularly it is tinged with blood, and loses its proper colour before it falls into the sea: it dyes the sea, to a large space, red: and thus announces their time of mourning to the Byblians. Their story is that during these days Adonis is wounded, and that the river's nature is changed by the blood which flows into its waters; and that it takes its name from this blood. Such is the legend vulgarly accepted: but a man of Byblos, who seemed to me to be telling the truth, told me another reason for this marvellous change. He spoke as follows: "This river, my friend and guest, passes through the Libanus: now this Libanus abounds in red earth. The violent winds which blow regularly on those days, bring down into the river a quantity of earth resembling vermilion. It is this earth that turns the river to red. And thus the change in the river's colour is due, not to blood as they affirm, but to the nature of the soil." This was the story of the Byblian. But even assuming that he spoke the truth, yet there certainly seems to me something supernatural in the regular coincidence of the wind and the colouring of the river.

I went up also from Byblos into the Libanus, a single day's journey, as I had heard that there was an ancient temple of Aphrodite there founded by Cinyras. I saw the temple, and it was indeed old. These then are the ancient great temples of Syria.

123

Lucian tells us that the women of Byblos beat their breasts and wailed to lament the death of Adonis, shaving their heads as a sign of grief as the Egyptians did on the occasion of the death of Apis. As an alternative the women could for the period of one day offer themselves to strangers. The proceeds from this type of temple prostitution were used to pay for sacrifices to Aphrodite (Astarte).[49] After a period of mourning sacrifices were made to Adonis and his effigy was exposed proving that he was alive again.

Of interest is the fact that some inhabitants of Byblos believed that the Egyptian Osiris was buried in their town and that the public mourning was performed in memory of Osiris, not of Adonis. This belief was probably based on Plutarch's account of Isis and Osiris in which Isis made a trip to Byblos in search of the body of her lover which had floated there in a wooden chest and was cast ashore.[50] Osiris was not originally a vegetation deity in the Osiris myth. During the Hellenistic age he took on the attributes of a vegetation god and was connected with Adonis in popular belief at Byblos.

Byblos and Afka were closely associated in the cult of Adonis. It was believed that when Adonis was chasing the wild boar in the mountains near the source of the river of Byblos (Afka), the animal he was hunting turned on him and gored his thigh. He died of the wound. On the anniversary of his death the women of Byblos formed an emotional procession to Afka, where the temple of Aphrodite stood, and wailed and lamented his death. The river changed color in spring and it was thought to flow red with the blood of Adonis. Not everyone in Byblos believed this miraculous event. A sceptic explained to Lucian that violent winds brought down into the river quantities of red earth from the mountains and it was this earth that turned the river red. At the end of the seventeenth century A.D. another traveller to Jebeil recorded the phenomen of the change in color of the waters of the Adonis River (called the Nahr Ibrahim today). Maundrell reports: "The water was stained to a surprising redness and as we observed in travelling had discoloured the sea a great way into a reddish hue, occasioned doubtless by a sort of minium, or red earth, washed into the river by the violence of the rains."[51] To the present day this phenomenon can be observed in Lebanon, usually during the month of April after heavy rainfall.

[49] Lucian § 6. During the seventh century B.C. Ezekiel 8.14 describes how a parallel cult was practiced in Jerusalem. "Then he brought me to the entrance of the north gate of the house of the Lord; and behold, there sat women weeping for Tammuz. Then he said to me 'Have you seen this, O son of Man? You will see still greater abominations than these!'"

[50] Plutarch, *On Isis and Osiris* 357.15.

[51] H. Maundrell, *A Journey from Aleppo to Jerusalem*, 6th ed., Oxford, 1749, p. 153. The first edition was printed in 1699 two years after his visit to the Adonis River during the month of April, 1697.

The cult of Adonis spread from Byblos throughout the Graeco-Roman world. As early as the fifth century B.C. there is evidence that Adonis was worshipped in different places in Greece. Plutarch in the *Life of Nicias* relates that during the Peloponnesian War Alcibiades' expedition to Syracuse coincided with the celebration of the festival of Adonis at Athens and this was considered an ill omen:[52]

[52] Plutarch, *The Life of Nicias* 13. This was during the year 415 B.C.

> Others were also disturbed by the season of the year at which it was decided to despatch the fleet. It was the moment when the women of Athens were celebrating the festival of Adonis, and in many parts of the city little images of the dead youth were being carried in funeral processions, accompanied by the wailing cries of the women, so that all who paid attention to such omens were filled with misgivings for the fate of the men setting out. A sudden dread seized them that this mighty expedition, fitted out with such magnificence and expense, might in its very prime be blasted and come to nothing.

A passage in Thucydides, referring to the expedition to Syracuse, states that the departure of the fleet for Sicily took place in the summer.[53] From this testimony it would appear that the festival of Adonis, in Greece at any rate, was a summer festival.

[53] Thucydides 6.30.

During the Hellenistic age the worship of Adonis spread to Alexandria where it was practiced on an elaborate scale under royal patronage. Theocritus, a poet born in Syracuse (ca. 315 B.C.), lived in Alexandria during the reign of Ptolemy Philadelphus. In his *Idyll* 15, he tells us how two middle class women of Alexandria go out into the crowded streets accompanied by their maids to see the procession. The god, according to popular belief, was permitted to return annually from Pluto's region to the upper world for a brief reunion with Aphrodite. The festival celebrating his return lasted two days at least. On the first day his reunion with Aphrodite was celebrated; the second day was one of mourning as the women bewailed his departure for the underworld. Little pots of rapidly growing herb called "gardens of Adonis" were planted on the occasion of the festival. The stalks of wheat or barley which grew and died swiftly symbolized the brevity of youth.[54] In Alexandria Adonis was represented by a statue reclining on a silver couch in

[54] *The Idylls and Epigrams of Theocritus* with English notes by Herbert Kynaston, Oxford, Clarendon Press, 1892, p. 181, line 113. The custom of planting rapidly growing herbs is still practiced today by Christians in Lebanon and Cyprus on the occasion of Christmas.

a temporary bower ornamented with birds and cupids. Part of these ceremonies were staged in the royal palace and praises to the queens Arsinoë and Berenice were sung. This was one way of eulogizing the family of Ptolemy who patronized the festival. A dirge was then sung for Adonis' departure. At the end of the festival the statue of Adonis was carried outside the city and flung into the sea amidst the wailing and lamentations of the women.

Apollodorus, author of *The Library,* was a contemporary of Hadrian and lived in the early part of the first century A.D. His work is of interest as it is a summary of Greek myths and heroic legends as these were recorded in literature. The writer makes no statement that he is drawing on oral tradition.[55] *The Library* can be considered an accurate record of what the Greeks in general believed.

According to Apollodorus, Adonis was the son of the Syrian king Theias by his daughter Myrrha. She had been inspired by Aphrodite with unnatural lust for her father and by concealing her identity conceived Adonis by him. When Theias discovered the truth he would have killed her but the gods in pity changed her into a tree of the same name. After ten months the tree burst asunder and from it Adonis came forth.

In another passage Apollodorus relates that Io came to Byblos. In Greek mythology Io was the daughter of Inachus, king of Argos. Zeus fell in love with her and to protect her from the wrath of his wife Hera, he changed her into a white heifer. Maddened by a gadfly sent by Hera, Io wandered all over the earth, crossed the Ionian Sea and at last reached Egypt. She was restored to her original form and became the mother of Epaphus. She was identified with Isis and Epaphus with the bull god Apis. Epaphus, according to this myth, was carried off by the order of Hera to Byblos where he was found again by Io.[56] As Osiris was connected with Adonis in the minds of the ancients, so was Isis with Io. Herodotus states that the two goddesses were represented similarly in art; statues of Isis show a female figure with cow's horns *(Fig. 105)* like the Greek representation of Io.[57] Diodorus also identifies Io and Isis.[58] During the Hellenistic age Isis is said to have nursed the infant son of the king of Byblos.[59] These legends reflect intercourse between east and west and the identification of foreign gods with Greek gods. The real relationship between Byblos and Egypt goes back as far as the third millenium B.C. based on the timber trade.

[55] Apollodorus, *The Library*, Introduction xvii.

[56] Apollodorus 2.1.3.

[57] Herodotus 2.41. Many representations of Io are preserved on vases and wall paintings in Greece.

[58] Diodorus 1.24.8. Diodorus states: "The origin of Isis is transferred by the Greeks to Argos in the myth which tells of that Io who was changed into a heifer."

[59] Plutarch, *On Isis and Osiris* 357.15.

A close connection existed between Byblos and Afka in the cult practices of Adonis. During the pagan period, before Christianity received official permission to exist and develop, the temples of Byblos and Afka were centers of pilgrimage. Political considerations were of primary importance to Constantine the Great (A.D. 288-337) when he adopted an eastern religion and moved his capital eastwards to Byzantium on the Bosphorus.[60] Zosimus, a pagan writer contemporary with Constantine the Great, visited the temple at Afka:[61]

> There is a site called Afka, between Byblos and Heliopolis where stands a temple of Aphrodite Aphakatis. Near the temple is a pool, which resembles a hand-made cistern. In the neighborhood of this temple and the surrounding place, a light shows itself in the air resembling a ball of fire when meetings are held on that place on prescribed times. It showed itself even in our time.

The description above by Zosimus conforms with the pagan view. The Christian point of view can be seen in a text by Eusebius, Bishop of Caesarea (ca. A.D. 260-340).[62]

> This was a grove and a sacred enclosure, not situated as most temples are, in the midst of a city and of market places, and of broad streets, but far away from either road or path, on the rocky slopes of Libanus. It was dedicated to a shameful goddess, the goddess Aphrodite. A school of wickedness was this place for all such profligate persons as had ruined their bodies by excessive luxury. The men there were soft and womanish — men no longer; the dignity of their sex they rejected; with impure lust they thought to honor the deity. Criminal intercourse with women, secret pollutions, disgraceful and nameless deeds, were practiced in the temple, where there was no restraining law, and no guardian to preserve decency.

A comparison of this text with that of Lucian shows that similar practices in temple prostitution were practiced at Byblos during the Roman period. The temple of Afka was built on an esplanade which dominated the Adonis River (Nahr Ibrahim). The remains of the sacred pool described by Zosimus can be seen today at the base of the wall northeast of the esplanade.

[60] A.A. Vasiliev, *History of the Byzantine Empire* I, Madison, University of Wisconsin Press, 1952, p. 47.

[61] Ludwig Mendelssohn, "Zosimi Comitis et Exadvocati Fisci", *Historia Nova*, Leipzig, 1887, p. 42.

[62] Eusebius, *Vita Constantina Magni* 3.55, § 3.

Two passages in the history of Ammianus Marcellinus (fourth century A.D.) indicate that the annual festival of Adonis was still observed during the early part of the Byzantine period. Marcellinus relates that during the wars of Constantine (A.D. 337-361) against the Persians, the son of King Grumbates, an ally of the Persian king, was killed in battle. He describes the funeral ceremony:[63]

[63] Ammianus Marcellinus, *Res Gestae* 19.1.11.

> The women for their part, woefully beating their breasts and weeping after their wonted manner, loudly bewailed the hope of their nation cut off in the bloom of youth, just as the priestesses of Venus are often seen to weep at the annual festival of Adonis, which, as the mystic lore of religion tells us, is a kind of symbol of ripened grain.

Ammianus Marcellinus makes an analogy between the mourning rites occasioned by the death of the young prince to the annual festival of Adonis as practiced in his day.

The second passage refers to the reign of Julian (A.D. 361-363). Julian's visit to Antioch coincided with the festival of Adonis and this was considered a bad omen. Ammianus Marcellinus describes the arrival of Julian in the city:[64]

[64] Ammianus Marcellinus 22.9.15.

> Now it chanced that at the same time the annual cycle was completed and they were celebrating in the ancient fashion, the festival of Adonis (beloved by Venus, as the poet's tales say), who was slain by the death-dealing tusk of a boar — a festival which is symbolic of the reaping of the ripe fruits of the field. And it seemed a gloomy omen, as the emperor now for the first time entered the great city, the residence of princes, that on all sides melancoly wailing was heard and cries of grief.

In comparing this passage with that of Plutarch's *Life of Nicias* 13, it can be seen that from the fifth century B.C. to the fourth century A.D., any event which coincided with the mourning rites of the Adonis festival was considered a bad omen.

Nonnus, a poet living during the fifth century A.D., wrote the *Dionysiaca* which can be considered a compendium of pagan information about Byblos. The poem professes to be the history of Dionysos. Nonnus includes all the stories of Greek mythology he could find in earlier collections. In Book 4, Harmonia sails together

with Cadmus over the seas. Nonnus presupposes that Cadmus was a Byblian:[65]

[65] Nonnus, *The Dionysiaca* 4.81.

> That must be his (Cadmus) home, beside the river of that enchanting Adonis, for that lovely young man came from Libanos where Cythereia dances. No, I was wrong! I don't suppose any mortal womb bred Cadmus; no, he is sprung from Zeus and he has concealed his stock!

Another reference to Adonis and Byblos is found in the following text:[66]

[66] Nonnus 20.142-145.

> But this Lord Bacchus was not to do for a long time to come. Now he marched past Tyros and Byblos, and the wedded water of the scented river of Adonis, and the rocks of Libanos where Cyprogeneia loves to linger.

The name of this god whose cult during the fifth century B.C. spread from Byblos to the Greek world and who continued to be worshipped until the fourth century of our era is not known. Adonis, the name given to him by classical authors, is actually a title derived from Phoenician *adon,* "lord". The title was applied, in lieu of their proper name, to kings and gods alike and is found frequently in the Semitic dialects of Syria-Palestine.

Adonis has been identified with Tammuz, Attis and Baal. In the Graeco-Roman age he was identified with the Greek god Dionysos and the Roman god Bacchus.

During the reign of Constantius (A.D. 337-361) a persistent policy against paganism was carried out. A decree ordered the temples closed, forbade entrance to them and prohibited the offering of sacrifices. A brief revival of paganism occurred under the rule of Julian the Apostate (A.D. 361-363) the successor of Constantius. He ordered the temples to be opened and victims to be brought to the altars for the worship of the gods.[67] With the accession to the throne of Byzantium of Theodosius the Great (A.D. 379-395) decisive steps were taken against paganism. Many temples were closed, some of which were then used for government purposes while others were almost completely destroyed and their rich treasures demolished by fanatical mobs. The last decree against the pagans was issued by Theodosius in the year 392. It prohibited the offering of sacrifices, burning of incense, hanging of garlands,

[67] Ammianus Marcellinus 22.5.1-2. Ammianus Marcellinus (A.D. 330-391), a pagan, was a friend of Julian and his companion in military campaigns.

libations, divinations and so forth. Those who disobeyed were liable to severe penalties.[68] Sometime during this period the Roman temple of Aphrodite at Afka was destroyed. Afka however continued to have a religious significance in popular belief. Even today this place is still venerated and it is thought that the waters have a healing property. Among those wishing a cure are barren women who hang offerings and lamps on a tree near the ancient walls of the Temple of Aphrodite.

With the destruction of her temples, Byblos no longer enjoyed the fame she had formerly known as an important temple city of Phoenicia. The testimony of Ammianus Marcellinus illustrates her inferior status in comparison to Tyre, Sidon and Beirut. Byblos is not mentioned among the cities of Phoenicia in this description:[69]

> After this comes Phoenicia, lying at the foot of Mount Libanus, a region full of charm and beauty, adorned with many great cities; among these in attractiveness and the renown of their names Tyre, Sidon and Berytus are conspicuous, and equal to them are Emissa and Damascus, founded in days long past.

Deforestation of the Mountains of Lebanon

The cedars of Lebanon have been frequently mentioned in ancient inscriptions, the Old Testament and classical texts. Throughout the ages pharaohs of Egypt, kings of Assyria and Babylonia cut down this precious timber from the mountains of Lebanon. On the walls of temples and palaces in their capital cities, these conquerors gave accounts of their expeditions to Syria and Palestine and recorded detailed descriptions and lists of the cedar and cypress trees which they had carried off. The prophet Isaiah in a taunt against Nebuchadnezzar, king of Babylon, predicting his death and going down to Sheol, sums up the extent and significance of these logging expeditions:[70]

> The whole earth is at rest and quiet; they break forth into singing. The cypresses rejoice at you, the cedars of Lebanon saying: "Since you (Nebuchadnezzar) were laid low, no hewer comes up against us."

[68] *Codex Theodosianus* 16.10.12.

[69] Ammianus Marcellinus 14.8.9.

[70] Isaiah 14.7-8.

130

[71] *Mission de Phénicie*, pp. 258-281. See R. Mouterde, s.J., "Les Inscriptions d'Hadrien à Tarchich et au Wadi Brissa", *Mélanges de la Faculté Orientale de l'Université Saint-Joseph* XXXIV, 1957, pp. 230-234. Mouterde states that over one hundred inscriptions have been reported defining the limits of the imperial forest preserves. At present it is believed that two hundred inscriptions exist throughout the mountains of Lebanon but have yet to be published.

[72] *Mission de Phénicie*, p. 262.

[73] *Mission de Phénicie*, p. 264.

[74] *Mission de Phénicie*, pp. 264-265, 274-275.

There have been no inscriptions found in Phoenicia prior to the Roman period showing the boundaries of the vast forested areas successive conquerors exploited or took over as royal domains. In 1860 Ernest Renan was told that there were many inscriptions engraved on rock in various regions of the mountains. In the region between Sannin and the Cedars, and particularly near Akoura, Kartaba and Tannourin, Renan recorded eighty inscriptions.[71] They are found in practically inaccessible places, rarely in cultivated areas in the valleys. This is evidence that in antiquity these remote areas were heavily wooded. The peculiarity of these inscriptions is that they are all in Latin and always contain the name of Hadrian. They are inscribed deeply in the rock in letters thirty to forty centimeters high. Generally they are well engraved. However, in some cases an inscription starts on one rock and continues on another due to lack of space. Sometimes as the surface of the rock is unequal, the engraver was obliged to modify the size of the letters by making the ones at the end of the inscription smaller. According to Renan the inscriptions may have been thought to be marking places for hidden treasure. Invariably underneath each inscription he mentioned seeing a hole dug by "treasure hunters". On a rock at Jrapta approximately five meters high and four meters wide the following initials are inscribed to be read: "Imperatoris Hadriani Augusti" *(Fig. 119)*.[72] At Beidar-el-Hadjl on a series of rock forming a natural wall this inscription is seen:

ARBORUM GENERA IV CETERA PRIVATA *(Fig. 120)*.[73]

In other localities an inscription of the type mentioned above has the following letters: MFIADAVG

> (Boundary of the forests of the Emperor Hadrian Augustus; four species of trees; the remaining species are private).[74]

This is evidence that the forests were considered the private domain of the Emperor. The inscriptions specify that only four kinds of trees were allowed to be cut for use by the Roman state. It would appear that the boundary stones had been set up by order of Hadrian in this region, which was still heavily wooded at the time, to allow logging only by command of the Emperor or his procurators. In this way Hadrian was able to control exploitation of the forests in Lebanon.

An inscription is found on the road between Zahlé and Shoueir presumably on the western slope of the Lebanon. Unfortunately it is not known whether this marks the upper or lower limit of the forest. This inscription, presently in the American University of Beirut Museum, is engraved on a rough block of stone:[75]

> IMP. HAD. AUG. DEFINITIO SILVARUM
>
> (Property) of the Emperor Hadrian Augustus — boundary of the forests.

Another inscription is found near Laklouk and has been reconstructed and published by R. Mouterde:[76]

> IMP(ERATORIS) HAD(DRIANI) AUG(USTI) VIC(ENNALIBUS) C(AIUS) UMBRIUS PROC(URATOR) AUG(USTI) IMP(ERATORIS) IT(ERUM) S(ALUTATI) P(OSUIT).
>
> (Property) of the Emperor Hadrian Augustus, in the twentieth year. Caius Umbrius, procurator of Augustus acclaimed Imperator for the second time, placed (it).

Mouterde states that the twentieth year of Hadrian's reign coincided with the date on which his army proclaimed him *imperator* when he crushed the second Jewish revolt in the year A.D. 134.

The inscriptions of Hadrian are evidence that during the Roman period the forests of Lebanon extended over large mountainous regions. Boundary markers were set up specifying the kinds of trees allowed to be cut and to restrict exploitation of the forests by individuals. During the Roman period the fleet was often stationed off the Phoenician coast. Timber was necessary for maintainance of the fleet and building new ships. Therefore serious measures were taken by the Emperor for the protection and preservation of forested areas. In Hadrian's time the northern mountain ranges of Lebanon were heavily covered by cedars and other kinds of coniferous trees. Today these regions are barren. To what can be attributed the gradual deforestation of the mountains of Lebanon? Briefly the evidence is as follows.

The Palermo Stone tells us that during the reign of Senefru, a pharaoh of the Fourth Dynasty, ca. 2650 B.C., forty ships of timber were sent to Egypt. This was an important amount of cedar wood. Byblos benefited from an ideal geographical situation on the coast of Canaan where the timber-bearing mountains came down nearest

[75] L. Jalabert and R. Mouterde, "Les réserves forestières impériales dans le Liban", *Mélanges de la Faculté Orientale de l'Université Saint-Joseph* IV, 1910, pp. 201-212. Jalabert and Mouterde reconstruct this inscription as follows: "Imp(eratoris) Had(driani) Aug(usti) definitio silvarum." Acknowledgement is made to Dr. H.S. Bliss for allowing this text to be published.

[76] R. Mouterde, "Date des inscriptions forestières d'Hadrien au Liban", *Mélanges* XXV, 1942-1943, pp. 41-47, especially p. 44.

to the sea. Excavations at Byblos have shown that from a small rural settlement at the beginning of the third millenium B.C. Byblos was transformed into a city. Massive city walls, houses, streets, drainage make their appearance as well as the first monumental stone structure found on the coast — a temple built for the city goddess. This temple, when excavated, produced a large number of fragments of alabaster and diorite vases and plates with the cartouches of pharaohs of the Old Kingdom. Egypt had need for cedar wood and close trade relations developed between Egypt and Byblos, relations which the pharaohs of the Old Kingdom took all measures possible to maintain and cultivate. In addition, cedar products such as cedar oil were used in mummification which added a religious motive for the maintenance of close ties. The pharaohs of the Middle Kingdom sent costly gifts to the kings of Byblos, some of which have been preserved in tombs of the royal necropolis. They too wished to trade with Byblos and benefit from the timber trade.

Then came the period of the Empire and the conquests in Syria and Palestine of Thut-mose III of the Eighteenth Dynasty. Thut-mose III had inscribed on the walls of the Temple of Amon at Karnak: "When my majesty crossed over to the marshes of Asia I had many ships of cedar built on the mountains of God's Land near the Lady of Byblos."[77] He boasted: "When my army which is the garrison in Ullaza comes (they bring tribute) which is the cedar of the victories of my majesty, through the plans of my father (Amon-Rē), who entrusted to me all foreign countries. I have not given (any) of it to the Asiatics (for) it is a wood which he loves."[78]

During this period the Egyptians named their commercial carriers "Keftiu, Byblos and Sektu ships of cedar".[79] The temples of Egypt were enriched with cedar from Lebanon. During the reign of Rameses III (Twentieth Dynasty) the following amounts of cedar are mentioned in a single text: "Slabs of cedar: 6, a mast of cedar: 1, beams of cedar: 8, various logs of cedar: 336, various logs of cedar: 351."[80] As early as the Eleventh Dynasty Lebanon was called the "Plateau of Cedar",[81] and during the Empire it was referred to as the "mountains of God's Land".[82]

In the period of independence with the political decline of Egypt and before the arrival of the Assyrians in the west, timber trade and shipbuilding formed an integral part of the economy of Byblos.

[77] *ANET*, p. 240.

[78] *ANET*, p. 240.

[79] *ANET*, p. 241.

[80] *ANET*, pp. 261-262.

[81] W.C. Hayes, *JEA* XXXV, 1949, p. 49.

[82] *ANET*, p. 240.

In Zakar-Baal's boast of the independence and wealth of his city during the eleventh century, he said: "If I cry out to the Lebanon, the heavens open up and the logs are here lying on the shore of the sea."[83]

[83] *ANET*, p. 27.

The Assyrian texts furnish us with interesting material on the exploitation of the cedar forests of Lebanon. Cedar wood was taken to Ashur by Tiglath-Pileser I (1114-1076 B.C.) for the construction of the Anu-Adad temple. A reference to cedar in the royal palace of Ashurnasirpal II infers that the Assyrian king returned to his capital with precious cedar. During the reign of Sennacherib a passage in the Old Testament gives evidence of the extensive logging operations of the kings of Assyria. In 2 Kings 19.23 Isaiah prophesizes the destruction of the Assyrian armies in the west and speaking in the name of the God of Israel addresses Sennacherib:

> By your messengers you have mocked the Lord and you have said, "With my many chariots I have gone up the heights of the mountains, to the far recesses of Lebanon; I felled its tallest cedars, its choicest cypresses; I entered its farthest retreat; its densest forest."

Two other passages in the Old Testament are of interest in this context. In Isaiah 60.13 the trees of Lebanon are listed: "The glory of Lebanon shall come to you, the cypress, the plane, and the pine, to beautify the place of my sanctuary; and I will make the place of my feet glorious." Isaiah 40.16 states: "Lebanon would not suffice for fuel, nor are its beasts enough for a burnt offering." This is evidence that the mountains of Lebanon were considered the greatest resource possible for timber.

Esarhaddon II (680-669 B.C.) after his Syro-Palestinian campaign undertook a vast building program. He forced the tributary kings, including Milkiashapa of Byblos, to procure cedar and pine timber for him and to transport the logs to Nineveh. Nebuchadnezzar II (605-562 B.C.) cut through mountains and opened roads for the transportation of cedar logs to Babylon. Likewise in an inscription during the reign of Nabonidus (555-539 B.C.), the king of Babylon states that he was engaged in the repair of the temples of Esagila and Ezida. He tells us that he rebuilt the main door leaves of the temple gate with cedar wood and mounted them with bronze.[84]

[84] *ANET*, p. 310.

85 Jerome, Commentary on Ezekiel 27.4-5. Jean Paul Migne, *Patrologia Latina* 25.260. See also Philip K. Hitti, *Lebanon in History*, London, MacMillan & Co., Ltd., 1957, p. 69 for photograph of burial chamber of Senefru's pyramid (ca. 2650 B.C.) where cedar is found.

Why was cedar wood considered precious and specifically mentioned in records of the ancient conquerors? The answer may be seen in a text of Jerome (fourth century of our era) who wrote a commentary on Ezekiel (cf. Ezekiel 27.4-5). In the passage where Tyre is described as a ship and the materials are given from which a Phoenician ship was built, Jerome states: "The mast is of cedar from Lebanon, cedar, because its wood is not subject to decay."[85]

For the Persian period there is a building inscription of Darius I found at Susa which is evidence that cedar wood was transported as far away as southern Iran. The kings of Persia considered the forest regions in Lebanon as their royal domain. The word "paradise" is derived from the Greek *paradeisos* which in its turn is derived from Persian and means "king's park". Theophrastus (Hist. Plant. 5.8.1) states that in Syria the trees grow so large that three men could not stretch around them; and that the trees are even larger than those in the *paradeisos*. He could mean in this context the former royal preserves of the Persian kings. Further proof that the Persians had royal domains can be seen in two passages from the Old Testament. Nehemiah 2.8 furnishes a clear piece of evidence of the "king's park". Nehemiah departing for Jerusalem requests King Artaxerxes of Persia to give him a letter to Asaph, the keeper of the king's forest, for timber to make beams for the gates of the fortress of the temple, for the wall of the city and for his house. Ezra 3.7 refers to the rebuilding of the temple in Jerusalem after the return of the exiles and reports how cedar trees were shipped to Joppa "according to a grant by Cyrus".

The cedar forests of Lebanon continued to be cut down during the Hellenistic age. Arrian (1.20) states that it was of strategic importance for Alexander the Great to control the Phoenician seaboard and the Phoenician fleet then in the service of Persia. In addition to control of the seaports it is evident that the cedar forests had to be secured for the maintenance of the existing fleet and for the building of more ships.

Quintus Curtius (4.2.18-19) states that for the siege of Tyre Alexander had timber brought from the Lebanon mountains to make rafts and towers. Diodorus (17.42.6) tells us that when a northwest gale blew up and destroyed a large part of the mole, Alexander sent up to the mountains and brought down huge trees and placed them alongside the mole to break the forces of the waves.

135

Quintus Curtius (10.1.17-20) further tells us that Alexander towards the end of his conquest of Asia was determined to cross from Syria to Africa as he held a grudge against the Carthaginians for their help to Tyre during the siege. With this in view he ordered the governors of Mesopotamia to cut timber on Mount Lebanon, transport it to Thapsacus, a city in Syria, and lay the keels for seven hundred ships; all were to be septriremes and were to be taken to Babylon. This ambitious ship-building project, as far as we know, was not carried out because of Alexander's untimely death.

Another passage in Diodorus, relating to events following the death of Alexander, is the only detailed historical account of logging in the mountains of Lebanon found in the works of classical authors. It shows that Byblos at this period was still important as a center for processing timber. It also emphasizes that one reason for deforestation was the periodic mass cutting of trees for naval needs. This logging operation was undertaken by Antigonus in his wars against the Ptolemies for the purpose of supplying the shipyards of Tripolis, Sidon and Byblos with timber to make him a fleet. Diodorus also gives us the extent of the forest ranges during this period: "This mountain range extends along the territory of Tripolis, Byblos and Sidon and is covered with cedar and cypress trees of wonderful size and beauty."[86]

One piece of evidence that the Seleucids took over the royal forest preserves is seen in Josephus. Concerning the rebuilding of the temple, Josephus states that Antiochus III ordered that timber be brought from Lebanon free of charge. If timber were ordinarily purchased or taxed this implies that there was a royal forest domain under the control of the Seleucid kings.[87]

From this evidence there emerges a clear picture which shows the reasons for the gradual deforestation of the mountains of Lebanon. During the third millenium B.C. Byblos prospered from the timber trade with Egypt. Expeditions were made to the "cedar terraces" for shipbuilding, religious and funerary purposes. With the acquisition by Egypt of an Asiatic Empire under Thut-mose III, Egypt exacted timber as tribute. With the political decline of Egypt Byblos enjoyed several centuries of independence. Trade with neighboring kingdoms during the tenth century B.C. made Byblos prosper and the city was greatly enriched. Then came the Assyrians, the Babylonians, the Persians and the Seleucids, who undoubtedly

[86] Diodorus 19.58 and 19.58.3.

[87] Josephus, *Jewish Antiquities* 12.141.

were forest conservationists in this sense — they wanted to preserve the timber for their building programs and their fleets. They either controlled the mountainous forest regions or maintained royal domains. It was only Hadrian who thought of setting up forest markers to define the boundaries of the Roman state forest preserves. After the reign of Hadrian there was no restraining authority to prevent uncontrolled exploitation of the forests of Lebanon. Over a period of several millenia not once was thought given to replanting trees which were cut down. The mass cutting of cedars, pines and cypresses for trade, naval and building purposes allowed the inevitable process of erosion to set in. After Hadrian no competent measures were taken to protect the forests that remained. Today the few majestic cedars which are located at Becharré stand as living testimony to the ruthless exploitation through the ages by state and individual of the magnificent coniferous forests of Lebanon.

A view of the port and buildings of the Medieval period at Byblos

11   The Medieval Period
(A.D. 330-1300)

Byblos and the Byzantine Empire (A.D. 330-636)

With the decline of the Roman Empire the latent struggle between East and West became more apparent. Egypt and Syria were the richest and most populous provinces of the empire. They contained its main centers of industry, their ships and caravans controlled the trade routes with the Orient. Their culture, spiritual and material, was far higher than that of the West because of their long traditions. During the fourth century A.D. not only did the Roman Empire have to resist barbarian invasions but it faced dissolution due to internal decay. The pagan emperors had been tolerant of local cults; local gods were easily fitted into the Roman pantheon. Persecutions had been occasionally directed against obstinate monotheists such as the Christians and the Jews. Constantine the Great (A.D. 288-337) adopted an eastern religion and moved his capital to Byzantium making use of Christianity to bind all his subjects to the empire.

From an archaeological point of view the Byzantine period is poorly represented at Byblos. Remains of the buildings were found in an extremely delapidated condition. One factor to explain the poverty of the remains of the Byzantine levels can be attributed to the type of materials used. In that period builders were content with local sandstone and buildings on a modest scale. Some of the older walls on the site were incorporated in the Byzantine buildings, then shabby thin walls were added where needed. The shallow foundations and the poor quality building materials used in the constructions of the Byzantine period were such that if the building

139

stood at all it was due to the more ancient structures supporting them. Another factor to explain the poverty of the buildings could be that Byblos, deprived of her pagan temples, had gradually sunk into obscurity.

Several centuries later the Crusaders in their search for large stone blocks for their castle went through the Byzantine structures to reach the Roman levels below. Further disturbance of the levels occurred in more recent times. As the Byzantine levels at Byblos were buried under only two or three meters of debris in some areas they came to light when foundations for modern houses were made. The size of the Byzantine sandstone blocks suited the needs of modern engineers who did not hesitate to incorporate them in their buildings.[1]

Remains of the Byzantine levels have been found in three different areas which had miraculously escaped destruction at the hands of the Crusaders and later builders. The first area was located near the Temple of Baalat-Gebal and consisted of seven rows of flagstones.[2] The second area was found near the Roman colonnade and consisted of the remains of a circular basin and a wall running in a north/south direction.[3] To the north of these remains, between the colonnade and the Crusader castle, a third area revealed a street of the Byzantine period. The street ran in an east/west direction and was made of paving stones of different sizes and shapes placed in a haphazarded manner. Lining each side of the street were the foundations of buildings and the thresholds of shops.[4] The presence of a *pithos* measuring 1.80 meters in diameter in which there were ashes led Dunand to believe that this was an oven in a bakery shop. Under the paving stones a drainage system was found consisting of clay cylinders with lead joints. During the excavations various fragments of pottery of the Byzantine period were found in addition to a number of lamps.[5]

Byblos and the Arab Conquest (A.D. 636-1095)

With the coming of Islam the first important Arab invasion of the Eastern Mediterranean world took place. The strength of Islam lay in its simplicity. There was one God in Heaven, one Commander of the Faithful to rule on earth and one Law, the Koran, by which he should rule. Unlike Christianity which preached

[1] *Fouilles de Byblos* I, pp. 51-58. According to Dunand a small Greek Orthodox church situated one hundred meters to the west of the Crusader church of St. John at Byblos is a building dating to the Byzantine period. See *Byblos, son histoire, ses ruines, ses légendes*, p. 78.

[2] *Fouilles de Byblos* I, p. 52.

[3] *Fouilles de Byblos* I, p. 52.

[4] *Fouilles de Byblos* I, p. 52.

[5] *Fouilles de Byblos* I, p. 23.

a peace that it never achieved, Islam conquered by the sword. The Arabs subjugated the Persians and began a series of military conflicts with the armies of the Byzantine emperors. Gaining a foothold in southern Palestine, they followed the trade route east of the Jordan to Damascus. Damascus fell in August, 635. The Arabs quickly overran Egypt and North Africa; they occupied Spain eleven years later. In the year 717 their empire stretched from the Pyrenees to central India and Arab armies stood before the walls of Constantinople.

The entire Near East fell under the rule of the Omayyad and Abbasid caliphs. The decline of the Omayyads and the civil wars that led to the establishment of the Abbasid caliphs at Baghdad in 750 precipitated chaos in Syria, Phoenicia and Palestine. Early in the tenth century the Abbasid Caliphate began to decline. Local dynasties arose. Chief among these were the Hamdanids of Mosul and Aleppo and the Ikhshids of Egypt. A revival in Islam was led by the Fatimid dynasty which established itself in Egypt and southern Syria. Opposition to the Byzantine Empire was renewed. In 1001, a ten years' truce was made between the Byzantine Empire and the Fatimid Caliph effecting a peace that was not seriously broken for more than half a century.[6]

In the middle of the eleventh century Moslem rule was lenient along the Phoenician coast. The Persian traveller, Nassiri Khosrau, visited Tripoli in 1047 and described the number of Greek merchant ships to be seen in the harbor.[7] He then proceeded southward to Byblos.

Tranquillity in the Eastern Mediterranean world seemed assured for many years to come. Its two great powers, Fatimid Egypt and Byzantium, were on good terms with each other. Both wished to keep in check Turkish incursions on the borders to the east but invasion by the Turks was not long delayed. The Seljuk Turks of Asia Minor dealt a serious blow to the Byzantine Empire. The Battle of Manzikert in 1071 was the most decisive disaster in the history of the empire. The Seljuks took control of the Bekaa valley and parts of the Lebanese mountains. The Fatimites took control of the coastal cities of Lebanon. Tripoli became an independent principality. Ca. 1095 a Shiite clan at Tripoli, the Banu Ammar, set up an autonomous principality whose authority extended to the south including Byblos and the Nahr Ibrahim River. To the

[6] Steven Runciman, *A History of the Crusades* I, Cambridge, Cambridge University Press, 1951, p. 33.

[7] *History of the Crusades* I, p. 37.

141

travellers of the time it seemed that every city had a different master. Everywhere there were brigands on the roads. At each small town the local lord tried to levy a tax on passers-by.

Archaeological material from Byblos for the period covered by Arab occupation is fragmentary. At Anjar (Chalcis of the Graeco-Roman period) in the Bekaa valley the magnificent remains of a palace of the Omayyads is evidence that vast building projects were undertaken. Byblos during the Arab period had no doubt declined in importance. An inscription found in the debris at Byblos indicates that a tower was built in the general area, if not on the site of the later Crusader castle. This inscription was made during the period of Fatimid rule and before Byblos came under the control of the Emirs of Tripoli ca. 1095 B.C. The inscription on a fragment of a stele consists of six lines in raised relief separated by horizontal bands:[8]

[8] *Fouilles de Byblos* I, p. 33.

SUCCOUR COMES FROM GOD FOR HIS SERVANT AND HIS FRIEND . . . (SUCH A ONE) PRINCE OF THE BELIEVERS — MAY THE BLESSING (BE ON HIM, AS WELL AS ON HIS PURE ANCESTORS AND HIS NOBLE DESCENDANTS!) — HAS COMMANDED TO BUILD (OR — TO RE-BUILD) THIS TOWER . . . HE WHO UNITES THE TWO NOBILITIES, THE STRONG SUPPORT (OF THE DYNASTY?) . . . KHALAF SON OF AL-HASAN AS-SUF . . . UNDER THE SURVEILLANCE OF HIS SON, THE CADI . . . .

Dunand believes that part of a wall of the Crusader castle is of the Arab period. Under the tower in the southeast corner of the building several large stone blocks with a polished surface appear to be the remains of a construction of the Fatimids.[9] Sections of the medieval wall at Byblos are also believed to belong to the Arab period. Apart from the inscription and a few artifacts such as lamps and bracelets, there has been nothing published in *Fouilles de Byblos* I and II to throw light on Arab occupation of the city.

[9] *Byblos, son histoire, ses ruines, ses légendes*, p. 75.

Byblos under the Seigneurs de Gibelet (A.D. 1108-1300)

After the Battle of Manzikert in 1071 the Byzantine Empire was unable to put an effective army into the field. This stimulated the intervention of the West which took the form of the Crusades. By the end of the eleventh century the idea of the holy war caught the imagination. Christian knights and soldiers were encouraged

by authorities of the Church to journey to the frontiers of Christendom to fight the infidel. To reward them for their services they could take possession of the lands that they reconquered. Western knights responded readily to the appeal for both religious and material reasons. The Crusaders conquered Byblos in 1108; they called the city Gibelet and built the castle and fortifications. The Crusader castle at Byblos can therefore be considered one of the oldest examples of Crusader architecture in Syria and Lebanon *(Fig. 124)*.

We have an account which shows how Byblos fell to the Crusaders. The major source for this period is the history of William, Archbishop of Tyre from 1175 to 1185.[10] He was chancellor of the Latin Kingdom of Jerusalem from 1174 to his death. Although William of Tyre was important both as a churchman and a statesman, his fame rests almost entirely upon his work as a writer and historian.

Raymond VI of Saint Gilles, Count of Toulouse, was one of the knights who set out on the First Crusade in 1096. His goal was the conquest of Tripoli, the most important emirate on the coast. The Emirate of Tripoli, together with other Moslem emirates, was considered an obstacle to the Christians since it separated the Franks of Antioch and Edessa from those in Jerusalem. Raymond wished to establish a principality that would command both the coast road and the Orontes. He was victorious in a battle before Tripoli against the Banu Ammar and the Emirs of Homs and Damascus. His forces, however, were too small to conquer Tripoli itself. After exacting heavy tribute in money and horses he returned to Tortosa, his headquarters north of Tripoli, to plan his next campaign. He learned that a Genoese squadron of forty vessels lay at anchor at Lattakieh. He hired this squadron for an attack on Tripoli. The attack failed and so he moved southward and captured instead the port of Jebeil. The Genoese were rewarded with one third of the town.[11] This was the first step in the acquisition of Jebeil by the Genoese. On Raymond's death the barons of Toulouse accepted his illegitimate son, Bertrand, as a successor. Bertrand had already governed for nearly ten years prior to his father's death during his absence in the East. Bertrand arranged for a Genoese squadron to accompany him when he set out for the East in 1108 to claim his father's inheritance and to round off his future prin-

[10] William, Archbishop of Tyre, *A History of Deeds Done Beyond the Sea* I, New York, Columbia University Press, 1943, Introduction p. 4.

[11] *History of the Crusades* II, p. 60.

143

cipality by the conquest of Tripoli. Genoa had promised to aid Bertrand take over his father's conquests. In return they wished to receive a favored commercial position. Bertrand landed with the Genoese squadron near Tripoli. The following is an account of the capture of Jebeil:[12]

[12] William of Tyre Book 11.9. William probably received this account of the surrender of Jebeil from Ugo Embriaco, the grandson of Hugh Embriacus.

> The Genoese fleet with which he had come consisted of seventy galleys, under the command of two noble Genoese, Ansaldus and Hugh Embriacus. It was soon apparent that they were wasting their efforts in the siege of Tripoli at that time. It was therefore deemed advisable, in the meantime, to attempt something worthy of remembrance. Accordingly they begged Bertram in a friendly way to accompany them to Jubail by land, and they themselves directed the fleet thither.
>
> Jubail is a city on the coast of Phoenicia, one of the dependent cities which are recognized as subject to the metropolitan of Tyre, with metropolitan right. Ezekiel the prophet mentions it, saying "The ancients of Gebal (Jubail) and the wise men thereof were in thee thy calkers." Again, in the first book of Kings, it is written thus concerning the same city: "So they (the Jubailites) prepared timber and stones for the building of the house (of the Lord)." The ancient name of this place was Eve, for Eveus, the sixth son of Canaan, is believed to have been its founder.
>
> On arriving before Jubail, the armies invested the city both by land and by sea. The citizens were thrown into a state of panic, for they had no confidence in the strength of their defenses. A deputation was accordingly sent to the commanders of the fleet, Ansaldus and Hugh Embriacus, to announce that under certain conditions the citizens were willing to unbar the entrances and admit them as lords. It was stipulated that those who desired to leave be given an opportunity to do so unhindered, with their wives and children, but that those who did not wish to abandon their homes in the city be permitted to remain under favorable conditions. The terms asked were granted, and they therefore surrendered the place to the two

commanders. One of these, Hugh Embriacus, received the city for a definite time on consideration of a fixed annual payment to the treasury of the Genoese. The same man was the grandfather of the Hugh who rules that city today and bears the same name and surname.

King Baldwin I of Jerusalem and Bertrand became allies in the attack on Tripoli. The city was taken on June 10, 1109. The Genoese were rewarded by a quarter in Tripoli and by a castle known as the Castle of the Constable ten miles north of Tripoli. Bertrand was installed as the Count of Tripoli and reaffirmed his vassalage to the Kingdom of Jerusalem. Thus did Jebeil, ancient Byblos, come into the hands of the Genoese as a hereditary fief, controlled by the descendants of Hugh Embriacus.

On June 29, 1170 a terrible earthquake devastated Syria. Many fortresses were ruined including the Krak des Chevaliers and the castles of Tripoli and Jebeil.[13] It took many months to repair the ruined fortresses. In the meantime the great warrior Saladin succeeded in uniting Islam and drove the Crusaders to a narrow strip on the coast of Phoenicia. In 1187 after Palestine surrendered he moved up the coast. Tyre was well fortified and well garrisoned. His first attack failed and so Saladin passed on. Sidon surrendered without a blow on July 29. Beirut capitulated on August 6 and Jebeil surrendered a few days later on the orders of its lord, Hugh Embriaco, whom Saladin released on that condition.[14] Once again the city of Jebeil came under Moslem control. During the Third Crusade early in 1197 Jebeil was recovered by the Crusaders.[15]

On July 1, 1198 a peace was negotiated between al-Adil, leader of the Ayoubites, and Almaric, king of Jerusalem. It gave Jaffa to the Moslems and the Crusaders took possession of Jebeil and Beirut. Sidon was divided between them. The peace was to last for five years and eight months.[16]

During the thirteenth century Italian merchants controlled important investments in the Near East. The three great Republics of Genoa, Venice and Pisa with their colonies in every Levantine port dominated Mediterranean trade. Various conflicts arose. In the conflict between the interests of the Venetians and the Genoese in Acre the head of the Embriaco family in Jebeil, true to his Genoese origin, defied the prohibition of his suzerain, Bohemond VI

[13] *History of the Crusades* II, p. 389.

[14] *History of the Crusades* II, p. 462.

[15] *History of the Crusades* III, p. 92.

[16] *History of the Crusades* III, p. 98.

of Antioch-Tripoli, and sent troops to help the Genoese in Acre.[17] This disobedience to his order and the personal hatred of Bohemond for his vassal, Henry of Jebeil, soon developed into war. Not only did Henry defy Bohemond's suzerainty and maintain his independence with the help of the Genoese, but Henry's cousin Bertrand, head of the younger branch of the Embriaco family, attacked Bohemond in Tripoli. At the instigation of Bohemond, Bertrand Embriaco, who owned large estates in and around Jebeil, was beheaded by peasants while riding through one of his villages. This resulted in a blood feud between the Houses of Antioch-Tripoli and the Embriaco.[18]

In 1277 Bohemond VII of Tripoli quarreled with the most powerful of his vassals, Guy II Embriaco of Jebeil. Guy allied himself with the Templars and Bohemond responded by destroying the Templars' buildings at Tripoli and cutting down a forest they owned nearby. The Master of the Temple led the knights of the Order against Tripoli and burned the castle at Batroun. When the Templars had moved back, Bohemond set out to attack Jebeil. Guy, with a contingent of Templars, went to meet him. A fierce battle took place a few miles north of Batroun resulting in the loss of many lives on both sides.[19] After one year's truce Guy and the Templars attacked Bohemond again. Another truce was arranged between the Grand Master of the Hospital and Bohemond. Guy however had ambitions to capture Tripoli. In January 1282 with his brothers and his friends, he smuggled himself into the Templar quarters in Tripoli. A misunderstanding with the Templar commander started a panic and Guy and his companions fled to a tower in the Hospital of the Templars where they were besieged by Bohemond's troops. After a few hours they agreed, at the request of the Hospitallers, to surrender on condition their lives be spared. Bohemond broke his word, all of Guy's companions were blinded. Guy himself and his brothers and cousin were taken to Nephin and there they were buried up to their necks in a ditch and left to starve to death. This deed shocked the vassals of Bohemond. The allies of Guy in Tyre planned to move up from Tyre to avenge the deaths, but Bohemond reached Jebeil before them and took over the city temporarily.

In 1289 Tripoli fell to the Mameluke forces. Qalawun, the Mameluke Sultan, had the city razed to the ground lest the Crusaders

[17] *History of the Crusades* III, pp. 283-284.

[18] *History of the Crusades* III, p. 288.

[19] *History of the Crusades* III, pp. 388-389.

[20] *History of the Crusades* III, p. 407.

[21] *Byblos, son histoire, ses ruines, ses légendes,* p. 74.

with their command of the sea try to recapture it. Mameluke troops went on to occupy Batroun and Nephin. No attempt was made to defend these cities. Peter Embriaco, lord of Jebeil, offered his submission to the Sultan. He was allowed to keep his city under strict surveillance for another decade.[20]

The medieval city of Jebeil covered an area 275 meters long and 200 meters wide.[21] The city was surrounded by a wall. The walls which are seen today belong to the Arab period (1289-1516) and the period of the Ottoman Empire (1516-1918). The masonry, which in several sections of the walls belongs to the Crusader period, can be identified here and there in the lowest rows forming the foundations. A large tower in the northeastern corner of the fortifications is of the Crusader period and was re-used by the Turks. On the northern side of the city square guard towers were built for defense. The Crusader castle served as military headquarters and a place of refuge in time of siege. It was surrounded by a moat. Many of the large stone blocks in the castle obviously were found on the site and incorporated in the construction. They come from the temples of the Roman period.

The Crusader castle has an elevated central castle-keep surrounded by a court in a quadrilateral enclosure. In each corner of the enclosure square guard towers had been built for defense. A fifth tower had been built in the middle of the wall facing north to ensure better protection of the drawbridge. Sections of the enclosure facing east and south are of the Crusader period. The walls of the other two sides of the enclosure are of the Arab period. The castle-keep was built with large stone blocks of the Roman period, some of which are five meters long. The castle-keep is composed of three floors. In the underground section a large area contains reservoirs. On the ground floor of the keep which is on the level of the court there is a large hall with a vaulted ceiling. A narrow window was built high up in the wall facing east to provide light.

The gate of the Crusader castle dates to the Arab period. Large steps lead down to the small square in front of the castle. From this square a road leads to the port, another to the Crusader Church of St. John *(Fig. 126)*. This church is situated in the center of the old Crusader town. It was built ca. 1215 and is in the Romanesque style. A beautiful baptistry was built against the

northern wall of the church at the end of the twelfth century *(Fig. 127)*. Italian influence is seen in the design. Its three arches have different decorative motifs. The north and west arches have *coussinets* and zigzags as decoration. On the arch facing east there is a combination of a design of zigzags and rosettes. At this period Jebeil was under the control of the Genoese. This cathedral of the Latin bishops of Gibelet was dedicated to St. John the Baptist and still serves the people of Jebeil as their principal church.

During the twelfth century the bishopric of Jebeil, together with Tripoli and Tortosa, fell under the jurisdiction of the patriarch of Antioch. In order that these bishoprics return to their mother church at Tyre, Pope Innocent addressed a letter dated January 17, 1139 to the Bishops of Tripoli, Tortosa and Jebeil and to the Patriarch of Antioch. He admonished them to observe obedience and unity. The Pope restored them and their churches to the church of Tyre which he considered as their metropolis. In this way the Pope also absolved the bishops of Tripoli, Tortosa and Jebeil of the oath of fidelity by which they had been bound to the patriarch of Antioch.[22]

With the departure of the Crusaders Jebeil sank into obscurity. Travellers to the Near East during the eighteenth and nineteenth centuries invariably passed by Jebeil with hardly a look at the Crusader castle half buried by accumulated debris. Several nineteenth century travellers to Syria and the Holy Land such as Henry Bartlett, Keepsake, Léon de Laborde, Cassas, Victor Guérin and Count Joseph d'Estourmel barely mention Jebeil as they give accounts of their journeys southward from Tripoli to Beirut. They passed on and at the Dog River they stopped and admired the beauty of the river gorge and marvelled at the stelae on the rock cliffs of the ancient kings of Egypt and Assyria. One traveller, Eugène Flandin, stopped at the entrance of Jebeil in 1840 and made a drawing of the Crusader castle and the mosque.[23] But Byblos itself remained forgotten and neglected until in 1860 Ernest Renan came to Jebeil and located the ancient city situated on a height only a slight distance from the sea.

[22] William of Tyre Book 14.13.

[23] Eugène Flandin's lithograph "Entrée de Jebeil", in *l'Orient,* Paris, Gide Éditeur, 5 Rue Bonaparte, 1840-1841, has been reproduced for the end sheets of this book.

Plates

149

1

1   A view from the air of the ancient seaport
of Byblos. The Crusader castle is seen
to the right in the photograph

2   A view of the excavations of Byblos in 1939
showing the Early Bronze Age city walls,
the Middle Bronze Age royal necropolis
and the Temple of Baalat-Gebal.

On the following pages an aerial view of Byblos
taken on May 17, 1968. From left to right:
the Temple of Baalat-Gebal,
the Early Bronze Age city walls,
the *Temple en L*, the Land Gate of Byblos
(to the right of the Crusader castle),
the Temple of the Obelisks and to the extreme right
the foundations of a building of the Persian period

150

151

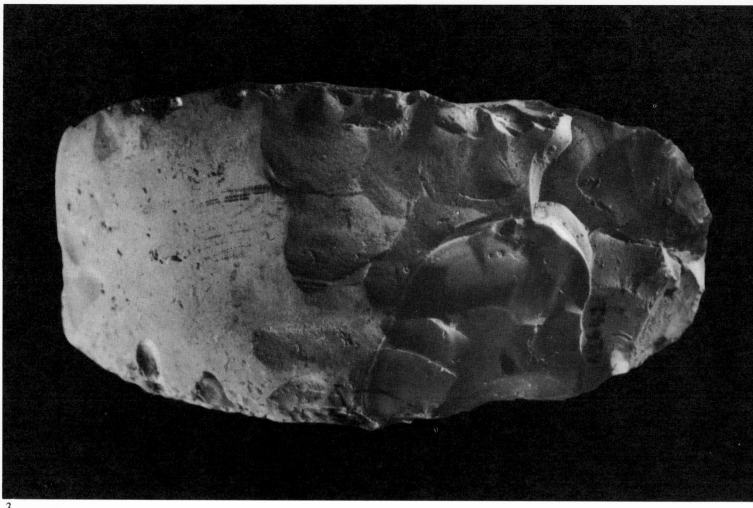

3

4

3   Stone hand axe of the Neolithic
      settlement at Byblos (ca. 4500 B.C.)

4   Pottery bowl with incised decoration
      of the Neolithic Age

5   Pottery jars of the Neolithic Age
      illustrating the herringbone pattern
      and the reed design

6   Clay figurine of the Neolithic Age. The
      figurine measures 4 centimeters in height

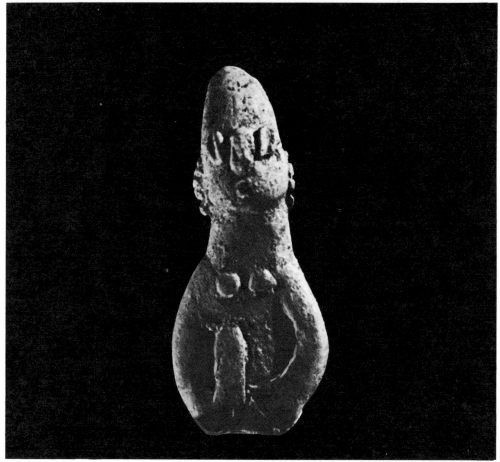

6

7

8

7   Crushed limestone floor of a monocellular hut
    of the Neolithic settlement

8   Foundations of two houses of the Chalcolithic
    settlement

9   Chalcolithic jar burial *in situ*. A globular pot
    can be seen near the skull of the skeleton

10 A burial jar of the Chalcolithic period illustrating
    how a flap was removed on the shoulder of the jar
    to allow the insertion of the body.
    Reproduced from *Fouilles de Byblos*,
    Atlas (1926-1932), Plate CLXXXIX

10

11

11 A building of the proto-urban period
illustrating slabs of sandstone
laid in the herringbone pattern

12 Plan of the different architectural
stages of the Temple of Baalat-
Gebal. *Fouilles de Byblos,*
Atlas (1926-1932), Plate CCXII

13 Foundations of the Temple of
Baalat-Gebal

14 Drawing of the Temple of
Baalat-Gebal during the Old
and Middle Egyptian Kingdoms.
Fouilles de Byblos,
Atlas (1926-1932), Plate CCX

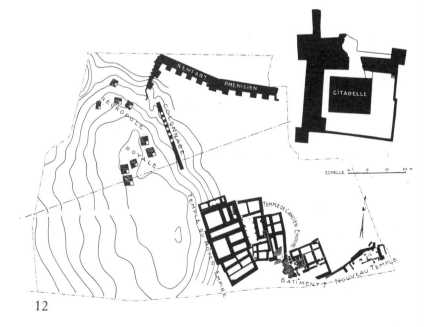

12

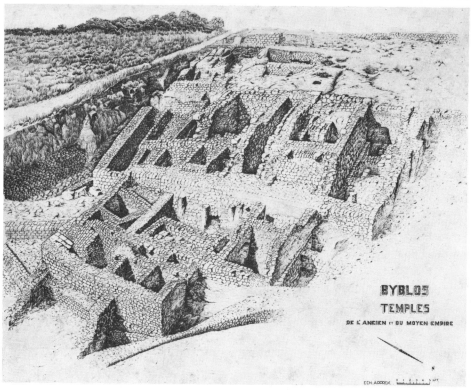

BYBLOS
TEMPLES
DE L'ANCIEN ET DU MOYEN EMPIRE

ECH. APPROX.

N

14

15

15 Cylinder seal of a ruler of Byblos
of the third millenium B.C. This is
the first representation of Baalat-Gebal
(or her Egyptian counterpart Hathor)
found at Byblos. The goddess is wearing
the solar disc between cow's horns
on her head

16 Egyptian stone vase found at Byblos

17 Fragments of alabaster plates
with the cartouche of Pepi I,
a pharaoh of the Sixth Dynasty,
found in the Temple of Baalat-Gebal

18 Statuette of monkey with young
with part of the cartouche of Pepi I
inscribed on her arm

16

17   18

19

20

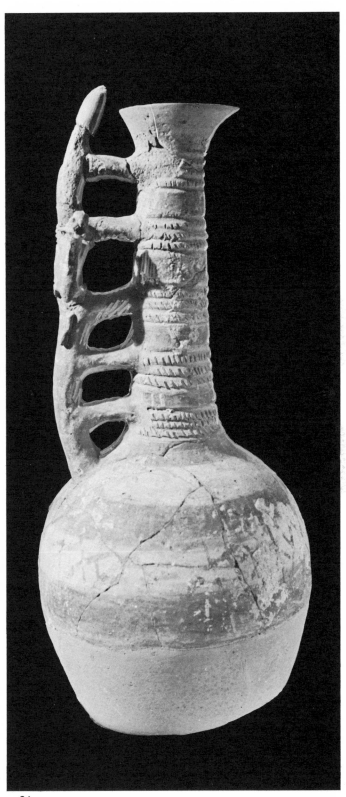

21

19 Egyptian stone vase found at Byblos

20 Egyptian stone vase found at Byblos

21 Third millenium B.C. pottery jar
    with exotic handle decorated with animals

22 Third millenium B.C. figurines
    which may have inspired the axiom
    "I see no evil, I say no evil, I hear no evil"

23 Third millenium B.C. figurines

24 Third millenium B.C. pottery figurine

22

23

24

25

25 Foundations of the
Early Bronze Age *Temple en L*

26 Charred stone at the entrance
of the sacred court of the
Temple en L which is evidence that
the temple was destroyed by fire
at the end of the Old Kingdom

27 Foundations of the sanctuary
of the *Temple en L*

28 Clay vessels set in a ledge of the
north-eastern building
of the *Temple en L*

26

29

30

31

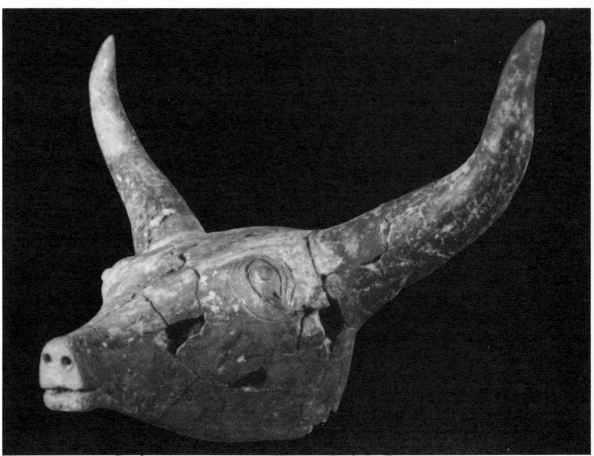

32

33   Second millenium B.C.
       black diorite statue
       of an Egyptian scribe

34   Metal toggle pins found in the
       "Montet jar"
       in the foundations of the
       Temple of Baalat-Gebal

35   Metal torques found at
       Byblos in the "Montet jar"

33

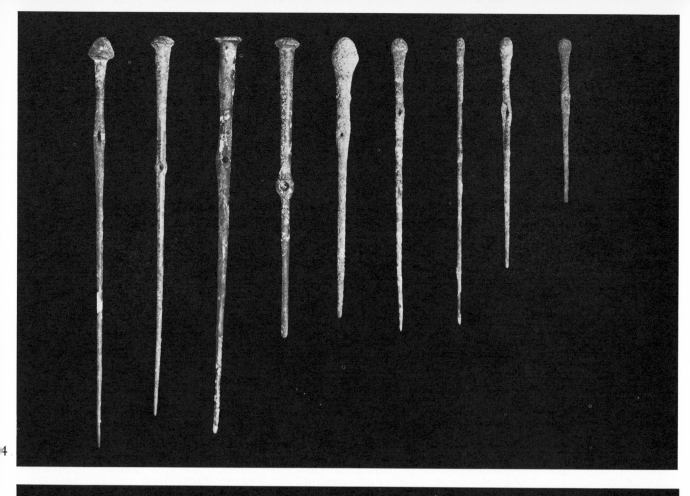

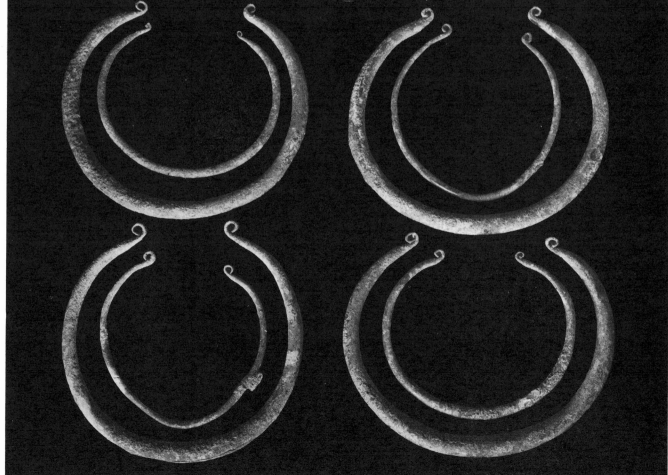

36

36 The royal necropolis

37 White limestone sarcophagus
    of King Abishemu (Tomb I)

38 Position of sarcophagus and
    funerary equipment (Tomb I).
    Charles Virolleaud,
    Syria III (1922), p. 277, Fig. 2

39 Sarcophagus of King Abishemu
    showing the position of the funerary
    gifts laid beside the body
    at the time of burial.
    Charles Virolleaud, *Syria* III, (1922),
    p. 283, Fig. 4

37

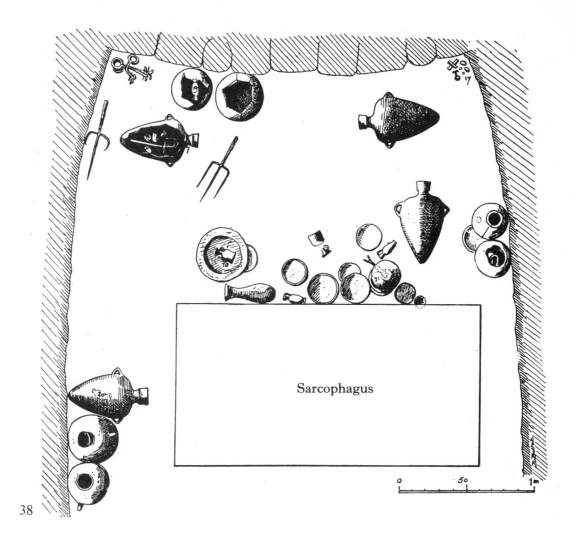

Sarcophagus

38

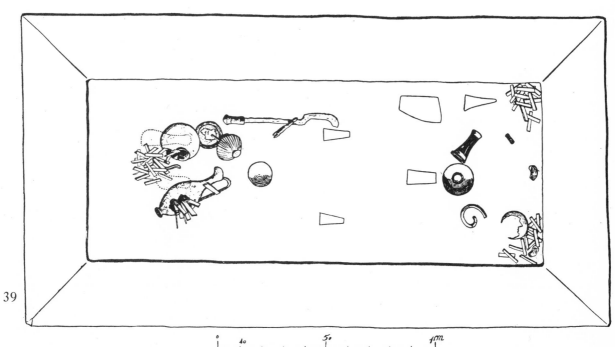

39

40

40 Silver "tea pot" from the tomb
    of King Abishemu (Tomb I)

41 Silver "tea pot" from the tomb
    of King Ibshemuabi (Tomb II)

42 Bronze trident from Tomb I

43 Obsidian vase with an inscription
    in hieroglyphic of Amenemhat III,
    a pharaoh of the Twelfth Dynasty

44 Bronze trident from Tomb I

45 Pottery goblet from Tomb I

41

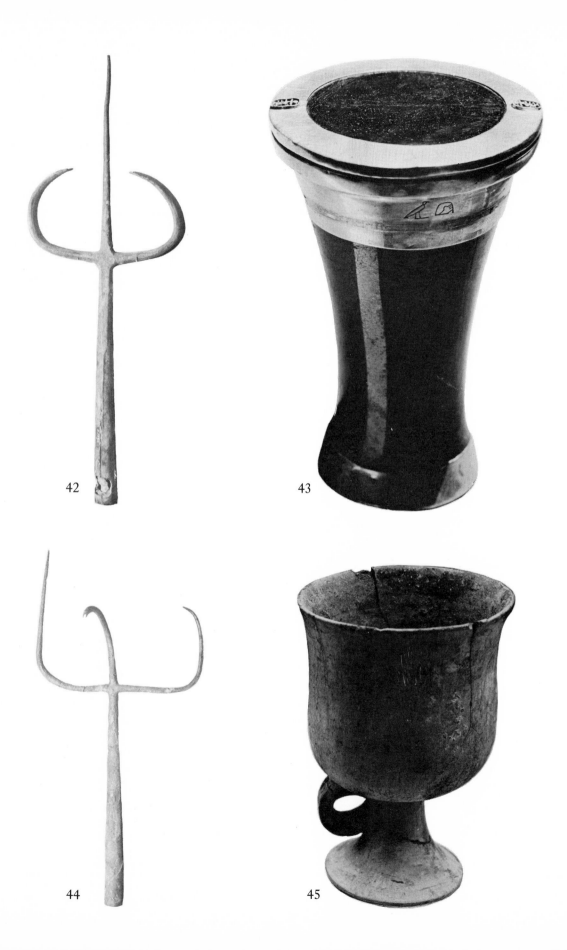

42

43

44

45

46   Silver mirror with gold ornamentation
on the handle from Tomb II

47   Obsidian box set in gold
with an inscription in hieroglyphic
of Amenemhat IV (Tomb II)

48   Grey stone vase with an inscription
in hieroglyphic of Amenemhat IV
on the cover (Tomb II)

49   Gold pendant set with precious stones
(Tomb II)

50   Gold pectoral set with inlaid polished
stones with a gold chain (Tomb II)

46

47

48

49

50

51

52

51 Bronze lotus leaves inlaid with silver

52 Gold duck's head which served
    as a spoon-handle from Tomb II

53 Gold bowl from Tomb II

54 Gold necklace from Tomb II

55 Scimitar of King Ibshemuabi (Tomb II).
    The inscription is evidence that
    Ibshemuabi is the son of King Abishemu
    of connecting Tomb I

56 Ornamental dagger (Tomb II)

57 Gold diadem with uraeus (Tomb II)

58 Gold bracelet with amethyst scarab
    (Tomb II)

59 Gold earring (or brooch) from Tomb II

53

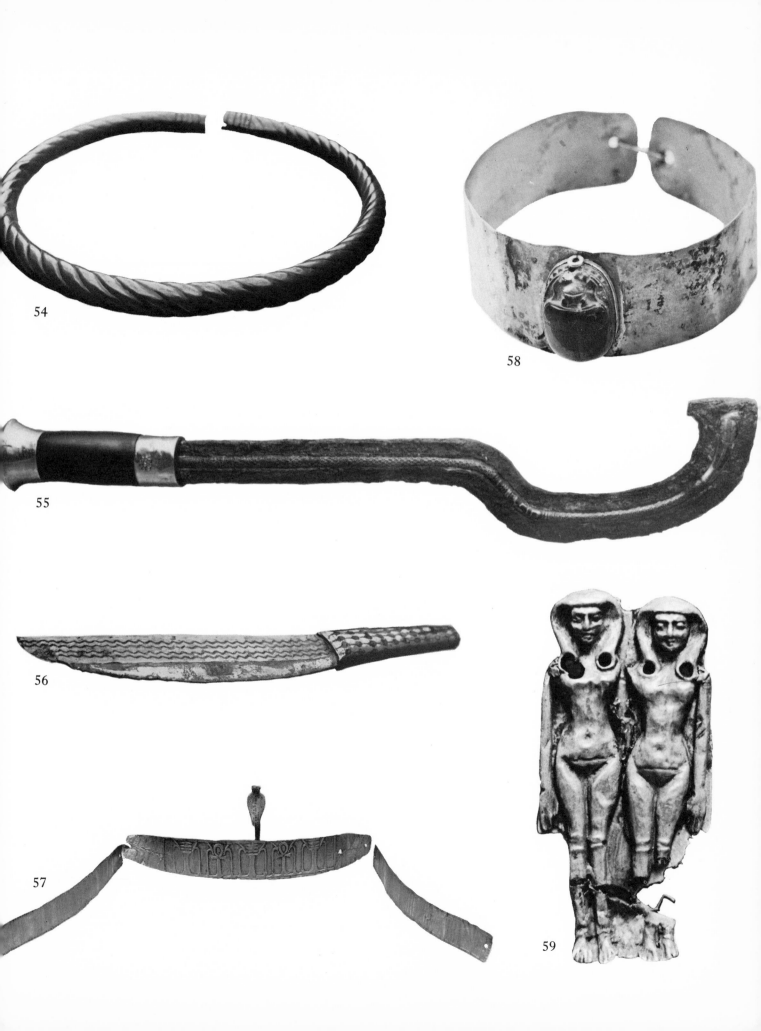

60

61

60 Gold statuette
of the Egyptian god Horus

61 Gold pectoral of the goddess Hathor

62 Pectoral in gold leaf representing
a falcon with extended wings
(Tomb III)

63 The Temple of the Obelisks

64 Stone work table
associated with the jewelers' workshop
of the Temple of the Obelisks.
The work table is presently located
in the Early Bronze Age *Temple en L*

62

65

66

65   The first appearance of the obelisks. *Fouilles de Byblos,* Atlas (1933-1938), Plate XXI

66   General view of the Temple of the Obelisks. *Fouilles de Byblos,* Atlas (1933-1938), Plate XXII

67   Stone anchor in the courtyard (Temple of the Obelisks)

68   Inscribed obelisk of Abishemu, king of Byblos (Temple of the Obelisks)

68

69

69 Place of sacrifice (Temple of the Obelisks)

70 Shrine for a god (Temple of the Obelisks)

71 Pottery jar in which a deposit was
    buried during the Middle Bronze Age
    in the *Champ d'offrandes*.
    Fouilles de Byblos, Atlas (1933-1938),
    Plate LXIII, Fig. 9686

72 Bronze figurine of a bull from the
    Champ d'offrandes. Fouilles de Byblos,
    Atlas (1933-1938), Plate LXIII, Fig. 9687

73 Gold fenestrated axe
    from the Temple of the Obelisks

70

71

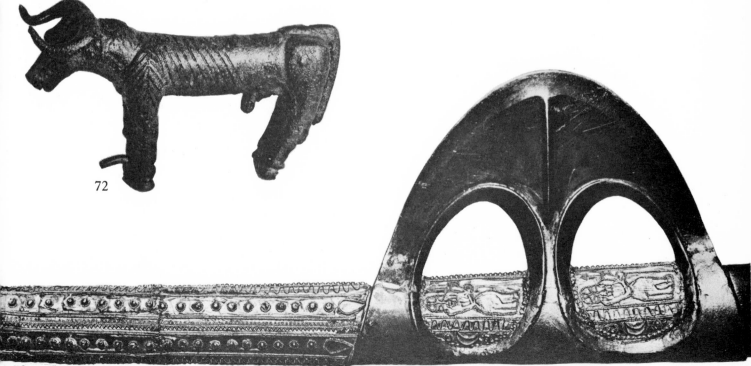

72

73

74

74 Bronze figurines covered with gold leaf
from the Temple of the Obelisks

75 Gold fenestrated axe
from the Temple of the Obelisks

76 Head of a bronze statuette covered in
gold leaf from the Temple of the Obelisks

77 Bronze figurine (front view)
from the Temple of the Obelisks

78 Bronze figurine (back view)
from the Temple of the Obelisks

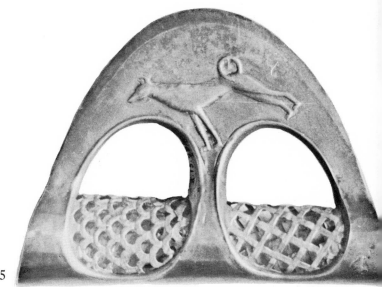

75

76

78

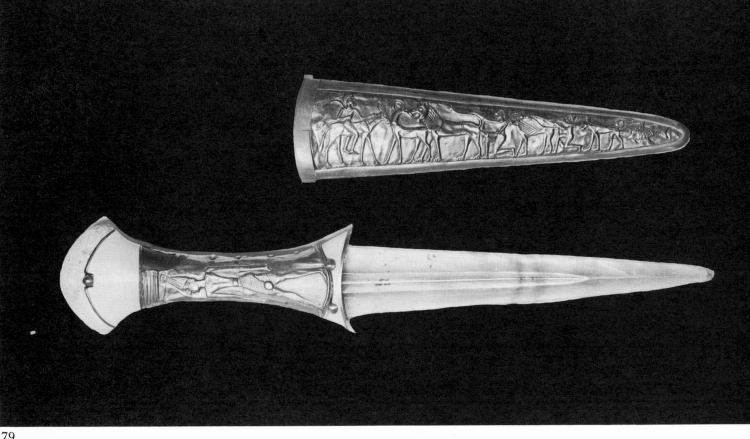

79

79 Gold dagger from the Temple of the Obelisks.
The decorative motif on the scabbard is evidence
of Mesopotamian influences which flooded Byblos

80 Detail from the handle of the gold dagger.
The figure on the handle is evidence
of Egyptian influence seen in the art of Byblos

The faience figurines on the following pages
were found buried under the floor
of the *pro-cella* of the Temple of the Obelisks

81 Faience figurine of a hippopotamus

82 Faience statuette of a composite human and animal figure

83 Faience statuette of a composite human and animal figure

80

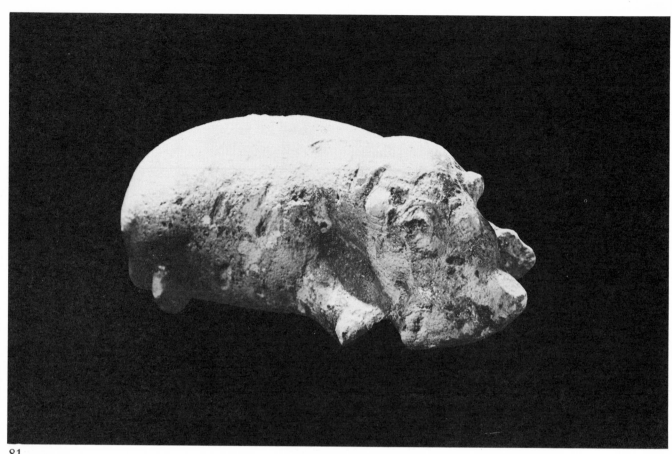

81

82

83

84

85

84 Kneeling faience figurine

85 Standing faience figurine

86 Faience figurine of a hippopotamus

87 Standing hippopotamus
with a crocodile on his back

88 Standing hippopotamus
with a crocodile on his back

89 Faience figurine of a baby crocodile

90 Faience figurine of a cat

91 Faience figurine of a panther

86

87

88

89

90

91

92

92   The sarcophagus of Ahiram
     in the burial chamber of Tomb V.
     Byblos et l'Egypte, Atlas (1928), Plate XVI

93   Shaft of the tomb of Ahiram
     showing the niches which probably
     held wooden poles supporting
     a second protective roof.
     Byblos et l'Egypte, Atlas, Plate CXXVI

94   King Ahiram seated on his throne
     (see frontispiece for the inscription)

95   Scene from the sarcophagus of Ahiram
     showing the procession of courtiers

93

96

96   Lid of the sarcophagus of Ahiram.
Byblos et l'Egypte, Atlas,
Plate CXXIX

97   Scene from the sarcophagus
of Ahiram
showing the mourning women

98   Alabaster vase with the cartouche
of Rameses II found in the shaft
of the tomb of Ahiram

99   Fragment of an alabaster plate
with the cartouche of Rameses II
found in the burial chamber
of Ahiram

100   Fragment of a Mycenaean
ivory plaque found in the shaft
of the tomb of Ahiram

97

101

𐤏𐤍𐤂𐤏𐤋𐤌𐤋𐤊𐤉𐤂𐤋

102

[𐤋𐤂𐤉𐤍𐤊𐤊]𐤊𐤋𐤊[𐤓𐤓𐤀]

103

[𐤂𐤋]𐤉𐤊𐤋𐤊𐤋𐤀𐤀𐤍𐤏

101   Reverse of silver coin of Ozbaal,
      king of Byblos ca. 350 B.C.

102   Reverse of silver coin of Adramelek,
      king of Byblos ca. 340 B.C.

103   Reverse of silver coin of Ayinel (Enylos),
      king of Byblos ca. 333 B.C.

104   Stele of Yehawmilk, king of Byblos.
      Baalat-Gebal is wearing the solar disc
      between cow's horns characteristic of the
      Egyptian Hathor-Isis. Compare with
      goddess on third millenium B.C.
      cylinder seal in Fig. 15

105   Drawing of the Egyptian goddess Isis

106   Drawing of the goddess on the
      "Renan bas-relief" (sixth century B.C.).
      Mission de Phénicie, p. 179

105

106

04

107

108

109

110

111

112   The Roman colonnade
seen today at Byblos

113   The theater at the time
of discovery
during the excavation
of the Roman levels.
In the background
modern houses built over
ancient Byblos

114   The theater rebuilt
by the sea

13

14

115

115 The spring at Byblos
called "Ayin-el-Melek"
(the spring of the king)
In the Isis and Osiris myth,
Isis met the queen's
maidservants here

116 Water conduit
of the Roman period

117 Statue of the goddess Hygeia

116

117

118

119

120

ARBORVMGENERAINCETERAPRIVATA

121

122

122   Cedars of Lebanon. Victor Guérin, *La Terre Sainte* II, Paris, Librairie Plon, 1884

123   The waterfall at Afka, source of the Adonis River

124

124   The Crusader castle built ca. 1108

125   Detail of a wall of the
      Crusader castle showing
      granite columns of the
      Roman period used as
      binders in the construction

126   The Crusader church of St. John
      at Jebeil

127   The baptistry of the church
      of St. John

125

128

128   Fishing boats of Byblos today

129   The Neolithic fisherman's village
       of Byblos 4500 B.C.

129

The Byblos King-List

The known rulers of Byblos with their approximate dates are given below. This tentative king-list is drawn from the available written sources in cuneiform, Egyptian and Phoenician. Main studies on the kings of Byblos during the second millenium B.C. are found in K.A. Kitchen, "Byblos, Egypt and Mari in the Early Second Millenium B.C.", *Orientalia* XXXVI (1967), Part 1, pp. 39-54; and W.F. Albright, "The Eighteenth-Century Princes of Byblos and the Chronology of Middle Bronze", *BASOR* No. 176 (1964), pp. 38-46. See H. Donner and W. Röllig, *Kanaanäischen und aramäische Inschriften* II (Wiesbaden: Harrassowitz, 1964), pp. 9-10 for Byblos king-list Ahiram to Ayyin'el; and W.F. Albright, "The Phoenician Inscriptions of the Tenth Century B.C. from Byblus", *JAOS* LXVII (1947), pp. 153-160 for Byblos king-list Zakar-Baal to Ayyin-El.

Name	Approximate dates	References and notes
Ba'alat-rūm's son . . . rūm, the chief of the (foreign) land of Byblos.	2350 B.C.	H. Goedicke, *Journal of the American Research Center in Egypt* V (1966), pp. 19-21. The name of this ruler appears on a cylinder seal found at Byblos which Goedicke has placed during the reign of Unas (Fifth Dynasty). P. Montet has dated this seal in the Third Dynasty. See *Byblos et l'Egypte*, pp. 62-68.
Ibdâdî	2050 B.C.	E. Sollberger, *Archiv für Orientforschung* XIX (1959-1960), pp. 120-122. Ibdâdî's name appears on a cuneiform text in the Drehem archives, contemporary with Amar-Suen of the Third Dynasty of Ur.
Abishemu	1820-1795 B.C.	*ANET*, p. 229 and n. 5. *Byblos et l'Egypte*, p. 174. Abishemu (Tomb I of the royal necropolis) is the father of Ibshemuabi and is contemporary with Amenemhat III (Twelfth Dynasty).
Ibshemuabi	1795-1780 B.C.	*ANET*, p. 229. *Byblos et l'Egypte*, p. 174. Ibshemuabi (Tomb II of the royal necropolis) is the son of Abishemu and is contemporary with Amenemhat IV (Twelfth Dynasty).

Name	Approximate dates	References and notes
Reyen or Yakin-el	1780-1765 B.C.	*ANET*, p. 229. See also *Fouilles de Byblos* I, pp. 197-198. W.F. Albright, *BASOR* No. 176 (1964), p. 43 reads *Yakin-el* and makes him a vassal of Seḥetep-ib-re' II of the Thirteenth Dynasty. Reyen (or Yakin-el) is the father of Yantin-ḫamu, Inten or Entin, prince of Byblos.
Yantin-ḫamu, Inten or Entin	1765-1735 B.C.	*ANET*, p. 229. The name of Inten, "Count of Byblos", appears on a relief found at Byblos that names Neferhotep I of the Thirteenth Dynasty, contemporary with Zimri-Lim of Mari. His name also appears on two scarabs purchased by P. Newberry and published in *JEA* XIV (1928), p. 109. See W.F. Albright, *BASOR* No. 99 (1945), pp. 9-17.
Ilima-yapi (?)	1735-1720 B.C.	W.F. Albright, *BASOR* No. 176 (1964), pp. 40-41. The name of this ruler appears on an amethyst scarab probably from Tomb IV (presently in the LeClerq collection at the Louvre). See *Byblos et l'Egypte*, pp. 196 ff. and p. 203.
		In addition to the inscription found in Tomb II of the royal necropolis, the name of Abishemu is found on the following inscriptions at Byblos:
Abishemu II	1720-1700 B.C.	P. Montet, *Kemi* XVI (1962), pp. 89-90. The name of this ruler appears on an inscribed obelisk found in the Temple of the Obelisks. He was contemporary with Néhesy of the Fourteenth Dynasty. See also *Fouilles de Byblos* II, Part 2, p. 878.
		Byblos et l'Egypte, pp. 212-213, Nos. 852 and 853. Abishemu's name appears on a fragment of a blue faience vase found in Tomb IX of the royal necropolis. The name Abi, prince of Byblos, appears on the cover of a blue faience vase and was also found in Tomb IX. See also P. Montet, *Kemi* XVII (1964), pp. 61-68.
		Fouilles de Byblos II, Part 1, pp. 174-175. Abishemu's name appears on a plaque found at Byblos.
		It is not known whether these inscriptions refer to the same or different rulers of Byblos bearing the name of Abishemu.
Yapa-shemuabi	1700-1690 B.C.	P. Montet, *Kemi* XVII (1964), p. 66. Yapa-shemuabi is the son of Abishemu, prince of Byblos. His name appears on a hieroglyphic inscription found at Byblos.
'Akery	1690-1670 B.C.	P. Montet, *Kemi* XVII (1964), p. 64. 'Akery, prince of Byblos, is the son of Abishemu. His name appears on a stele in hieroglyphs from Byblos.
Akäy	1670-1650 B.C.	P. Montet, *Kemi* XVII (1964), p. 62. The name of Akäy appears on a stele in hieroglyphs from Byblos concerning repairs made to the temple of Nut by this prince.

Name	Approximate dates	References and notes
Rib-Addi	1375-1355 B.C.	J.A. Knudtzon, *Die El-Amarna Tafeln* (1907-1915). Rib-Addi was ruler of Byblos contemporary with Amenhotep III and Akh-en-Aton (Eighteenth Dynasty). There are fifty-four letters written by him to the Egyptian court during the Tell-el-Amarna period.
Ahiram Ittobaal (son of Ahiram)	In the period 1250-1000 B.C.	See above, Chapter 4, pp. 29-33.
Zakar-Baal	1075 B.C.	*ANET*, pp. 25-29. Zakar-Baal was king of Byblos during the reign of Herihor and Nesubanebded, founder of the Twenty-first Dynasty, and is known from the Wen-Amon papyrus.
Yehimilk	950 B.C.	W.F. Albright, *JAOS* LXVII (1947), p. 160. Yehimilk, king of Byblos, is known from a stele found at Byblos concerning repairs done to the Temples of Baalat-Gebal and Baal-shamen.
Abibaal (son of Yehimilk ?)	930 B.C.	W.F. Albright, *JAOS* LXVII (1947), p. 160. Abibaal (son of Yehimilk ?) is known from an inscription on a statue base of Sheshonk I, founder of the Twenty-second Dynasty.
Elibaal	920 B.C.	W.F. Albright, *JAOS* LXVII (1947), p. 160. Elibaal was the son of Yehimilk and is known from an inscription on the bust of Osorkon I, son of Sheshonk I.
Shipit-Baal I	900 B.C.	W.F. Albright, *JAOS* LXVII (1947), p. 160. Shipit-Baal I is the son of Elibaal; the grandson of Yehimilk. His name appears on a stele from Byblos concerning a wall built by him for the Temple of Baalat-Gebal.
Shipit-Baal II	740 B.C.	*ANET*, p. 282. Shipit-Baal II (Sipitti-be'l in the Assyrian records) is contemporary with Tiglath-Pileser III, king of Assyria.
Ormilk	701 B.C.	*ANET*, p. 287. Ormilk (Uru-milki in the Assyrian records) is contemporary with Sennacherib, king of Assyria.
Milk-asaph	670 B.C.	*ANET*, p. 291. Milk-asaph (Milki-asapa in the Assyrian records) is contemporary with Esarhaddon, king of Assyria.
Shipit-Baal III	500 B.C.	*Fouilles de Byblos* I, pp. 31-32. Shipit-Baal III is known from three fragmentary pieces of a funerary stele of his son. The son's name has not been preserved.
Ormilk II	480 B.C.	*ANET*, p. 502. Grandfather of Yehawmilk.
Yehar-Baal	470 B.C.	*ANET*, p. 502. Father of Yehawmilk.
Yehawmilk	450 B.C.	*ANET*, p. 502. Yehawmilk is known from a stele from Byblos concerning repairs made to the Temple of Baalat-Gebal. He is the son of Yehar-Baal and the grandson of Ormilk II.

Name	Approximate dates	References and notes
El-Paal	362 B.C.	G.F. Hill, *Catalogue of the Greek Coins of Phoenicia*, p. 94-96. King El-Paal's name appears on quarter-stater coins minted at Byblos. Hill has established the chronology for the kings of Byblos of the Persian period as follows: El-Paal (before 362 B.C.), Azbaal (350 B.C.), Ainel, identified with Enylos (333 B.C.), and Adramelek (late 4th century B.C.).
Ozbaal (Azbaal)	348 B.C.	*Fouilles de Byblos* I, p. 407. Ozbaal may be the son of Batno'am *(Fouilles de Byblos* I, p. 31). His name appears on one-stater coins minted at Byblos.
Adramelek	340 B.C.	*Fouilles de Byblos* I, p. 407. Adramelek's name appears on 1/16-stater coins minted at Byblos.
Ayinel (Ainel)	333 B.C.	*Fouilles de Byblos* I, p. 407. Ayinel's name appears on 1/16-stater coins minted at Byblos. Ayinel is identified with Enylos, contemporary with Alexander the Great.

Bibliography

Classical and Medieval Sources

Aelian. *Varia Historia*. Leipzig: B. G. Teubnerl, 1887.

Arrian. *Anabasi Alexandri* I & II. Trans. E. Iliff Robson. London: W. Heinemann Ltd., 1929-1933 (The Loeb Classical Library).

Athenaeus. *The Deipnosophists* I. Trans. Charles Burton Gulick. Cambridge: Harvard University Press, 1951 (The Loeb Classical Library).

Curtius, Quintus. *History of Alexander* I & II. Trans. John C. Rolfe. Cambridge: Harvard University Press, 1956 (The Loeb Classical Library).

Diodorus Siculus. *Diodorus of Sicily* I, VI, VIII, IX. Trans. C. H. Oldfather. Cambridge: Harvard University Press, 1954-1963 (The Loeb Classical Library).

Geographi Graeci Minoris II. Ed. Muller, "Tautios Orbis Descripto", Paris, 1861; reprinted Hildesheim, 1965.

Guilelmus of Tyre. *A History of Deeds Done Beyond the Sea*. By William, Archbishop of Tyre. Trans. Emily Atwater Babcock and A. C. Krey. New York: Columbia University Press, 1943 (in two volumes).

Herodotus. *The Histories* I-IV. Trans. A. D. Godley. Cambridge: Harvard University Press, 1957-1963 (The Loeb Classical Library).

Homer. *The Iliad* I & II. Trans. A. T. Murray. Cambridge: Harvard University Press, 1962 (The Loeb Classical Library).

— *The Odyssey* I & II. Trans. A. T. Murray. Cambridge: Harvard University Press, 1966 (The Loeb Classical Library).

Inscriptiones Graecae. Ed. Maior XII. Berolini Apvd Georgivm Reimervm MCMVIII, Fascicle 7.

Jerome. *Commentary on Ezekiel* 27.4-5; Jean Paul Migne. *Patrologia Latina* 25.260.

Josephus, Flavius. "Against Apion", *Josephus* I. Trans. H. St. J. Thackeray. Cambridge: Harvard University Press, 1961 (The Loeb Classical Library).

— "Jewish Antiquities", *Josephus* V & VII. Trans. H. St. J. Thackeray. Cambridge: Harvard University Press, 1950-1961 (The Loeb Classical Library).

— "The Jewish War", *Josephus* II & III. Trans. H. St. J. Thackeray. Cambridge: Harvard University Press, 1957 (The Loeb Classical Library).

Justin. *Abrégé des histoires philippiques de Trogue Pompée*. Trans. E. Chambry and L. Thely-Chambry. Paris: Librairie Garnier Frères (Classiques Garnier).

Lucian. *De Dea Syria*. The Syrian Goddess. Trans. Herbert Strong. London: Constable & Co. Ltd., 1913.

2 Maccabees. *The Apocrypha*. New York: Thomas Nelson & Sons, 1894 (Nelson Series).

Malalae, Ioannis. *Chronographia*. Corpus Scriptorum Historiae Byzantinae. Bonn: L. Dindorf, 1931.

Marcellinus, Ammianus. *Res Gestae* I-III. Trans. John C. Rolfe. Cambridge: Harvard University Press, 1950 (The Loeb Classical Library).

Nassiri Khosrau. *Sefer Nameh*, Relation des voyages de Nassiri Khosrau. Trans. C. Schefer. Paris, 1881.

Nonnus. *Dionysiaca* I-III. Trans. W. H. D. Rouse. Cambridge: Harvard University Press, 1955-1956 (The Loeb Classical Library).

Philo of Byblos. Edited in fragments in Eusebius' *Praeparatio Evangelica* by Felix Jacoby in *Die Fragmente der Griechischen Historiker*. Leiden: E. J. Brill, 1958.

Pliny. *Natural History* II. Trans. H. Rackham. Cambridge: Harvard University Press, 1957 (The Loeb Classical Library).

Plutarch. "On Isis and Osiris", *Moralia* V. Trans. Frank Cole Babbitt. Cambridge: Harvard University Press, 1956 (The Loeb Classical Library).

— "Life of Lucullus", *Plutarch's Lives* II. Trans. Bernadotte Perrin. Cambridge: Harvard University Press, 1959 (The Loeb Classical Library).

— "Life of Nicias", *Plutarch's Lives* III. Trans. Bernadotte Perrin. Cambridge: Harvard University Press, 1958 (The Loeb Classical Library).

Polybius. *The Histories* III & V. Trans. W. R. Paton. Cambridge: Harvard University Press, 1960 (The Loeb Classical Library).

Strabo. *The Geography of Strabo* V & VII. Trans. Horace Leonard Jones. Cambridge: Harvard University Press, 1954 (The Loeb Classical Library).

Stephanus of Byzantium. *Ethnica*. Ed. A. Meineke. Berlin, 1859; reprinted Graz, 1958.

Supplementum Epigraphicum Graecum XVIII. Leiden: A. W. Sythoff, 1962.

Theocritus. "Love of Cynisca", *Idyll* XIV; *The Greek Bucolic Poets*. Trans. J. M. Edmonds. Cambridge: Harvard University Press, 1950 (The Loeb Classical Library).

— "The Women at the Adonis Festival", *Idyll* XV; *The Greek Bucolic Poets*. Trans. J. M. Edmonds. Cambridge: Harvard University Press, 1950 (The Loeb Classical Library).

Theophrastus. *Enquiry into Plants* I & II. Trans. Sir Arthur Hort. Cambridge: Harvard University Press, 1916 (The Loeb Classical Library).

Thucydides. *The Peloponnesian War* III. Trans. Charles Forster Smith. Cambridge: Harvard University Press, 1966 (The Loeb Classical Library).

Zosimus. Mendelssohn, Ludwig (ed.). "Zosimi Comitis et Exadvocati Fisci", *Historia Nova*. Leipzig, 1887.

Studies on Byblos

Albright, William F. "An Indirect Synchronism Between Egypt and Mesopotamia ca. 1730 B.C.", *BASOR* No. 99 (1945), 9-17.

— "The Eighteenth-Century Princes of Byblos and the Chronology of Middle Bronze", *BASOR* No. 176 (1964), 38-46.

— "The Phoenician Inscriptions of the Tenth Century B.C. from Byblus", *JAOS* LXVII (1947), 153-160.

Chehab, Maurice. "Un trésor d'orfèvrerie syro-égyptien", *BMB* I (1937), 7-21.

Contenau, G. *La civilisation phénicienne*. Paris: Payot, 1949.

Dunand, Maurice. *Byblos, son histoire, ses ruines, ses légendes*. Beyrouth, 1963.

— *Fouilles de Byblos* I & II. Paris: Librairie Orientaliste Paul Geuthner, 1939.

— "Rapport préliminaire sur les fouilles de Byblos en 1948", *BMB* IX (1949), 53-64.

— "Rapport préliminaire sur les fouilles de Byblos en 1949", *BMB* IX (1949), 65-74.

— "Rapport préliminaire sur les fouilles de Byblos en 1950", *BMB* XII (1955), 7-12.

— "Rapport préliminaire sur les fouilles de Byblos en 1951", *BMB* XII (1955), 13-20.

— "Rapport préliminaire sur les fouilles de Byblos en 1952", *BMB* XII (1955), 21-23.

— "Rapport préliminaire sur les fouilles de Byblos en 1954", *BMB* XIII (1956), 73-78.

— "Rapport préliminaire sur les fouilles de Byblos en 1955", *BMB* XIII (1956), 81-86.

— "Rapport préliminaire sur les fouilles de Byblos en 1957", *BMB* XVI (1964), 69-73.

— "Rapport préliminaire sur les fouilles de Byblos en 1958", *BMB* XVI (1964), 75-79.

— "Rapport préliminaire sur les fouilles de Byblos en 1959", *BMB* XVI (1964), 81-85.

— "La sixième campagne de fouilles de Byblos", *Syria* IX (1928), 1-5, second article 173-186.

— "La septième campagne de fouilles de Byblos", *Syria* X (1929), 206-216.

Dussaud, René. "Les inscriptions phéniciennes du tombeau d'Ahiram, roi de Byblos", *Syria* V (1924), 135-155.

— "Dédicace d'une statue d'Osorkon par Elibaal, roi de Byblos", *Syria* VI (1925), 101-110.

— "Inscription phénicienne de Byblos de l'époque romaine", *Syria* VI (1925), 269-273.

— "Le sanctuaire phénicien de Byblos d'après Benjamin de Tudèle", *Syria* VII (1927), 247-256.

— "Les quatre campagnes de fouilles de M. Pierre Montet à Byblos", *Syria* XI (1930), 164-187.

Frazer, James G. *The Golden Bough, A Study in Magic and Religion* 3rd ed., IV, Adonis Attis Osiris Vol. I, Chapter II "Adonis in Syria", pp. 13-30. London: MacMillan & Co., Ltd., 1955.

Goedicke, Hans. "A Cylinder Seal of a Ruler of Byblos of the Third Millenium", *Mitteilungen des Deutchen Archäeologischen Instituts Abteilung Kairo* XIX (1963), 1-5.

— "The Cylinder Seal of a Ruler of Byblos Reconsidered", *Journal of the American Center in Egypt* V (1966), 19-21.

215

Hayes, William C. "Career of the Great Steward Henenu under Nebḥepetre Mentuḥopte", *JEA* XXXV (1949), 43-49.

Hill, George F. *Catalogue of the Greek Coins of Phoenicia*. London: Longmans & Co., 1910. Introduction lxi-lxxi.

Hubert, Henri. "De quelques objets de bronze trouvés à Byblos", *Syria* VI (1925), 16-29.

Jalabert, Louis, S.J. "Inscriptions grecques et latines de Syrie", *Mélanges de la Faculté Orientale de l'Université Saint-Joseph* I (1906), 132-188.

Jalabert, L. et Mouterde, R. "Les réserves forestières impériales dans le Liban", *Mélanges de la Faculté Orientale de l'Université Saint-Joseph* IV (1910), 209-215.

Kitchen, K. A. "Byblos, Egypt and Mari in the Early Second Millenium B.C.", *Orientalia* XXXVI (1967), Part 1, 39-54.

Knudtzon, J. A. *Die El-Amarna Tafeln*. Vorderasiatische Bibliothek. Leipzig: 1907-1915.

Mercer, Samuel B. (ed.). *The Tell-el-Amarna Tablets* I & II. Toronto: MacMillan Company of Canada Ltd., 1939.

Montet, Pierre. *Byblos et l'Egypte*, Quatre campagnes de fouilles à Gebeil 1921, 1922, 1923, 1924. Paris: Librairie Orientaliste Paul Geuthner, 1928.

— "Dépôts d'offrandes à Byblos et à Tod", *Kemi* XVI (1962), 89-90.

— "La IVe dynastie à Byblos", *Kemi* XVI (1962), 86-89.

— "Quatre nouvelles inscriptions hiéroglyphiques trouvées à Byblos", *Kemi* XVII (1964), 61-68.

— "Le pays de Negaou près de Byblos et son dieu", *Syria* IV (1923), 180-182.

— "Un Égyptien roi de Byblos sous la XIIe Dynastie", *Syria* VIII (1927), 85-92.

— "Sur quelques objets provenant de Byblos", *Syria* X (1929), 12-15.

Mouterde, R. "Date des inscriptions forestières d'Hadrien au Liban", *Mélanges de la Faculté Orientale de l'Université Saint-Joseph* XXV (1942-1943), 41-47.

— "Reliefs et inscriptions de la Syrie et du Liban — VIII. Les inscriptions d'Hadrien à Tarchich et au Wadi Brissa", *Mélanges de la Faculté Orientale de l'Université Saint-Joseph* XXXIV (1957), 230-234.

Naville, Édouard. "Le vase à parfum de Byblos", *Syria* III (1922), 291-295.

Neghbi, Ora and Moskowitz, S. "The Foundation Deposits or Offering Deposits of Byblos", *BASOR* No. 184 (1966), 21-26.

Nelson, Harold H. "Fragments of Egyptian Old Kingdom Stone Vases from Byblos", *Berytus* I (1934), 19-22.

Newberry, Percy E. "A Middle Kingdom Mayor of Byblos", *JEA* XIV (1928), p. 109.

Pauly's Real-Encyclopädie (1899). Article on "Byblos", pp. 1099-1102.

Pillet, Maurice. "Le temple de Byblos", *Syria* VIII (1927), 105-112.

Renan, Ernest. *Mission de Phénicie*. Paris: Imprimerie Impériale, 1864.

Rouvier, Jules. "Gébal-Byblos; son histoire dans l'antiquité et sa nécropole phénicienne". Conférence donnée à l'Association Bibliographique de Beyrouth le 23 mars 1899.

— *Numismatique des villes de la Phénicie*. Beyrouth, 1900.

Seyrig, Henri. "Le grand prêtre de Dionysos à Byblos", Antiquités Syriennes: 55, *Syria* XXXI (1954), 68-73.

Sollberger, E. "Byblos sous les rois d'Ur", *Archiv für Orientforschung* XIX (1959-1960), 120-122.

Tufnell, O. and Ward, W. A. "Relations between Byblos, Egypt and Mesopotamia at the End of the Third Millenium B.C.", *Syria* XLIII (1966), 165-241.

Virolleaud, Charles. "Découverte à Byblos d'un hypogée de la XIIe dynastie égyptienne", *Syria* III (1922), 273-290.

Ward, William A. "Egypt and the East Mediterranean from Pre-Dynastic Times to the End of the Old Kingdom", *Journal of Economic and Social History of the Orient* VI (1963), 1-57.

General Works

Albright, William F. "Remarks on the Chronology of Early Bronze IV-Middle Bronze IIA in Phoenicia and Syria-Palestine", *BASOR* No. 184 (1966), 26-35.

— "Some Remarks on the Archaeological Chronology of Palestine before about 1500 B.C." in Robert W. Ehrich (ed.), *Chronologies in Old World Archaeology*. Chicago: University of Chicago Press, 1954.

Baramki, Dimitri C. *The Archaeological Museum of the American University of Beirut*. Beirut: The American University of Beirut, 1967 (Centennial Publications).

— *Phoenicia and the Phoenicians*. Beirut: Khayats, 1961.

Barnett, R. D. *A Catalogue of the Nimrud Ivories*. London: The Trustees of the British Museum, 1957.

Breasted, James H. *Ancient Records of Egypt* I-IV. Chicago: University of Chicago Press, 1906-1907.

Bruin, Frans. "Royal Purple and the Dye Industries of the Mycenaeans and Phoenicians", *American University of Beirut Festival Book* (Festschrift) Beirut, 1967 (Centennial Publications).

Diringer, David. *Writing*. London: Thames and Hudson, 1962.

Donner, H. and Rölling, W. *Kanaanäischen und aramäische Inschriften* II. Wiesbaden: Harrassowitz, 1964.

Drioton, Étienne and Vandier, Jacques. *L'Egypte*. Paris: Les Presses Universitaires de France, 1938.

Dussaud, René. *Topographie Historique de la Syrie Antique et Médiévale*. Paris: Librairie Orientaliste Paul Geuthner, 1927.

Dunbabin, T. J. *The Greeks and Their Eastern Neighbors*. John Boardman (ed.). London: The Society for the Promotion of Hellenic Studies, 1957.

Frisk, Hjalmar. *Griechisches Etymologisches Wörterbuch*. Heidelberg: Carl Winter, 1960.

Gardiner, Sir Alan. *Egypt of the Pharaohs*. Oxford: The Clarendon Press, 1961.

Grollenberg, L. H. *Atlas of the Bible*. Trans. and ed. Joyce M. H. Reid. London: Thomas Nelson & Sons Ltd., 1957, p. 143.

Harden, Donald. *The Phoenicians*. London: Thomas and Hudson, 1962.

Hitti, Philip. *Lebanon in History*. London: MacMillan & Co. Ltd., 1957.

James, E. O. *The Ancient Gods*. New York: G. P. Putnam's Sons, 1960.

Kalayan, Haroutune Y. *L'habitation au Liban* I. Beirut: Syco Press, 1966.

Kantor, Helene. *The Aegean and the Orient in the Second Millenium B.C.* Bloomington, Indiana: Principia Press, 1947.

Kenrick, John. *Phoenicia*. London: B. Fellowes, 1855.

Kenyon, Kathleen M. *Amorites and Canaanites*. London: Oxford University Press, 1966.

Laessoe, Jorgon. *The People of Ancient Assyria*. Trans. I. S. Leigh-Browne. London: Routledge & Kegan Paul Ltd., 1963.

Lucas, Alfred. *Ancient Egyptian Materials and Industries*. 3rd ed. London: Arnold, 1948.

Luckenbill, Daniel. *Ancient Records of Assyria and Babylonia* I & II. Chicago: University of Chicago Press, 1926.

Maundrell, H. *A Journey from Aleppo to Jerusalem*. 6th ed. Oxford, 1749.

Movers, F. C. *Die Phönizier* I & II. Berlin: Ferd. Dümmler's Berlagsbudhandlung, 1856.

Posener, G. *Princes et pays d'Asie et de Nubie*. Bruxelles: Fondation Égyptologue Reine Elizabeth, 1940.

Pritchard, James B. (ed.). *Ancient Near Eastern Texts Relating to the Old Testament*, 2nd ed. Princeton: Princeton University Press, 1955.

Rawlinson, George. *History of Phoenicia*. London: Longmans & Co., 1889.

Runciman, Steven. *History of the Crusades* I-III. Cambridge: University Press, 1951-1954.

Saggs, H. W. F. *The Greatness that was Babylon*. London: Sidgwick and Jackson, 1962.

Säve-Söderbergh, T. "The Hyksos Rule in Egypt", *JEA* XXXVII (1951), 53-71.

Schaeffer, Claude F. A. *Stratigraphie comparée et chronologie de l'Asie occidentale, Syrie, Palestine, Asie Mineure, Chypre, Perse et Caucase*. Londres: Oxford University Press, 1948.

— *Ugaritica* II. Paris: Librairie Orientaliste Paul Geuthner, 1949.

Schwabe, M. "Greek Inscriptions Found at Beth She'arim in Fifth Excavation Season", *Israel Exploration Journal* IV (1954), 250.

Vasiliev, A. A. *History of the Byzantine Empire* I & II. Madison: University of Wisconsin Press, 1952.

Ward, William A. "Relations Between Egypt and Mesopotamia from Prehistoric Times to the End of the Middle Kingdom". *Journal of Economic and Social History of the Orient* VII, Parts 1 and 2 (1964), 1-45, 121-135.

Watson, Patty Jo. "The Chronology of North Syria and North Mesopotamia from 10,000 B.C. to 2000 B.C." in Robert W. Ehrich (ed.), *Chronologies in Old World Archaeology*. Chicago: University of Chicago Press, 1954.

Weill, Raymond. *Phoenicia and Western Asia to the Macedonian Conquest*. London: George Harrap & Co. Ltd., 1940.

Wilson, John A. *Signs and Wonders Upon Pharaoh*. Chicago: The University of Chicago Press, 1964.

Weissbach, F. H. *Die Dankmäler und Inschriften an Der Mündung Des Nahr el Kelb*. Berlin: Vereinigung Wissenschaftlicher Verleger Walter de Gruyter & Co., 1922.

— *Die Inschriften Nebukadnezars II im Wadi Brisa und am Nahr El-Kelb*. Leipzig: J. C. Hinrichs'sche Buchandlung, 1906.

Index

219

Printed at
the Imprimerie Catholique
Beirut, Lebanon

June 1968

Layout by
Joseph Gébara

Published in the same series:
The Roman Temples of Lebanon
Portrait of a People, Lebanon